ARAB MiGs, Volume 3, The June 1967 Wa

Tom Cooper and David Nicolle, with Lon Nordeen and

ARAB MiGs
Volume 3

The June 1967 War

To David with special thanks and best wishes,

Tom Cooper
11 NOV '12

Tom Cooper and **David Nicolle**, with **Lon Nordeen** and **Patricia Salti**

HARPIA
PUBLISHING+

Consulting and inspiration by Kerstin Berger
Artworks by Tom Cooper and Jameel Patel
Maps and diagrams by James Lawrence
Editorial by Thomas Newdick
Layout by Norbert Novak, www.media-n.at, Vienna

Printed at Grasl Druck & Neue Medien, Austria

ISBN 978-0-9825539-9-2

Harpia Publishing, L.L.C. is a member of

Contents

Introduction

Arab MiGs Volume 3 continues the story of specific Arab air forces that was initiated by the previous two volumes in this series. While *Volume 1* explained the background to how various Arab air forces acquired and flew MiG-15s and MiG-17s during the late 1950s and through the 1960s, *Volume 2* completed the coverage through researching the circumstances under which the same air forces acquired MiG-19s and MiG-21s – together with a host of other Soviet-made aircraft and helicopters, as well as various British-made types. In discussing these topics, these two volumes described the political manoeuvring that was taking place in the background, in turn explaining details such as why Iraq became the first Arab country to receive MiG-19s and MiG-21s (as well as Tupolev Tu-16 bombers); how Egypt continued its purchases of MiGs through the 1960s – although not at the rate usually reported; the true story of the supposed defection of an Iraqi MiG-21 pilot to Israel; and the reality behind Egyptian MiG-21 missions over Israel in May 1967, which some recent publications attempted to use as a justification for subsequent Israeli aggression. *Volume 2* concluded with a detailed description of the chaotic status of the Egyptian Air Force resulting from a series of incorrect decisions by its political and military leadership.

Volume 3 begins right where *Volume 2* ended – with a detailed description of Egyptian Air Force operations during the June 1967 War with Israel. It continues in a similar fashion by providing an insight into the status of the Iraqi, Jordanian and Syrian air arms – together with an overview of general military planning – shortly before the June 1967 War, and their participation in that conflict.

Even more than the previous two works, this volume relies entirely upon original, primarily first-hand sources, and particularly upon narratives provided by pilots and other officers, but also on extensive original documentation that has recently become available in Egypt. Some of these documents and narratives have already been published in Arabic, but most remain entirely unknown in the West. Taken together, they shed an entirely new light upon a particularly controversial – indeed, an incendiary – part of Arab history that is so critical that it continues to define the entire Middle East to this today.

As such, *Arab MiGs Volume 3* provides the most comprehensive account of the June 1967 War fought between Israel and its Arab neighbours as seen from the standpoint of the officers and airmen who served with five crucial Arab air arms during that conflict.

In the minds of a great many, the story of Israel's Operation Moked (Focus) and the seemingly total destruction of the Egyptian, Jordanian and Syrian air arms seem to sum up the whole conflict. However, this does not reflect the true and overall picture. Although the destruction of the Arab air forces was a primary objective of Operation Moked, as already revealed in previous volumes of this series, it was neither as complete nor as easily achieved as is often claimed. Although mauled by the opening Israeli strike, the Egyptian Air Force did not suffer on such a large scale as claimed by Israel at the time and since. Instead, its pilots not only scored a number of aerial victories on the first day of the conflict, indicating how much could have been possible if the entire United Arab Republic Air Force had been properly led, but they also kept on fighting, delivering blows upon unsuspecting Israeli airmen and ground troops. Furthermore, while the Egyptian Air Force received the brunt of the blow delivered by Israeli air power on the opening day of the June 1967 War, Syria and Jordan also became involved, followed by Iraq. Eventually, even Algerian elements appeared on the scene, though most of the aircraft they deployed to the combat zone arrived too late to have a significant impact.

In order to provide the best possible, but also the most balanced account, our team of authors has been aided considerably through the addition of new and particularly valuable material provided by researchers from several countries.

As in previous volumes, this work can claim to provide the first correct identities for most of the relevant Arab pilots and units, as well as factually correct data concerning the quantity and quality of the equipment at their disposal. For these reasons, we are confident that this book represents a significant advance over anything previously published on this topic, even though the non-availability of specific original documents as well as the inability to locate and contact specific participants still prevent us from presenting the 'full picture'.

When studying the June 1967 War it is important to keep in mind contemporary time zones, which were different at the time. Between 1940 and 1967, Egypt used Daylight Saving Time (DST), and was therefore within the time zone GMT +3 (this practice was discontinued on 1 October 1967, after which Egypt was within the time zone GMT +2). As of June 1967, Jordan was within the time zone GMT +2: DST was only introduced from 6 June 1973. Between 22 September 1957 and 7 July 1974, Israel did not use DST, and was thus within the same time zone as Jordan. Finally, Iraq introduced DST only on 1 May 1982 (a practice discontinued from 1 April 2005), such that as of June 1967 it was within the time zone GMT +3.

Tom Cooper and Dr David Nicolle, September 2012

Acknowledgements

Meeting and talking with the participants, or corresponding with them via e-mail, has always been an interesting experience for all the authors and researchers involved. It came as something of a surprise to discover how very differently the various protagonists took in their surroundings. At one end of the scale, many seemed to possess a scrupulously accurate knowledge of places, people or aircraft, while others gave the impression that they only had very superficial contact with the events and actors throughout this entire period. There are those who could recall events vividly, and others for whom, naturally, the passage of time or advancing years has caused memories to fade or whose recollections have become confused. The latter was often a result of what they had either read about or seen on television during the intervening years.

Several of the people we talked to had intriguing personal stories or eyewitness accounts to recount, and occasionally we met or were put in contact with somebody who was able to throw an especially interesting light on a particular event that had taken place. Irrespective of how many of their own recollections various sources provided, the authors would like to express their gratitude to all those persons who contributed to this book. Foremost are the officers and pilots of various Arab air arms, particularly in Algeria, Egypt, Iraq and Syria, but also members of their families, friends and colleagues who kindly shared recollections and documentation with us. They include the late Air Marshal Taher Zaki (EAF, ret.), the late Air Marshal Mustafa Shalabi el-Hinnawy (EAF, ret.), the late Air Marshal Alaa Barakat (EAF, ret.), Lieutenant General Arif Abd ar-Razzaq (IrAF, ret.), Air Marshal Badr Domair (EAF, ret.), Air Vice-Marshal Qadri Abd el-Hamid (EAF, ret.), Air Vice-Marshal Mohammad Okasha (EAF, ret.), Air Vice-Marshal Nabil el-Shuwakri (EAF, ret.), Air Vice-Marshal Mamdouh Taliba (EAF, ret.), Major General Ihsan Shurdom (RJAF, ret), Brigadier General Ahmad Sadik (IrAF, ret.), Brigadier General Faysal Abdul Mohsen (IrAF, ret.), Brigadier General Farouk Abdeen (RJAF, ret.), Air Commodore Farouk el-Ghazawy (EAF, ret.), the late Air Commodore Mustafa Hafez (EAF, ret.), Air Commodore Fikry al-Gindy (EAF, ret.), Air Commodore Fuad Kamal (EAF, ret.), Air Commodore Gabr Ali Gabr (EAF, ret.), Air Commodore Abdel Moneim el-Tawil (EAF, ret.), Group Captain Kapil Bhargava (IAF, ret.), Group Captain Saif-ul-Azam (BAF and ex-PAF, ret.), Wing Commander Kamal Zaki (EAF, ret.), Wing Commander Talaat Louca (EAF, ret.), Wing Commander Usama Sidqi (EAF, ret.), and others.

We would like to thank Mr Tarek el-Shennawy, Mr Ahmed Keraidy, Mr Ahmad Turaiba, Mrs Leila, the late Mrs Khouda and the late Mrs Mona Tewfik, for their kind permission to use their family archives.

We would also like to specially thank a number of other researchers for their kind help during the research for this book, in particular: Group 73 in Egypt, including Dr Abdallah Emran, Nour Bardai and Ahmed Zayed, who provided extensive transcriptions from their interviews with a number of leading Egyptian fighter pilots, including Major General Zia el-Hefnawi (EAF, ret.), Major General Mamdouh Heshmat (EAF, ret.), Major General Samir Aziz Mikhail (EAF, ret.) and Major General Medhat Zaki (EAF, ret.); to Mohammad Hassan, Abdul Salam al-Maleki, and Hayder Aziz in Iraq who provided plenty of their own documentation, photographs, publications as well as contacts to a number of former IrAF pilots and officers, and who helped with additional translations of original documents and publications; to Yasser al-Abed and other friends in Syria for their selfless sharing of documentation concerning SyAAF officers and pilots; to Yawar Mazhar and Usman Shabbir in Pakistan, as well as Jagan Mohan in India, for kindly sharing the results of their research and helping with contacts relating to the Pakistan and Indian Air Forces, respectively; to Albert Grandolini and Marc Koelich in France for their endless kind help and provision of materials from their immense archives; to Yoav Efrati, Zvi Kreissler and other friends in Israel; to Mark Lepko in the United States for selflessly providing the results of their relevant research, based on plenty of hard work and extensive knowledge; to Sherif Sharmi, Franz Vajda, Jeroen Nijmeijer, Menno van der Wall, Frank Olynyk, and Peter Weinert for their kind permission to use some of their research, and to Hicham Honeini from Lebanon for his patience and kind help with the translations of various publications and documentation from Arabic.

Sadly, we do not feel free to reveal in public the names of many other individuals and have therefore expressed our gratitude personally.

Last but by no means least, we would like to thank a number of friends who have helped with additional information, commentary, translations or encouragement over a prolonged period, foremost Farzad Bishop, Adrian Roman, Christof Hahn, Ugo Crisponi, Adrian deVoe and Tom Long. All of them have consistently supported our work with the greatest enthusiasm, and our special thanks are due to each one of them.

Abbreviations

AA-2 Atoll	ASCC codename for R-3S, Soviet short-range AAM
AA	anti-aircraft
AAA	anti-aircraft artillery
AAM	air-to-air missile
AB	air base
AdA	Armée de l'Air (French Air Force)
Air Cdre	air commodore (military commissioned officer rank, equivalent to brigadier general)
AM	air marshal (military commissioned officer rank, equivalent to lieutenant general)
An	Antonov (the design bureau led by Oleg Antonov)
AS-5 Kelt	ASCC codename for KSR-2, Soviet air-to-surface missile
ASCC	Air Standardisation Coordinating Committee
AVM	air vice-marshal (military commissioned officer rank, equivalent to major general)
BAF	Bangladesh Air Force
Brig Gen	brigadier general (military commissioned officer rank)
CAP	combat air patrol
Capt	captain (military commissioned officer rank)
CAS	close air support
C-in-C	commander in chief
c/n	construction number
CO	commanding officer
COIN	counter-insurgency
Col	colonel (military commissioned officer rank)
Col Gen	colonel general (top military commissioned officer rank)
CZK	Czechoslovak Koruna (currency)
DM	Deutschmark
EAF	Egyptian Air Force (official designation from 1952–58)
EFUAC	Eastern Front United Arab Command
ELINT	electronic intelligence
FAL	Force Aérienne Libanaise (Lebanese Air Force)
Flg Off	flight officer (military commissioned officer rank, equivalent to lieutenant or first lieutenant)
Flt Lt	flight lieutenant (military commissioned officer rank, equivalent to captain)
FM	field marshal (top military commissioned officer rank)
GBP	British Pounds Sterling
Gen	general (military commissioned officer rank)
GOC	general officer commanding
GP	general-purpose (bomb)
Gp Capt	group captain (military commissioned officer rank, equivalent to colonel)
IAF	Indian Air Force
IAP	international airport

IDF	Israeli Defence Force
IDF/AF	Israeli Defence Force/Air Force
IrAF	Iraqi Air Force (official designation since 1958)
Il	Ilyushin (the design bureau led by Sergey Vladimirovich Ilyushin, also known as OKB-39)
KIA	killed in action
KSR-2	Soviet air-to-surface missile, ASCC codename AS-5 Kelt
Lt	lieutenant (military commissioned officer rank)
Lt Col	lieutenant colonel (military commissioned officer rank)
1st Lt	first lieutenant (military commissioned officer rank)
2nd Lt	second lieutenant (lowest military commissioned officer rank)
Maj	major (military commissioned officer rank)
Maj Gen	major general (military commissioned officer rank)
MBT	main battle tank
MiG	Mikoyan i Gurevich (the design bureau led by Artyom Ivanovich Mikoyan and Mikhail Iosifovich Gurevich, also known as OKB-155 or MMZ 'Zenit')
NWC	National Water Carrier (in Israel)
OC	officer in command
OCU	Operational Conversion Unit
OCU	Operational Training Unit
Plt Off	pilot officer (military commissioned officer rank, equivalent to 2nd lieutenant)
PoW	prisoner of war
QJJ	al-Quwwat al-Jawwiya al-Jaza'eriya (Algerian Air Force)
R-3S	Soviet short-range AAM, ASCC codename AA-2 Atoll
RAF	Royal Air Force (of the United Kingdom)
RJAF	Royal Jordanian Air Force
RSAF	Royal Saudi Air Force
SA-2 Guideline	ASCC codename for S-75 Dvina, Soviet SAM system
SAM	surface-to-air missile
SIGINT	signals intelligence
Sqn	squadron
Sqn Ldr	squadron leader (military commissioned officer rank, equivalent to major)
Su	Sukhoi (the design bureau led by Pavel Ossipovich Sukhoi, also known as OKB-51)
SyAAF	Syrian Arab Air Force
THK	Türk Hava Kuvvetleri (Turkish Air Force)
UAC	United Arab Command
UARAF	United Arab Republic Air Force – designation of Egyptian and Syrian air arms 1958–62, and of Egyptian air arm until 1969
UARAF	United Arab Republic Air Force (official designation 1958–69)
USAF	United States Air Force
USAFE	United States Air Forces in Europe
Wg Cdr	wing commander (military commissioned officer rank, equivalent to lieutenant colonel)

ADDENDA/ERRATA: ARAB MIGS, VOLS 1 & 2

The authors would like to make the following amendments and corrections to *Arab MiGs, Volumes 1 and 2.*

Volume 1, Chapter 1: First Egyptian MiGs

As in the case of *Volume 2*, *Volume 3* opens with a photograph of a Supermarine Spit-fire in Egyptian markings. Nour Bardai kindly provided another photograph from his collection – probably taken by the Egyptian military photographer Osman Mahmmoud and originally published in the *Egyptian Armed Forces* magazine – showing one of the Spitfire F.Mk 22s ordered by the then Royal Egyptian Air Force on 1 May 1950. Deliveries began later that year.

An EAF Spitfire F.Mk 22 photographed in 1954. At the time, this aircraft – serial number 700 – served with the Air Force Academy at Bilbeis and still wore the EAF national insignia in green and white. (Nour Bardai Collection)

Volume 1, Chapter 2: Early Syrian Jets, pp29–31

With the help of readers from Croatia, the authors managed to identify a group of foreign instructors that formerly served with the Syrian Arab Air Force (SyAAF) during the early years of its existence. Germany and Italy occupied the former Yugoslavia in 1941 and a pro-Axis government was installed to rule Croatia as the Nezavisna Drzava Hrvatska (NDH, or Independent State of Croatia). The NDH maintained its own armed forces, including an air force – Zrakoplovstvo NDH (ZNDH, Air Force of the NDH). During the summer of 1941, part of the ZNDH was trained in Germany, organised into the Kroatische Luftwaffen Legion (KLL, Croatian Air Force Legion), equipped with German aircraft and deployed on the Eastern Front against the USSR. Although reasonably well equipped and trained, the ZNDH and the KLL mainly consisted of former Royal Yugoslav Air Force personnel, many of whom disagreed with the official policies of their new superiors. This situation resulted in numerous defections to the anti-fascist side between 1941 and 1945, some pilots flying their aircraft to the parts of Yugoslavia held by Communist Partisans, others to parts of Italy held by the Allies, the USSR, or even to Turkey. Among the pilots who defected to the Soviet Union was the leading Croatian ace, Capt Mato Dukovac, who served with the KLL and scored 44 kills before defecting with his Bf 109 to the Soviet side, in September 1944. Dukovac served as a flight instructor with the Soviet Air Force before being handed over to the Partisans, in December of the same year. Back in Yugoslavia, he was instrumental in establishing and running the main Pilot Training Centre of the newly established Jugoslovensko Ratno Vazduhoplovstvo (JRV, Yugoslav Air Force), but was exposed to frequent abuse by Serbian officers, almost arrested and eventually defected to Italy, in August 1945. Late in 1947, Dukovac was contracted by the Syrian authorities to help train the future SyAAF. He gathered a small group of former ZNDH airmen from several detention camps and reception centres in Italy and then travelled to Lebanon, where they were based at the former RAF Estabel. Together with pilots named Josip Krasnik, Majetic and Corkalo, he served with the SyAAF as an instructor and also as an operational pilot during the first phase of the war with Israel, flying North American T-6 Texan trainers and various other aircraft. Dukovac emigrated to Toronto, Canada later the same year, and became a wealthy entrepreneur, while other pilots took to the Israeli side before returning to Italy in 1950.

Volume 1, Chapter 3: Suez War, 1956, p49

Our report in *Volume 1* concerning interceptions of RAF Canberras under way over Egypt by EAF MiGs, during the night to 30 October 1956, prompted the relative of one of the Egyptian pilots involved to contact the Group 73 historians. According to the recollection of the relative, one of two Canberras intercepted and damaged by Egyptian MiGs that night – either the bomber flown by Flt Lt Hunter or the example flown

 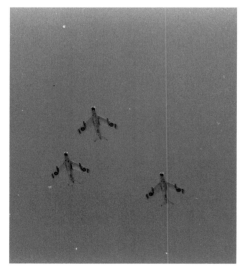

Taken in the course of a military parade in Cairo in June 1956, these two photographs show details of the lower surfaces of early EAF MiG-15bis. Notable are the very large roundels and the usual identification stripes. (Albert Grandolini Collection)

by Flg Off Campbell – was hit by the MiG-15bis flown by Flt Lt Sayd el-Qadi. Sadly, his superiors deemed el-Qadi's post-mission report untrustworthy and he was punished for 'lying'. It was only once the former British Prime Minister Anthony Eden published his memoirs – including the statement regarding intercepted and damaged Canberras, cited on p49 of *Volume 1* – that el-Qadi was rehabilitated and received a decoration. While it is certain that el-Qadi flew MiG-17s after the Suez War, nothing is known about his subsequent career.

Volume 1, Chapter 3: Suez War, 1956, p50

Albert Grandolini kindly provided the following photograph from an unknown IDF publication, showing the wreckage of the Piper PA-18 Super Cub light aircraft hit while on the ground in the course of an attack by Egyptian MiG-15s on Israeli forces near the Parker Memorial, at the eastern entrance to Mitla Defile, on the morning of 30 October 1956.

This photograph of Israeli Piper Cub serial number 47 (applied in white on the underside of the left wing) shows that the aircraft in question was not only 'damaged', as usually reported by Israeli sources in the West, but was completely destroyed. (IDF via Albert Grandolini)

Volume 1, Chapter 3: Suez War, 1956, p55

According to the book *Historique de l'Escadron de Chasse 1/3 'Navarre' de 1915 à 2000*, by Denis Albin, on the morning of 1 November 1956 Commandante André Pichoff of the French Air Force (Armée de l'Air – AdA), encountered a Gloster Meteor fighter of the Egyptian Air Force over Abu Suweir airfield while flying a Republic F-84F-51-GK Thunderstreak based in Israel. Pichoff did not manage to shot down his opponent, but quickly forced him to land. Nevertheless, AdA units equipped with F-84Fs and based in Israel seem to have scored one kill against an Egyptian Ilyushin Il-28 bomber later the same day. More precise details concerning both claims are unlikely to become available as it is understood that all documentation relating to AdA operations from Israeli bases has been destroyed in order to preserve the secrecy of this affair.

Further to the topic of air combats during the Suez War, the article 'USAFE's 38th TRS, 1952 to 1991', by Doug Gordon, published in *Air Enthusiast* in July/August 2007, reported the following:

'*On the fifth day of our rest* [after the 'gruelling' 40-minute flight from Brindisi to Larissa; authors' note], *we were taken to the Athens Int'l Airport, to be picked up by Maj Rufus Barnes (10th Tactical Recon Wing Ops) in* [a Douglas] *RB-26. While we were waiting to be picked up, standing in the shade of the US Naval Attaché's* [Grumman] *SA-16, 21 MiG-15s landed and were refuelled by Royal Dutch Petroleum's fuel trucks (with white sidewall tires, no doubt bought with US dollars …). The Russian pilots were wearing flight suits without insignia or other markings. After refuelling, they took off, bound for Cairo. Over the Med, British and French pilots, flying NATO fighters based on Cyprus, intercepted the Russians. Nineteen MiGs were shot down en route, one was shot down on final approach to Cairo Airport, and the other MiG landed and was strafed on the taxiway. While that was happening, we were making the turn over Marseille, heading home, when we got a radio call to proceed directly to Spangdahlem* [NATO air base in then West Germany], *and go directly to 38th TRS operations. (At that time, we did not know about the shoot-downs: we found that out after landing at Spang). For three days, 'the buzz' was that World War III was about to start. The Israeli Army had crossed the Suez, and was advancing toward Cairo. The Russian MiGs were supposed to assist the Egyptians, and counter the Israeli advance.*'

Whether something of this kind indeed ever happened, or if this story was based on (hugely exaggerated) claims for Egyptian MiGs actually destroyed by the British and French pilots on the ground, remains unclear.

Volume 1, Chapter 4: Follow-Ups, p95

According to an article in the contemporary Egyptian press, one of the crucial figures involved in the coup in Syria that resulted in the collapse of the union between Egypt and Syria (United Arab Republic), launched on 28 September 1961, was SyAAF/UARAF pilot (rank unknown) Haider el-Kasbary. El-Kasbary apparently recruited a group of around 500 Syrian officers and soldiers that participated in the plot (each officer was paid 5,000 Syrian Pounds and each solider 1,000 Syrian Pounds for participation; the source of the money was not mentioned) and flew the aircraft that bombed the residence of FM Amer in Damascus (Amer was not there at the time), which signalled the start of the coup. Next to nothing is currently known about el-Kasbary's subsequent fate.

Volume 1, Chapter 4: Follow-Ups, pp99–108 & Volume 2, Addenda/Errata, p29

The first photographs of the initial MiG-15UTI and (at least four) MiG-15bis that arrived in Algeria appeared on the Algerian Internet recently. They belong to a series taken in late 1962 at an unknown airfield in Libya, and depict aircraft donated to newly independent Algeria by Egypt.

Haider el-Kasbary in uniform before 1961, and as seen a few years later, while serving as a politician in Damascus. With the MiG-17F being the only combat aircraft type in service with the UARAF in Syria at the time, it is very likely that el-Kasbary flew such an aircraft when leading the coup of 28 September 1961. (Nour Bardai Collection)

A rear view of (freshly overhauled) MiG-15UTI serial number 6002, clearly showing the original form of the Algerian national markings – as well as the fact that these were applied at least on the upper surface of the left wing.
(Karim S. via Ahmed)

A fine view of the starboard side of MiG-15UTI serial number 6002, together with one of the Egyptian MiG-15bis donated to Algeria on the same occasion.
(Karim S. via Ahmed)

This photograph shows the scene to the left of MiG-15UTI serial number 6002, revealing three additional MiG-15bis.
(Karim S. via Ahmed)

During their flight to Algeria, the MiGs were 'escorted' by these two Egyptian Il-14s, which transported the associated ground equipment and weapons. They also acted as 'pathfinders' – providing navigation during the long journey over the vast deserts between Egypt and Algeria.
(Karim S. via Ahmed).

Volume 1, Chapter 4: Follow-Ups, p94; Volume 1, Chapter 5: Water War, p116; Volume 2, Chapter 3: Political Games, pp113–115 & Volume 2, Chapter 4: Mixed Fortunes, pp154–158

Patricia Salti, widow of 1st Lt Muwaffaq Salti of the Royal Jordanian Air Force (RJAF), and a leading historian of the RJAF, provided us with a number of additional facts concerning the history of that service, as collected from official files (including the No. 1 Squadron Diary, RJAF Yearly Diary and the Records of the Hashemite Dynasty, Transjordan 9), as well as interviews with dozens of participants.

- The first C-in-C of what was then the Arab Legion Air Force (ALAF, re-designated as the RJAF on 1 April 1956) was Wg Cdr Fisher (RAF). Fisher remained in charge from 1950 until 1953 (the first budget for the ALAF was granted in January 1951). Although Queen Zein of Jordan and the British authorities attempted to prevent Fisher from helping the youthful Crown Prince Hussein to develop an interest in flying, he continued doing so during his tenure in Jordan – on condition that the future King keep this strictly to himself.
- Wg Cdr Jock Dalgleish was posted as C-in-C ALAF in June 1953, replacing Fisher, but returned to the UK in January 1956. Like Fisher before him, Dalgleish had great influence over the young King and had therefore been told to do all he could to discourage him from taking up flying. However, Hussein persisted and successively soloed on an Auster, a de Havilland Dove and then a de Havilland Vampire under Dalgleish's supervision. Indeed, the King of Jordan subsequently demanded Dalgleish's secondment to the RJAF to be extended, but Glubb Pasha, then in command of the Arab Legion (as the Jordanian Army was named until 1956), demurred. Dalgleish was replaced by the first Jordanian C-in-C, Maj Ibrahim Othman. He did return to Jordan subsequently, but as commander of a detachment of six Hawker Hunters from No. 208 Squadron RAF, deployed to Amman during the Jordan Crisis in 1958.
- The first three Gomhouria trainers donated to Jordan by Egypt had arrived by 6 April 1956. These were followed by five Vampire FB.Mk 52s that arrived on 25 October 1956.

This rare photograph taken at Amman International Airport on 25 October 1956 shows five Vampire FB.Mk 52s of the Egyptian Air Force shortly after their donation to Jordan – which took place before the Suez Crisis. The aircraft at the front has the serial number 1548, the second in the row 1545. Sadly, the serial numbers of the other three examples remain unknown.
(Nour Bardai Collection)

- Following the Suez War of 1956 an attempt was made to establish a type of pan-Arab fighter jet unit, consisting of Algerian, Egyptian, Jordanian, Saudi Arabian and Syrian pilots. Five Jordanians were sent for this purpose to the SyAAF Academy in Aleppo, including Nasri Jumean, Firas Ajlouni, Marwan Zakkaria, Sharif Ghazi Sa'adeddin and Hussein Oweideh, where they trained together with eight Syrians (including the future President Hafez al-Assad), four Egyptians and an Algerian. Additionally, five Jordanian pilots were sent to Egypt for basic pilot training. However, following a coup attempt against King Hussein, plotted by pan-Arabist Gen Ali Abu Nowar (appointed as head of the Jordanian Army only few weeks before), on 10 April 1957, relations between Jordan and Syria cooled and all the Jordanians were recalled, returning home in June and July of the same year.

- When two UARAF MiG-17s flown by Syrian pilots intercepted the de Havilland Dove of the Royal Flight RJAF, flown by Wg Cdr Dalgleish and King Hussein of Jordan, on 14 November 1958, they opened fire, forcing Dalgleish to enter a series of very tight turns, and finally descend to critically low levels in order to escape back towards Jordanian airspace. Curiously enough, just six months later, in May 1959, both of the Syrian pilots involved defected to Jordan and requested political asylum. They said they had been told not to open fire without permission, and when they had requested this, Damascus remained silent. On returning to their base, they were accused of allowing King Hussein to escape – and were ostracised. Jordan provided them with shelter, but only a week later one of the Syrians pleaded to return home to see his family. Dalgleish warned him of the probable consequences but the young pilot crossed the border by night, illegally. In the words of Dalgleish, *'he never saw the sunrise'*.

- In August 1960, following the assassination of Jordanian Prime Minister Hazza'a al-Majali, King Hussein wanted to launch a reprisal attack on Syria (then the 'Eastern Province' of the United Arab Republic). In the course of preparations for this operation, he entered secret negotiations with Israel, in order to secure his western flank, while RJAF Hunter and Vampire pilots were redeployed to H-5 airfield and briefed for attacks on the UARAF air bases in Syria. No. 3 Squadron was scheduled to attack Almazza and Aleppo, while No. 1 Squadron was to hit Dmeyr. Jordanian pilots flew corresponding practice sorties, with training flights over similar distances and ground-attack work. The planning for this operation was largely complete by 8 September 1960, when two brigades of the Jordanian Army were concentrated on the border, together with armour and artillery support. This operation was cancelled under British pressure, several days later, but RAF pilots seconded to the RJAF at the time later said they had no idea of what was going on and never received any corresponding briefings.

- A UARAF MiG-17 that took off from Syria crash-landed in northern Jordan on 27 September 1960, followed by another that came down in the desert southwest of Amman on 4 October 1960. The pilot of the first fighter had been injured and was taken into custody, but later returned to Syria. The pilot of the second MiG – which, according to the Records of the Hashemite Dynasty, was equipped for photo-reconnaissance – Adnan Madani (or Adnan Malki, according to other sources), said he was on a training flight from Dmeyr airfield and mistook the old Kirkuk-Haifa pipeline for its Kirkuk-Banias branch, thus becoming entirely disoriented. The pilot was taken into custody and handed over to the RJAF, where he requested political asylum. He was housed in one of No. 1 Squadron's rooms at Mafraq airfield (or at Amman IAP, according to other sources) for several months. Unfortunately, because of pressure upon his family in Syria, he committed suicide while there, as recalled by Zeid Toukan, a former RJAF Hunter pilot:

'*Adnan Malki crash-landed his MiG-17 southwest of Amman. He told me that he had got lost and followed heading 140 instead of 040. He was in the Officers' Mess for a couple of months. I often used to see him sitting and thinking. He died in a strange way. I was flying, the rest of the guys were in the Old Officers' Mess where there was a tennis court. Every pilot carried a gun with him. They decided to go and play tennis so left everything in their rooms. Adnan went with them to the tennis court, then said he wanted to go back to his room to read. He went into Kamal Haddad's room, took his gun and killed himself. Everybody was thoroughly investigated and I was asked if I knew the man before ... Kamal was fired from the Air Force; he joined Alia Airlines and was killed in the* [Handley Page] *Dart Herald that exploded in the air on the way to Beirut ... Radio Cairo later said that we killed the pilot. Actually, the Syrians had no idea what had happened, and Adnan said that he definitely did not want to defect ... His MiG was recovered, put into a hangar, dismantled* [both the British and the Americans had

These two photographs, provided by Air Cdre John Greenhill RAF (OC RAF Training Team and Air Adviser to King Hussein) via Patricia Salti show the scene of what is now a forgotten drama that occurred southwest of Amman on 4 October 1960, when a UARAF MiG-17F flown by Adnan Madani made a belly-landing. The aircraft is obviously wearing full UARAF markings – including identification stripes around the wingtips and the rear fuselage – but also still has its original Syrian serial number, 48, applied in black on the forward fuselage.
(Greenhill via Patricia Salti)

a chance to thoroughly examine it], *then put together again and returned to Syria by road, something like a year later.'*

- The last official flight of a single-seat RJAF Vampire took place on 17 April 1962, followed by the last flight of a two-seat Vampire T.Mk 11 on 14 July 1962. Subsequently, No. 3 Squadron was disbanded and its former mounts sold for scrap.
- The defection of a number of RJAF pilots to Egypt occurred on 10 November 1962. The affair began with King Hussein's decision to deploy 62 Jordanian troops together with a shipment of 12,000 Lee-Enfield rifles to the Saudi-Yemeni frontier, in support of the Yemeni Royalists. This was despite the lack of public support for such an action in Jordan. Additionally, on 10 November 1962, eight Hunters and a single Dove of the RJAF were deployed to Taif in Saudi Arabia. This decision backfired badly when the recently appointed C-in-C RJAF, Col Sahel Hamzeh, flew the Dove, while pilots Sandoukah and Saima flew two Hunters, not to Taif, but to Egypt instead. Barely 24 hours later, two other pilots – including al-Shra' – defected in their Hunters, flying these straight from Amman to Egypt. The following account from one of the RJAF Hunter pilots involved was provided on condition of anonymity:

'Nasri Jumean, Firas Ajlouni, Jihad Irsheid, Wasfi Ammari, Kamal Haddad and Zeid Toukan ferried six Hunters to Taif and were briefed for an attack sortie expected to be flown the next morning. Before leaving Jordan we were not allowed to talk to anyone about this mission ... I thought it a bit ridiculous as the only weapons for our aircraft were guns: we had only rockets with dummy warheads. Furthermore, when we calculated the route to the targets, we found out we could get there – but not get back. Therefore, our superiors told us to continue for Aden, as the RAF had been briefed to accept RJAF aircraft. Alternatively, we could bail out over friendly tribes ... Jamal Said, who was going to Amman the next day, then told us he would try and persuade our superiors to change the plans: if they did, he would stay in Amman the next day, and if not, he would be back in the afternoon. In the meantime, we continued planning our mission, and flew some orientation flights around Taif [his logbook shows a 55-minute flight; authors' note]. *The afternoon came and Sahel did not return, and we all thought, 'Thank God'. Then, between 18.00 and 19.00 a message came from Amman asking if Sahel had arrived. They thought he must have crashed somewhere under way ... then we heard on the radio that Sahel had defected to Egypt. Our attack was postponed for 48 hours ... The Royal Saudi Air Force was not allowed to fly for political reasons and we were subsequently surrounded by Saudi troops as they thought that all the RJAF pilots in Saudi Arabia would defect too. The CO of the Jordanian Army contingent in Saudi Arabia, Brig Omar al-Madaneh, came in the evening after Sahel's defection and gave us a speech about loyalty, etc. The next evening, after the other two pilots defected, he came back to give us the same speech again. Prime Minister Wasfi Tell had to fly to Taiz to urge the other pilots to fly our planes to Jordan, not to Egypt. Eventually, we returned back to Mafraq on 21 November, feeling like dirt ...'*

Eventually, King Hussein offered amnesty to the pilots that defected while Nasser, on Hussein's request, released all three aircraft. As mentioned in *Volume 2*, at least three of the pilots nevertheless joined the UARAF: one served as a fighter-controller, Tahsin Saima reached the rank of major general, while Harib Arif Sandoukah retired as a colonel due to illness.

- No. 2 Squadron was disbanded as a Hunter-equipped unit on 11 April 1964, and all of its personnel, aircraft and equipment joined No. 1 Squadron, then under the command of Capt Firas Ajlouni, with Capt Nasri Jumean as deputy CO. This unit was further reorganised into the Prince Abdullah Flight (CO 1st Lt Zeid Toukan) and the Prince Feisal Flight (CO 1st Lt Jihad Irsheid).

- After a series of coups in Iraq in 1963, a number of Iraqi Air Force pilots defected to Jordan in the same year. At least one of them, Aboud Salem, joined the RJAF and served as the C-in-C from 1973 until 1976.

- In 1964 the RJAF began assembling its own napalm tanks. These were created by using old drop tanks (apparently left behind from RAF times, and previously used by de Havilland Venoms). According to Zeid Toukan and Hamid Anwar, all the pilots of No. 1 Squadron refused to fly aircraft equipped with such weapons, considering them too dangerous – until Anwar not only did so, but also performed aerobatics with these weapons attached. Later on, these weapons were demonstrated to Egyptian representatives on two occasions – the Egyptians thinking that the pilots flying the Hunters were British.

- The four RJAF Hunter pilots involved in an air combat with four Israeli Dassault Mirage IIICJs on 21 December 1964 were:
    - Red Section
      1st Lt George Matta
      1st Lt Bader Zaza
    - Blue Section
      Capt Firas Ajlouni
      1st Lt Ghazi Smadi

They claimed a total of no fewer than three kills, as George Matta explains:

'At 11.15, the phone in the ops room rang and an order to scramble was given from GOC [general officer commanding]. We were airborne five minutes later. The radar took control and directed us to the Hebron area … at medium altitude. At 11.40 another pair was scrambled and [was] asked to go to the Amman area. Meanwhile, Red Section was told by the GCI that a pair of bogies was inside the border, at their 6 o'clock. Red Section turned hard to face the enemy. During the turn, the enemy fired at Red 2 but missed. I called the Blue Section to head in their direction and informed them that they were engaged with a pair of enemy Mirages. After the enemy fired, and since the enemy fighters were at high speed, the deflection was too much for us to hold and they passed through my line of flight. I saw them turning so I reversed into them. Enemy no. 2 split – their split was disorganised: the one that went low, the enemy formation leader, started to turn which helped us and I tried to get him in a scissors, although I knew a Mirage could handle very well at low speed. I dropped my speed fairly rapidly and asked my no. 2 to watch the high one. I had too much deflection at 600ft [183m] distance but the enemy reversed and helped me close the distance and reduce the deflection angle. I aimed and fired at 400ft [122m] and saw him go out of control – or that is what I thought. His wings rocked and suddenly the aircraft went down in a screaming dive, vertically. I followed him but he disappeared in a patch of stratus … At 3,000ft [914m] above the ground his angle of dive was still vertically down, so I reversed to see what happened to the other one. I saw him climbing and my no. 2 behind him, but knowing the speed of my no. 2 was low, I knew he

could not remain behind the enemy. Bader Zaza fired as the range increased. By then we were low on fuel and Bader also out of ammo, and thus we disengaged … Firas and Ghazi meanwhile reached the Dead Sea approaching from northeast. They sighted another pair of Mirages. Post mission debrief brought a conclusion that we shot down three of them and one force-landed at Lydda …'

The following day Israeli newspapers reported that Jordanian fighters had penetrated Israeli airspace. An RAF flight lieutenant was in Ajloun radar station (installed and equipped by the Marconi company of the UK and officially named 'Prince Mohammed') at the time, and he confirmed that the Israeli jets were actually over the West Bank, and thus within Jordanian airspace. As Matta later explained, the IDF/AF pilots often 'cut the corner' over the southern West Bank when returning from exercises flown over the Negev Desert.

- During 1964 the RJAF painted the noses and large portions of the fins of its Hunters red. The reason for this was the establishment of the United Arab Command (UAC) and related measures, one of which was to make Arab aircraft easier to identify in air combat – especially if different Arab air arms were to encounter each other in combat over Israel. It was for these reasons that the Iraqis, the Lebanese and Syrians also painted large parts of the noses, fins, and wingtips of their aircraft in red.
- Regarding the loss of two Hunters in 1964 and 1965, the first of these occurred during the course of an air combat training sortie involving Pakistani Air Force instructor Hamid Anwar. The RJAF pilot killed in this incident was 1st Lt Amer Zaza. According to Anwar:

  'We were up to 10,000ft [3,048m]. *He went into a jerky motion and then went into a spin, came out, went into a dive and pulled back much too hard. The aircraft stalled and I told him to bail out. He was at 4,000–5,000ft [1,219–1,524m] by then. He kept on going. Finally, he bailed out but too late. When the aircraft hit the ground, the debris flew up and hit him …'*

  The Hunter T.Mk 66 that crashed in 1965 came down near the road from Amman to Mafraq airfield, shortly after the first RAF Red Arrows display in Jordan. The aircraft hit the ground with such force that there were barely any recognisable pieces of aircraft wreckage or human remains.
- On 28 March 1965 two RJAF Hunters – piloted by Firas Ajlouni and Jihad Irsheid – flew a reconnaissance sortie over Syria, to investigate the extent of damage caused by previous Israeli attacks on the construction site for the diversion of the River Jordan. Syrian ground units opened fire but neither aircraft was hit. The Syrians 'returned the favour' in a much more provocative style – and on at least two occasions. On 21 September 1966 four MiG-17s passed over Mafraq airfield, and on 16 October 1966 a pair of MiG-17s attacked the dummy radar station nearby.

Volume 1, Chapter 6: Yemen

Martin Smisek, who is himself working through files in the National Archives of the Czech Republic, as well as various local publications related to arms deliveries to the Middle East (including 'Ilyushin Il-10/Avia B.33 Ground Attack Aircraft in the Czechoslovak Air Force, 1950–1963', by M. Irra, published in *Jakab* magazine, Volume 2/2009), has kindly provided the following insight into Czechoslovak cooperation with the Imamate of Yemen (later North Yemen, now the Yemen Republic) during the 1950s and 1960s:

On 23 February 1956 a Czechoslovak business delegation left Cairo and arrived in Yemen via Djibouti. During their stay in Sana'a, Czechoslovak representatives were, among others, asked about possible deliveries of weapons for the Yemeni Army. Around the same time, the Yemenis discussed the same topic with Moscow. Thus, in March 1956 the Soviets officially informed the Czechoslovak prime minister that they would deliver arms to Yemen and would like to repeat the 'Egyptian pattern' on this occasion. Czechoslovakia should play the role of Soviet middleman again. Prague gave consent to its function in April 1956. In June of the same year Moscow informed Czechoslovak officials that the USSR would fulfil all Yemeni requests and Czechoslovakia would secure the 'camouflage' only.

The situation changed abruptly in July 1956 when Soviet representatives at the meeting in Prague announced that Moscow would provide only 60 per cent of the requested weapons. The rest would be obtained from Czechoslovakia. Theoretically, Prague would have had no issue with this decision, apart from the fact that the Soviets offered very 'exclusive' conditions – in terms of very lucrative prices and terms of payment – to Imam Ahmad Ben-Yahya Hamid. The essence of the problem was that the price Yemen was to pay was lower than the manufacturing costs. The original value of all the equipment, armament and ammunition ordered was put at 52.9 million CZK (or 10.8 million Soviet Roubles) – but Yemen was to pay only around 15 million CZK (or 3.1 million Roubles), which equated to no more than 30 per cent of the entire value of the consignment.

Unsurprisingly, such conditions led to some dissent in Prague, but this was pushed aside by Soviet pressure. A corresponding contract with Sana'a was signed in Prague on 11 July 1956 (a contract for the re-export of Soviet arms between Czechoslovakia and the USSR was signed on 14 August 1956). This envisaged the delivery of the following items:

- 24 Avia B-33 attack aircraft (Czechoslovak-manufactured Ilyushin Il-10s), together with spare parts, ammunition and ground support (for a photograph of one of these aircraft, see *Volume 1*, p129)
- Zlin Z-126 Trener 2 training aircraft
- 30 T-34/85 tanks (licence-built in Czechoslovakia)
- 50 SD-100 self-propelled guns (Soviet SU-100 assault guns, licence-built in Czechoslovakia)
- 100 BTR-40 armoured personnel carriers (manufactured in the USSR)
- 100 M1939 anti-aircraft cannon of 37mm calibre
- 100 M1942 field guns of 76mm calibre
- 12 M1931/37 field guns of 122mm calibre
- Large quantities of rifles, machine guns, mortars, bazookas and ammunition

As expected in Prague, Sana'a soon proved unable to pay its dues. The contract of 11 July 1956 was to be paid in several instalments between 1957 and 1966. However, Yemen paid only 15.9 million CZK and thus in March 1966 an amendment to the original contract was signed in Prague, according to which Yemen was to pay the full price by 1972. This payment never materialised, prompting the Central Committee of the

Czechoslovak Party to decide that any future deals with Yemen could only be realised if the Yemenis were to pay in advance.

Nevertheless, the above-mentioned weapons were delivered to Yemen during the first half of 1957. Specifically, a total of 20 B-33s and four CB-33 conversion trainers arrived on 18 May 1957. Right from the start, this type proved entirely unsuitable for operations under local conditions. High temperatures and the high altitude of the local airfield presented nearly insurmountable obstacles and by 4 June the officers who arrived together with the aircraft reported that the Avias were unsuitable for operations under 'hot and high' conditions, and not a single aircraft became operational. An additional problem was the fact that the delivered aircraft had already been crated for some time. Furthermore, there was a latent lack of support materials and equipment, as well as spare parts. Taken together, these factors had a very negative effect upon the introduction to service and on the technical status of the delivered aircraft. Unsurprisingly, as of 13 December 1957, only nine B-33s and two CB-33s had been assembled.

Because of a lack of any operational and maintenance experience on the Yemeni side, Czechoslovakia and the USSR decided to send an additional team of 28 Czechoslovak and 12 Soviet advisors to Yemen in September 1957. The instruction of Yemeni officers was quite short-lived, however. Czechoslovak specialists then became primarily the repairmen for the military material that had been delivered. In January 1958 a new Czechoslovak team arrived, together with materiel and equipment necessary to complete the assembly of all the delivered aircraft. However, according to the recollections of one of the participants, Maj Jiři Sedlář, once again, they proved unable to bring any of the aircraft to operational condition. Indeed, a number of airframes remained stored within their transport crates.

Around the same time, Imam Ahmad requested delivery of additional equipment, including four Il-14 transports, 100 trucks, 40 cars and 10 buses – and an extension and expansion of the presence of Czechoslovak advisors. Prague promptly informed Moscow of this request, but no response was forthcoming and no such transfer materialised.

A delegation of the new Yemeni government visited Prague in November 1962 and – among other things – requested the delivery of 20 Yakovlev Yak-11 training aircraft and additional armament. Once again, a corresponding deal did not materialise.

A row of B-33s as delivered by Czechoslovakia to Yemen in 1956, and found by the Egyptians following their intervention in 1962. As revealed by official Czechoslovak documentation, hardly any of these aircraft was ever flown and none ever became operational.
(Nour Bardai Collection)

A new Czechoslovak military mission arrived in Yemen in January 1963. In its report, the leader of this mission stated that the delivered arms were '... *fully deployed and serve in combat against foreign interventionist forces ...*' This was not entirely true, however, at least not in regard to the B-33 attack aircraft, which proved entirely unsuitable for conditions in Yemen. Furthermore, the operations of the other types of major armament provided were greatly hampered by a lack of spare parts.

In March 1964 a delegation from Sana'a led by Abed Abdullah al-Sallal, President of Yemen, arrived in Czechoslovakia to present a new request for arms. In the course of corresponding negotiations, it became obvious that the remaining Z-126 trainers were non-operational. Eventually, Czechoslovakia agreed to provide a shipment of obsolete arms as a gift to the Yemeni armed forces, including:

- 3,000 Type 41S machine guns (Soviet-made PPSh-41, 7.62mm calibre)
- 18 Type 52 cannon (Czechoslovak-made anti-tank guns, 85mm calibre)
- 12 Type 43 mortars (Soviet-made mortar, 160mm calibre, licence-built in Czechoslovakia) – as well as ammunition for these weapons, 20 tents and thousands of light aviation bombs

Because of the above-mentioned difficulties with payments, this proved to be the last such order for several years. More details relating to this topic will follow in future volumes of this series.[1]

Volume 1, Chapter 6: June 1967 War, pp164–166

An additional photograph of a UARAF MiG-17F destroyed by the Israelis in el-Arish, on the morning of 5 June 1967, surfaced recently. It shows the burnt-out hulk of MiG-17F serial number 2235 and construction number N3222 (not N1222, as previously reported). The latter was stencilled in blue near the top of the fin and on the rudder.

The burnt-out hulk of MiG-17F serial number 2235. A contemporary report published in *Flight International* magazine described the scene as follows: *'The two MiG-17s parked in front of two QRA pens flanking the runway threshold have been caught on the ground, their battery trolleys still hooked up, and destroyed. Several other MiGs were caught inside their revetments and destroyed. Dummy wooden MiGs were not hit. Captured at this airfield was one Yak-18, manually damaged by Egyptians during their withdrawal.'[2]* (IDF via Albert Grandolini)

Volume 1, Chapter 7: June 1967 War, p148 & Volume 2, Addenda, p40

Searching further through his archive, Nour Bardai found an article and the accompanying photograph of the crash site of John Mechan's C-82A Packet, as published in Egypt in late 1964. According to the article in question, Mechan's aircraft entered Egyptian airspace over Sinai after passing over Eilat, in Israel, at 10.05 on 23 December

1964 (not 10 December, as previously reported). It was intercepted by two MiG-21s, the pilots of which called the crew on international frequencies and requested them to land at Cairo IAP. The Americans failed to reply on radio but after seeing appropriate hand-signals, acted as if following instructions and lowered the landing gear. On finals to Cairo IAP the C-82 suddenly turned away, retracted the landing gear and attempted to flee in the direction of Alexandria. Although receiving an order to open fire and shoot down the intruder, the two UARAF MiG-21 pilots initially fired in front of the civilian transport. When it failed to react, they fired three times at the engines. According-ing to the same article, the badly damaged Packet crashed near the village of Halek al-Gamil, between Marbut and Abu Hamas, in northern Egypt.

The wreckage of John Mechan's C-82A Packet, as photographed for the Egyptian press on the afternoon of 23 December 1964. (Nour Bardai Collection)

Volume 1, Appendix VII, p219 & p229

Marc Koelich kindly provided the following photograph scanned by Marco Pennings from the book *Last Tiger Out: The True Story of Dan Maukar, Ace Pilot in the Indo-nesian Air Force*, by Jan S. Doward:

Three Indonesian cadets during their training at Bilbeis Air Force Academy in Egypt, in front of an Egyptian Air Force MiG-15bis with a full set of markings as previously explained in *Volume 1*. Daniel Maukar is probably first on the right (and is also to be seen at the top right of the photograph on p229 of *Volume 1*).
(Marco Pennings via Marc Koelich)

Volume 2, Addenda/Errata, p43

Several readers noted an error in the caption to the photograph on p43 in *Volume 2* showing the landing of an Egyptian Il-28 as well as a short take-off and landing aircraft in the foreground. The latter aircraft is not a Morane-Saulnier M.S.502 as indicated, but a Czechoslovak-built Aero L-60 Brigadyr. Developed by Ondrey Nemec in 1951 on the basis of the K-65 Cap – the Czechoslovak variant of the legendary German-made Fieseler Fi 156 Storch – the aircraft first flew in 1953 and was manufactured from 1955 well into the 1960s. At least a handful of the 273 Brigadyrs produced in total were exported to Egypt and Syria.

The L-60 Brigadyr still bore close resemblance to the design of the legendary Fi 156 Storch, from which it was developed. The upper artwork shows the livery of Egyptian Brigadyrs on their delivery in 1958, while the lower shows the colours and markings they wore during the 1960s. (Jameel Patel)

Volume 2, Chapter 1: Turbulent Times in Iraq, p49

Photographs of a FAL Savoia-Marchetti SM.79L taken during a visit by a Lebanese delegation to Iraq in 1957, provided by Vatche Mitilian and published in *Volume 2*, reminded Albert Grandolini of an incident that occurred on 19 November 1959. On that day Israeli jets intercepted FAL SM.79L L-112 and forced it to land in Haifa. The aircraft and its crew were released and returned to Lebanon two weeks later.

This photograph was taken when a replacement FAL crew was signing papers for the release of the SM.79L, minutes before they assumed responsibility for the aircraft, on 6 December 1959. (JSS/Keystone 1028/704889, via Albert Grandolini)

Volume 2, Chapter 2: Compromised Solutions, pp83–96

Two readers from the German language area made us aware that Austrian engineer Dr Ferdinand Brandner published his memoirs in the form of a now little-known book entitled *Ein Leben Zwischen Fronten: Ingenieur im Schußfeld der Weltpolitik* (Life Between the Front Lines: an Engineer in the Line of Fire; Wels-München: Verlag Welsermühl, 1973; ISBN 3-85339-125-7). Although not dealing with technical details in the depth that might be expected today, Chapter 5 of this work contains an extensive recollection of Brandner's experiences in Egypt.

At the start of that chapter, Brandner specifies that the first effort to develop an 'indigenous' Egyptian fighter was launched by the government of Gen Nequib, immediately after the revolution of 1952, when an appropriate contract was signed with Prof Ernst Heinkel. All the work was undertaken in Stuttgart, in the then West Germany, in the following two years. A large Egyptian team was also trained by Germans. However, this project was cancelled in 1954 (not in 1957, as originally reported), due to irrevocable differences between Heinkel and the Egyptians, and despite the fact that the then considerable sum of DM18 million (then around GBP1.515 million) had already been spent.

Regarding the acquisition of Hispano Aviacion HA-200 Saeta jet trainers, Brandner noted that Egypt originally purchased the licence for manufacture of this type in 1959 (as the HA-200B al-Kahira), together with 40 Turboméca Marboré II engines made in France, but that deliveries of the latter were subsequently cancelled due to pressure from Paris (evidently related to what were then excellent relations between France and Israel).

A scan from Brandner's book, showing the engine-testing facilities at Factory 135, constructed in Helwan in late 1960 and early 1961. (Courtesy Brandner Collection/ Verlag Welsermühl)

According to Brandner, Messerschmitt originally envisaged the use of Bristol Orpheus BOr 12 engines for the HA-300, until informed that the further development of this engine had been cancelled in 1959. In reaction to a corresponding Egyptian request, the Bristol company demanded an up-front payment of GBP5 million to resume this work, announcing that in such a case it would deliver the first two engines in 1962 at a unit price of GBP110,000.[3] The British then announced that they expected the Orpheus BOr 12 to be ready for series production by 1966, at a revised total price of GBP5.9 million – a licence contract was to be negotiated separately.

Since such conditions appear to have been entirely unacceptable for Egypt, Messerschmitt established contact with Brandner instead. In April 1960 he asked Brandner if he would be interested in developing engines for aircraft that were to be built in Egypt. During his first trip to Egypt, Brandner met AM Mahmoud Sidki Mahmoud, Defence Minister Abd el-Wahab el-Bishry, Col Mahmoud Khalil (chief of the UARAF Intelligence since 1952) and Hassan Sayed Kamil to discuss the chances of realising such an ambitious idea, and visited two military factories near Helwan that already manufactured small arms and ammunition.[4] Following additional negotiations a decision was taken by which Brandner and Kamil would establish a joint stock company named MTP, based in Zurich, Switzerland. Aided by this company, Brandner recruited a team of 150 experienced Austrian and German engineers in June 1960 (at least 10 of these were from East Germany, while some previously worked for the French company SNECMA). This team was expected to spend the following four years in Egypt, where it would develop a light turbojet designated E-200.

Brandner's team moved to Egypt from 1 October 1960 and immediately began work on establishing several developmental departments as well as supervising the construction of corresponding works and test sites in Helwan. These facilities became known as Factory 135. Within two months, advanced installations – equipped with more than 500 pieces of the best machinery, including an annealing furnace, instruments and rigs purchased from the US, UK, Germany and Switzerland – were constructed and in use. They employed a total of 350 foreign and Egyptian specialists.[5]

A rare colour photograph of the prototype HA-300V1, apparently taken on the day of its first rollout, in July 1963.
(Albert Grandolini Collection)

The first prototype of the E-200 turbojet entered its testing phase in July 1962, when Nasser visited Brandner's team and factory for the first time. Most of the developmental work was completed by the time Nasser visited the works for the second time, accompanied by Algerian President Ahmed Ben Bella, in July 1963. However, subsequent development proceeded at a much slower pace, mainly due to the effects of Cairo's newly introduced economic policies (which brought the country to the verge of bankruptcy by 1965), but also due to nepotism, favouritism and jealousy between various groups within the UARAF. Furthermore, there were a series of mistaken decisions by both the UARAF and the Messerschmitt team regarding the HA-300. For example, the original HA-300 was designed with a top speed of Mach 1 in mind and was test-flown as such in 1964. In a rush to get their airframe airborne and without consulting Brandner, Messerschmitt's team (Factory 36) purchased 25 unnecessary Bristol 705 engines at considerable expense. Only five of these were ever used while the rest were not even unpacked before ending up in a scrap yard, in 1969.

Furthermore, by the time Kapil Bhargava flew the prototype HA-300V1 for the first time, Egypt had increased the maximum speed requirement to Mach 2 and then to Mach 2.5. Construction of the corresponding variant, the prototype V3, was therefore only launched in 1964, with the intention of a first flight in 1969. Brandner's team had to adapt the E-200 correspondingly, but nevertheless planned to have the resulting E-300 turbojet with appropriate capabilities ready by 1965.

Finally, the 'pro-Soviet' clique within the UARAF began complaining about all manner of imaginary issues relating to the HA-200 and HA-300. In reality there were no such problems, and although by that time not a single Egyptian pilot had flown the HA-300, this intimidation campaign was eventually successful where both projects were concerned. As a result, the projects related to the development of E-200 and E-300 engines fell out of favour in Cairo.

It was under such circumstances that the original contract between MTP and the Egyptian government expired on 1 July 1965. Unnerved by negative reports he was receiving from Cairo, Kamil then unilaterally – without consulting Brandner – terminated MTP's contracts with all foreigners working in Factory 135, and bankrupted the company. However, the Austrian instead opened negotiations with the government, resulting in the conclusion of a new agreement with a term of four years (apparently, Messerschmitt's team subsequently did the same).

According to Brandner, Kamil's decision also brought severe disruption to cooperation between Factory 135 and India, although AM Sidki Mahmoud had already agreed to take one of the Hindustan HF-24 prototypes – together with an entire team of Indian engineers and support personnel – to Egypt, for testing purposes. The Soviets also attempted to force the MiG-21 on Cairo, in the same way that they were exercising pressure upon New Delhi to buy the same type instead of the HF-24 developed by Dr Kurt Tank. Nevertheless, the HF-24 made its first flight powered by the E-300 on 29 March 1967 (Brandner recalled the year as 1966), piloted by Sqn Ldr I. M. Chopra, in the course of an official visit by AM Sidki Mahmoud and Dr Kurt Tank.[6]

Meanwhile, to further the testing of the E-300, Brandner and his team adapted an Antonov An-12 transport as a test-rig. As photographs published on p94 of *Volume 2* show, the Ivchenko AI-20M no. 1 engine (left inboard) – co-developed by Brandner during his detention in the USSR, from 1946 until 1955 – was replaced by a nacelle incorporating one E-300 prototype. Lacking technical drawings and the necessary documentation, Brander and his engineers adapted the aircraft on their own.

Finally, in regards to the reasons behind the Egyptian decision to cancel the HA-300 and E-300 projects, as well as the Indian decision to cancel the project to re-engine the HF-24 with the E-300, Brandner concluded that this *'must'* have been related to *'corruption'* and *'Russian pressure'*. The Austrian stated that he could not understand either of these decisions, when in his opinion there were no technical reasons for them – nothing else but the Soviet wish to impress the MiG-21 upon India, and do something similar in the case of Egypt. As result, the June 1967 War *'only delivered the nail into the coffin'* of this massive effort for which the government in Cairo spent at least GBP6 million in total between 1960 and 1969.

The E-300 on a test rig. The prototype engine completed over 2,000 test-hours without any major problems, and Brandner was convinced that it could power the HA-300V3 up to the required speed of Mach 2.5 once the airframe became available for flight-testing in 1969. As described by Wg Cdr Bhargava in an interview published in *Volume 2*, that prototype never progressed beyond a few ground runs. (Courtesy Brandner Collection/ Verlag Welsermühl)

Volume 2, Chapter 3: Political Games, pp113–114 & pp117–121

Searching further through his extensive archive, Nour Bardai found a collection of articles and photographs related to the series of coup attempts that occurred in Iraq in 1963, and which saw extensive involvement of the IrAF, as described in *Volume 2*.

Scanned from a contemporary Egyptian newspaper, this grainy photograph shows the damage to the Ministry of Defence building in Baghdad caused by No. 6 Squadron Hunters and No. 7 Squadron MiG-17s of the IrAF in the course of some 60 attack sorties flown during the coup of 8 February 1963. (Nour Bardai Collection)

This photograph shows Capt Munthir al-Windawy while entering Baghdad to be greeted as a hero after playing a crucial role in the coup against Qasim's government. Following his participation in the February 1963 coup, al-Windawy became a kind of star – especially for the Iraqi youth – comparable to modern-day 'pop icons'. (Nour Bardai Collection)

Volume 2, Chapter 4: Mixed Fortunes, p160

Nour Bardai also found the following photographs published following the defection of a Royal Saudi Air Force (RSAF) C-123B Provider to Egypt on 1 October 1962. According to accompanying captions, the transport took off from Jeddah, shortly after midnight, and was under way for Ma'arab when the crew of three decided to fly it to Egypt.

RSAF pilot Hamad Zahrani flew the C-123B Provider to Aswan in Egypt.
(Nour Bardai Collection)

RSAF pilot Mohammad Abdel Wahab backed Zahrani's defection to Egypt and supported his effort to reach Aswan.
(Nour Bardai Collection)

Egyptian officials inspect the cargo of the RSAF C-123B flown to Aswan. This consisted of 110 US-made Garand rifles and ammunition destined for Yemeni Royalists.
(Nour Bardai Collection)

Volume 2, Chapter 4: Mixed Fortunes, p170

Maj Gen Ihsan Shurdom (RJAF, ret.) and Mrs Salti further provided their extensive notes about the air combat which occurred on 13 November 1966, during the Israeli raid on Samu village, some 60km (37 miles) southwest of Jerusalem. These are based on Shurdom's own recollections and logbook (Shurdom was 24 years old and a graduate of RAF Cranwell at that time), exclusive interviews with two of the pilots who were involved (Jasser Zayyad and Yasser Ajami) and official documentation:

'Ihsan Shurdom and my late husband, Muwaffaq Salti, were the duty pilots. Muwaffaq was the pair leader. They were strapped in their aircraft and ready to scramble from Mafraq AB immediately should the need arise. Jasser Zayyad was in the third Hunter, acting as spare, and Nasri Jumean was in the fourth Hunter. George Matta and Hanna Najjar manned the third pair of Hunters, but they were never ordered into the air.

'Muwaffaq was actually not scheduled to fly that morning. However, shortly before the order for take-off came, Nasri was told that the C-in-C RJAF – Col Saleh Kurdi – wanted him on the phone. He had to leave the aircraft and Muwaffaq took his place ... for unrelated reasons, Kurdi did not want Nasri to fly but ordered him to control from the ground instead.

'Capt Firas Ajlouni and 1st Lt Zohair Thabsum served as controllers at Ajloun that morning. Their radar detected the Israeli aircraft quite early and they reported accordingly to Kurdi in the HQ, but he replied that these must be clouds. Firas called Kurdi three more times, but every time received a reply that there was no information about Israeli activity over the West Bank. It was only once Prime Minister Wasfi Tell reported that Jordan was under attack that the RJAF went into action.

'This is a recollection of that air battle as provided by Jasser Zayyad:

'When the signal to scramble came – a green Verey light was used – Ihsan launched but Muwaffaq's aircraft would not start. Yasser had powered his engine already, so Muwaffaq jumped out of his cockpit, ran across the tarmac to Yasser's aircraft, got on the ladder, put his hand under Yasser's chin and asked to take over. Yasser was not happy, but he unstrapped and got out. Muwaffaq got in and they departed. Shurdom therefore took off as first and did one circuit before Muwaffaq joined him. Yasser meanwhile went to another aircraft, powered up and got another green Verey, so he immediately taxied out to the runway. Turning east abeam the tower, he saw another aircraft rolling in the same direction but did not know who it was; hoping it was someone junior in rank, he called for 'Blue 2' and Farouq el-Abdeen answered.

'Matta and Najjar wanted to take off but their scramble was cancelled when Ajloun station detected a large number of Israeli aircraft over the combat zone. Thus, there were now four Hunters controlled by Ajloun radar station approaching the battle zone that was full of enemy aircraft. They were at low level, but when under way that low they could not hear the ground control.'

Ihsan Shurdom recalled:

'My plane was Hunter F.Mk 6 serial number N/712, and I was assigned as no. 2 to Muwaffaq Salti ... We were given vectors to the Samu area and headed in that direction at low level in order to avoid Israeli radar. On reaching the battle area I saw four Mirages turning into us from the four o'clock position, at which point I shouted with excitement, 'There they are!' Then the combat discipline took over and I continued reporting, 'Four bogies, four o'clock, slightly high, closing in.'

Hunter F.Mk 6 N/712, flown by Ihsan Shurdom in air combat over Samu on 13 November 1966. At the time this photograph was taken, the aircraft was equipped with a nose containing reconnaissance cameras, which was not installed at the time of the combat.
(Albert Grandolini Collection)

'There was no answer from Red Lead but I saw his flaps coming to take-off position and I think that he either saw the Israelis or heard me, but I was not receiving any radio traffic from him.

'The Mirages kept closing in and I kept reporting their position to Muwaffaq until I saw them approaching the firing zone. I reported this to my leader and said, 'Red Leader, they are in firing position. I have to break right'. I broke right and after that I did not see or hear Red Lead.

'After breaking right and until my exit from the combat zone, I was in constant combat with Israeli Mirages, either evading an attack or trying to get my gunsight on one of them. It was like towing an aerial target at the aerial firing range, as every time I looked back there was a Mirage on the perch position, turning to dive in.

'I was turning hard left at one time when Jasser Zayyad, the leader of Blue Section that was scrambled after us called, 'Hunter turning left, there is a Mirage behind you!' I answered, 'Contact, help if you can'. But, he could not because of other Mirages. The Mirage fired what I thought was a Matra R.530 at me but I was flying very low and turning very hard and it missed me and hit the ground.

'During the battle, I managed to fire three bursts at a Mirage III that I managed to follow. The Mirage was at long range and I twisted my throttle grip to maximum to give maximum current to steady the gunsight. I turned left, cleared my tail and as my fuel was running low I took an opportunity to break off combat and I headed east at very low level.'

Ajami and Zayyad explained:

'When the first pair arrived on the scene, Ihsan was heard to say, 'Oh my God, plenty of aircraft!' on the radio. Muwaffaq told Ihsan to return to base, engaged two Mirages and was then caught by another pair of Mirages approaching from the south. These were four Mirages that came in a 'double attack system' – about which the RJAF pilots did not know at the time: it was quite a new development from US pilots.

'Ihsan recalled that the Israelis fired at least one missile right at the start of the battle. This was the first time the Israelis had ever fired Matra R.530 missiles in combat. Ihsan broke and he and Muwaffaq lost sight of each other. Muwaffaq scissored with an Israeli that came at Ihsan's line astern. He then tried to warn Muwaffaq that an Israeli fighter was tailing him, but lost the radio link and then Muwaffaq's aircraft disappeared out of sight in the direction of the Dead Sea.

'While manoeuvring to avoid multiple attacks by Israeli fighters, Ihsan lost count of his enemies: during the entire battle, he saw at least between four and eight aircraft over the area between Falluja and Beersheba – so many Israelis were airborne. He engaged and fired at one, and then another Israeli fired a Matra 530 missile at him – but this hit the ground because he was flying so low. Eventually, Ihsan got low on fuel and headed in direction of Wadi Mujib.'

Shurdom continued:

'Just before I crossed the shore of the Dead Sea I saw two Mirages pulling up and turning West and I also noticed smoke at the shore in a place called Ain Alfashkha. After that I headed to Wadi Mujib and returned to Mafraq from there. My total time in the air was 30 minutes, which indicates a long time in jet fighter combat considering the short flight time from Mafraq to Samu …'

Ajami and Zayyad added:

'While disengaging, Ihsan sighted at least two Mirages pulling up and trailing smoke behind them. Ihsan returned to the Dead Sea by flying through the deep and dramatic Wadi Mujib [sometimes called the 'Grand Canyon of Jordan'; authors' note], then flew to Mafraq.

'Upon the take-off of his pair, Yasser changed to the frequency of the Ajloun radar station and they gave them the heading in a good, calm voice. The two Hunters remained at low level while approaching the combat zone. West of Khirbet Samra, Jasser asked Farouq to raise his gunsight and fire to make sure his guns were working. The ground station then called Blue Section to say there were no contacts nearby and they could climb. Thinking, 'if our radars cannot see us, then hopefully the Israelis cannot either', Jasser replied, 'Negative: tell me the targets.'

'Minutes later, Yasser sighted four aircraft in combat formation heading north and one aircraft turning left with a Mirage closing in on him. Then he saw another Hunter. Concerned with the aircraft that was turning left with the Mirage, Yasser called on the radio, 'Red 2, are you turning left?' – and received an affirmative reply. Yasser told him to keep turning left as there was a Mirage behind. Ihsan replied, 'Can you help me?' Yasser pulled up and said, 'I cannot help you because of the other four!' Then he saw a white puff coming out of the Mirage and said, 'Red 2, break left, break left!' Yasser felt a huge lump in his throat as he thought that Ihsan would be killed, but the missile missed, hit the ground and exploded in a vineyard.

'Yasser was now climbing from 2,000 to 3,000ft [610-914m], when the four Israelis above sighted him as their no. 4 turned behind the others and dived. He took a look back at his wingman and noticed that Farouq was getting out of position. He ordered: 'Stay with me!' and Farouq answered, 'What the hell are you doing?'

'As Yasser turned his attention to the Israelis in front of him, he saw the Mirage approaching to 800 yards [732m] and opening fire, then flashing by while still firing, and thus he ordered to Farouq, 'Blue 2, watch him!' Jasser meanwhile engaged the leader who lit his afterburner shortly before the Jordanian opened fire. Then he heard Muwaffaq say, 'Hunter behind Mirage: break, break!' Because he could not see Farouq, he called, 'Blue 2, where are you?' Farouq answered, 'I am behind you' …

'Drop tanks from Israeli fighters were now falling down all around them, and all four Jordanians began talking to each other. Muwaffaq said, 'Sky is full of Mirages, let's get out of here!' Yasser sighted Muwaffaq and Ihsan behind him, and he heard Red Leader announcing he would be crossing into Jordan over the Dead Sea. Thus he led Farouq down to the deck. While diving, they opened their formation to provide mutual cover for each other. Then he heard Ihsan say, 'There are Mirages over Jericho!', and the ground control called, 'Can you raise the Red Section?' Jasser tried twice, but did not get a reply.

'Yasser exited the combat zone east of Jericho, via Salt, along the Naour Valley. While passing by, he saw a broadcasting station, antennae and the local university. Once over Mafraq, he saw only one aircraft on the downwind side and thus called Ihsan, 'Red 2: where is your leader?' – but got no reply. He thought maybe Muwaffaq had hit the ground or landed in Amman, but never thought he had been shot down. Ihsan landed first, followed by Yasser and Farouq.'

YEAR 1966		AIRCRAFT		PILOT, OR 1ST PILOT	2ND PILOT, PUPIL OR PASSENGER	DUTY (INCLUDING RESULTS AND REMARKS)	SINGLE-ENGINE AIRCRAFT				MULT	
MONTH	DATE	Type	No.				DAY		NIGHT		DAY	
							DUAL (1)	PILOT (2)	DUAL (3)	PILOT (4)	DUAL (5)	1ST PILOT (6)
—	—	—	—	—	—	— TOTALS BROUGHT FORWARD	171·50	443·45	13·35	20·05		
	•			SUMMARY FOR OCTOBER, 1966. UNIT:- NO'1 SQN. R.J.AF. DATE:- 21st Oct. 1966 SIGNATURE:- I. Shurdom		HUNTER F6 A/c TYPES	12·10	✓		20·55	TOTAL FOR MOV
NOV	2	HUNTER F6	E	SELF	SELF	L.L.B.		·55				
"	5	"	H	"	"	L.L.B.		·55				
"	7	"	K	"	"	OP. STRIKE. S.B.		·50				
"	8	"	F	"	"	L.L.B.		1·00				
"	9	"	D	"	"	OP. STRIKE. S.B.		·55				
"	13	HUNTER F6	N	"	"	OPERATIONAL SCRAMBLE AS NO 2 TO M/AW SALTI TO SAMU. FIRED THREE BURSTS AT A MIRAGE III FIGHTER. LEADER SHOT DOWN COMING BACK.		·30				
"	20	"	K	"	"	R & T		1·05				
"	23	"	V	"	"	OP. STRIKE. S.B.		·50				
"	26	"	B	"	"	R.Ps CINE		·35				
"	26	"	M	"	"	AIR TEST CONTROLS		·30				
"	26	"	M	"	"	AIR TEST CONTROLS		·30				
"	27	"	Y	"	"	OP. STRIKE. S.B.		·55				
				GRAND TOTAL [Cols. (1) to (10)] 658 Hrs. 45 Mins. 658 35 ✓		TOTALS. CARRIED FORWARD	171·50	453·15 452·15 ✓	13·35	20·05 20·55		

A scan from the pilot logbook of Ihsan Shurdom, documenting his mission in Hunter F.Mk 6 E/712 on 13 November 1966.

Shurdom recalled what happened after his landing:

'Muwaffaq had not returned and I told the squadron commander about the puff of smoke I had noticed and that was where they later found his body. King Hussein arrived to the squadron soon after that and I showed him my gun camera film, showing firing at the Mirage. I described him how I gave maximum current to the gunsight as we were taught by Capt Nasri Jumean, our fighter instructor pilot, who was also present.

'I strongly believe that Muwaffaq, in his haste to take off, forgot to attach his leg straps when he changed the airplane and as a result died on ejecting from his air-craft because of the forces on his legs and pelvis. I also do not think that he was shot down in a dogfight as he was a superb slow-speed and low-level combat pilot. We saw the Israeli gun film, later on, and his aircraft was in a gentle turn to the left when it was fired upon, so possibly he was unaware there was somebody behind him.'

Salti provides the following notes on the fate of her late husband:

'When the RJAF realised that Muwaffaq was missing, a search and rescue opera-tion was mounted. Marwan Nooreddin flew an Aérospatiale Alouette III helicopter, together with Zeid Toukan. They returned without success. During the second sortie, Nooreddin flew with Isam Malhas as co-pilot (Malhas was also a graduate of RAF Cranwell), and they found Muwaffaq's body – together with his parachute exactly next to him. Muwaffaq was buried in the Royal Cemetery, around 09.00, on the morning of 14 November 1966. To this day, Yasser remains convinced that in a hurry to scramble, Muwaffaq did not strap in properly after taking his place in Yasser's cockpit … Muwaffaq's body was found next to the 1948 Armistice line with Israel (not in the north of the Yarmouk Canyon, as sometimes reported). [In 2007;

authors' note] *the remnants of his aircraft were found by Israeli archaeologists, as the Dead Sea had retreated. They were inside the territory assigned to Israel/Palestine by the UN as of 1948. Muwaffaq's parachute did not fail to deploy but had no chance to deploy because of the angle at which he ejected while still inside the wadi.*

'*Ihsan was debriefed for hours. From his and Yasser's and Farouq's debriefs, the RJAF concluded that the combat looked to be against something like four Mirages for each of the Hunters. Jasser and Farouq each claimed one kill and Ihsan claimed a 'probable damaged'. Later on, Jasser, Ihsan and Farouk went with His Majesty King Hussein in a car to visit the wounded on the West Bank. The King invited them for dinner but they declined and went back to Mafraq instead. In front of the entrance there, the police had erected an unmarked barrier and the driver of the Land Rover in which they were travelling failed to see this. Thus the car crashed into the barrier ...*

'*All involved pilots were awarded the highest bravery medal.*

'*Later the RJAF learned that one Israeli fighter force-landed near Acre, on fire. The source was a UN person who spoke to a Jordanian representative in Jerusalem, not long after the battle.*'

Separately, in an interview with Group 73 in late 2011, Brig Gen Farouk Abdeen (ret.) added the following details:

'*The estimated number of Mirages that attacked our Hunters was between 14 and 16. Four Mirages engaged the late 1st Lt Salti alone; the Blue Section engaged a 'finger four' formation of Mirages, and there were other Mirages scattered in the sky, flying as singles or as twos.*

'*One of the tangible facts is that none of the RJAF pilots was shot down in the battle area: Salti was chased by a pair of previously unseen Mirage IIIs and shot down while climbing over a small hill near the Dead Sea. In comparison, we shot down two Mirages during the combat: Muwaffaq had shot down one before he went down, and I have shot down the other. This result speaks for itself, nicely showing the proficiency of the Jordanian pilots.*'[7]

The above recollections of RJAF pilots indicate that the claim that the Matra R.530 air-to-air missile achieved a '50 per cent success rate' – supposedly because out of two fired, one scored a kill (destroying an Egyptian MiG-19S on 29 November 1966, see *Volume 2*, p172) – is therefore unrealistic.[8] The Jordanians are certain that this weapon was deployed in combat during the air battle of Samu, when none of at least two rounds fired hit its target.

Volume 2, Chapter 5: Cutting the Lion's Tail

There is still considerable debate between academics regarding Soviet involvement and responsibility for the outbreak of hostilities in the Middle East on 5 June 1967. Some scholars argue that Moscow instigated the war in order to increase Arab dependence on Soviet aid, even though it had no desire to bring about the destruction of Israel. Others contend that the Soviet leadership was divided over the issue of Middle East policy as a result of a power struggle between members of the top political leadership in Moscow, with the 'adventurous' group – led by the Secretary of the Soviet Communist Party (CPSU) Leonid Brezhnev – being prepared to go to war and instigating a conspiracy to precipitate an armed conflict, while the other was sceptical about the Arabs being prepared for a war and therefore advocated a cautious policy.

A third variant contends that Moscow had no desire to encourage a war against Israel and only attempted to avert the danger of a potential Israeli attack on Syria. According to this variant, President Gamal Abd el-Nasser misinterpreted these intentions and blocked the Gulf of Aqaba without Moscow's knowledge.

New archival evidence, based on Brezhnev's secret report at a plenary session of the Central Committee of the CPSU on 20 June 1967 was obtained from the Polish archives as a part of a recent research project on the Cold War in the Middle East undertaken by the Chaim Herzog Center for Middle East Studies and Diplomacy at Ben-Gurion University of the Negev, in Israel, in cooperation with the Cold War International History Project (CWIHP) of the Woodrow Wilson International Center for Scholars.

The document in question shows that Moscow had no intention of inciting an armed conflict but also that the June 1967 War was the result of grave miscalculations by the top leaders of the Central Committee of the CPSU concerning their ability to control the Arabs. It confirms that there was no Soviet conspiracy to destroy Israel but that Moscow suspected that Israel was planning an act of aggression against Syria. Determined to rescue the government in Damascus, the Soviets informed Egypt about the (supposed) Israeli mobilisation, hoping to manipulate Nasser into assisting Syria through concentrating Egyptian armed forces on the border with Israel. While relatively apologetic in tone, the document in question does not shed light on the controversial information regarding the supposed concentration of Israeli troops on the Syrian border, as conveyed to the Egyptians by the Soviet government in mid-May 1967. Interestingly, it does not even link that action with the outbreak of hostilities.

Furthermore, the same document shows that Moscow mistakenly estimated that Israel was militarily weak and could not cope with a war on two fronts, and therefore Moscow consented to the ejection of United Nations (UN) peacekeeping forces from Sinai. However, from that point onwards, Moscow lost control of the crisis. The Soviets were taken aback by Nasser's blockade of the Gulf of Aqaba without having first consulted them, and then by Israel launching a swift attack that resulted in a victory within only six days. Even so, Moscow was not inclined to take any military action against Israel. It was only when the occupation of Damascus by the Israeli Defence Forces (IDF) seemed imminent that the Kremlin sharply increased pressure upon Israel and even resorted to military threats. These threats in turn forced the US President Lyndon B. Johnson to intervene and persuade the Israeli government to stop the fighting.[9]

1   Based on documents VÚA-VHA, MNO, 1969 and VÚA-VHA, MNO, 1970 from the Military Historical Archive, Prague, Czech Republic; as well as Zídek, P. and Sieber, K, *Československo a Blízký východ v letech 1948–1989, Ústav mezinárodních vztahů*, Prague, 2009 (ISBN 978-80-86506-76-0) and Púčik, M., 'Vývoz zbraní a špeciálnej techniky do záujmových krajín bývalej ČSSR v sedemdesiatych rokoch', *Apológia* magazine (exact volume unknown).

2   'The Bomb That Won a War', *Flight International*, 22 June 1967.

3   For comparison, it is notable that around the same time the price of a single Hawker Hunter fighter sold to Iraq was around GBP130,000. For details see *Volume 2*, p52.

4   According to Brandner, Col Mahmoud Khalil was the most influential Egyptian decision-maker in regards to the HA-300 and E-300 projects. Khalil became famous for acting as a double agent that 'cooperated' with the British MI6 and Mossad in a plot against Nasser instigated in the mid-1950s. In exchange for intelligence about Israel and GBP166,000 – 'sponsored' by the Saudis – he was to kill Nasser. Instead, Khalil delivered the money to the Egyptian President, thus reinforcing his position in the hierarchy of the UAR as the – de facto – third most powerful man in the UAR at the time.

5   Brandner stressed that all the equipment purchased by MTP (with Egyptian money, of course) was the 'most modern' available, that all of it was acquired together with all necessary spare parts and tooling, and that the company readily paid excesses in order to secure its earliest possible delivery – but not in order to avoid any kind of embargoes or political pressure. Furthermore, because MTP had planned from the outset to hand over the entire facility to the Egyptians, the company established training courses for local engineers lasting three years. The first group of 30 Egyptians recruited for training at the new facility joined the team in early 1961. In addition to engineers, the company also trained 120 Egyptian technical specialists annually during the period it operated in Helwan.

6   K. Chatterjee, *Hindustan Fighter HF-24 Marut*, Bharat-Rakshak.com website (extracted in November 2010). Brandner recalled Chopra as '… *a 55kg light, first-class engineer and a very careful pilot …*'

7   Abdeen, e-mail interview with Group 73, 17 December 2011.

8   Aloni, *Israeli Mirage and Nesher Aces*, p15.

9   For details on this document, see Uri Bar-Noi, *The Soviet Union and the Six-Day War: Revelations From the Polish Archives*, Cold War International History Project at the Woodrow Wilson International Center for Scholars, e-Dossier No. 8, based on *'On Soviet Policy Following the Israeli Aggression in the Middle East'*, by Comrade L. I. Brezhnev to the Plenum of the Central Committee of the CPSU, 20 June 1967, Archiwum Akt Nowych. (Polish document describing the speech given by Brezhnev to the Plenum of the Central Committee of the CPSU on the actions undertaken by the Soviet leadership before and during the 1967 Arab-Israeli War.)

Chapter 1

5 JUNE 1967, ATTACK ON EGYPT

Dozens of accounts of the Israeli attack on Arab air bases on 5 June 1967 have been published since the end of the June 1967 War. With only four exceptions, all concentrate almost exclusively on the Israeli side of this battle. While this is understandable considering the revolutionary nature of the Israeli planning and execution, not a single in-depth study of the Arab experiences, or an independent in-depth examination of true Arab losses, has become available in the last 50 years. The following account of what was happening in Egypt on that fateful day is based on interviews with dozens of participants as well as some of the official documentation that has become available in the meantime.

Operation Moked: Myths and Reality

Before looking at the Egyptian experiences from 5 June 1967, at least some of the cornerstones of Israeli planning and operations need to be discussed. In particular, a number of outright 'legends' that concern this enterprise are still considered 'facts' by the wider public.

Foremost – and in contrast to the Arab and particularly Egyptian war-planning, which was not only based on faulty intelligence but also envisaged somewhat sporadic attacks on Israeli air bases – the Israeli war-planning aimed at a massive and concentrated aerial campaign of sustained attacks on enemy air bases, right from the start of any war. This campaign was crucial for the outcome of the entire conflict and was therefore planned as the major effort for Israeli air power. Indeed, it would involve practically every available combat aircraft. The hammer blow it was expected to deliver was aimed at not only physically destroying the enemy air forces on the ground (in order to establish complete air superiority over the battlefield), but also to shock and crush the Arab will to fight. As such, Operation Moked was an all-out effort – very different from the 'sit and wait' position into which the United Arab Republic Air Force (UARAF) had been forced by the decisions of the top political and military leadership in Cairo.

The Israeli plan was originally developed in the early 1950s and – thanks to superb intelligence gathered during the following years – it was further refined and perfected during the 1960s. At a time when Egyptian pilots were threatened with arrest or were even forced to leave the service if they discussed the capabilities of enemy aircraft with their colleagues, all active Israeli fighter pilots received detailed knowledge of all major Arab air bases and constantly practiced attacks on them, until the geography and installations of their targets were imprinted in their minds.[1] Simultaneously, Israeli ground crews trained intensively in order to be able to refuel and re-arm every combat aircraft within the shortest possible period of time. Eventually, they proved able to 'turn around' all of their combat aircraft within seven to eight minutes, thus multiplying the relatively small force of fighter jets available to the Israeli Defence Force/Air Force (IDF/AF). In fact, the Israelis possessed only 206 fighter-bombers, of which around 197 were operational and 183 were manned as of the morning of 5 June 1967.[2] However, due to the excellent training of their ground crews, most of these were available to be flown – by different pilots, of course – up to eight times a day.[3]

The net result of this capability was that the planners of Operation Focus concluded that they could put another attack formation over each major Arab air base at intervals of between 10 and 15 minutes, and thus keep their enemy under constant pressure during daylight hours. This crucially important factor is very seldom put within the proper context in the various studies of the Arab reaction to the Israeli assault. However, when taken together with experiences of the US, British and French aircraft carriers that were used for interventions in the Middle East during the 1950s and 1960s (see *Volumes 1 and 2*), it serves to explain why many Arab leaders of the time, and most Arabs to this day, remain convinced that Israel was not alone in launching this attack. Thus, it is still widely believed that the Israelis were supported by (at least) British and US aircraft. The fact is that the Arabs were – and remain – stunned by the sheer number of aircraft the Israelis threw into the fray as they were hit by successive waves of IDF/AF fighter-bombers. Thinking in terms of their own insufficient military education and training, the military commanders in Cairo in particular could not imagine that the Israelis could put so many aircraft into the skies over Egyptian air bases. The pace of Operation Moked was therefore one of the decisive factors, and – considering the chaos it caused within the Egyptian military hierarchy – there is little doubt that the Israeli plan would have succeeded even if the first Israeli attack wave had not achieved the level of surprise it did: as explained in *Volume 2*, the fact is that the UARAF was unable to scramble enough fighters to intercept so many incoming Israeli formations.

The basic principle behind the Israeli planning was simplicity. Operation Moked aimed to destroy as many aircraft as possible and cause long-lasting damage to runways and taxiways at 20 different air bases in Egypt, Jordan and Syria. The Israelis found it necessary to increase the number of assigned targets during the course of 5 June, since the main targets of the first two waves included only some 15 air bases in Egypt. Due to the speed of the execution, the shock this attack caused to the Egyptian chain of command and to the UARAF itself, as well as the slow response from Iraq, Jordan and Syria, the Israelis found themselves free to focus upon Egyptian air power alone throughout the entire morning. This resulted in the IDF/AF swiftly achieving a more favourable numerical superiority over the other Arab air forces by noon.

The Israeli plan envisaged Arab air bases being attacked in several successive waves, only the first of which was pre-planned in detail. The planning for all subsequent waves was based on post-strike and intelligence reports concerning enemy activity, plus a considerable degree of improvisation.

For navigation to their targets the leaders of the Israeli formations depended on a compass, map, wristwatch, and their own skills and experience. All subsequent reports alluding to various 'traitors' guiding Israeli fighters to their targets, which were widely published in the Arab world, remain unconfirmed and, indeed, highly unlikely.

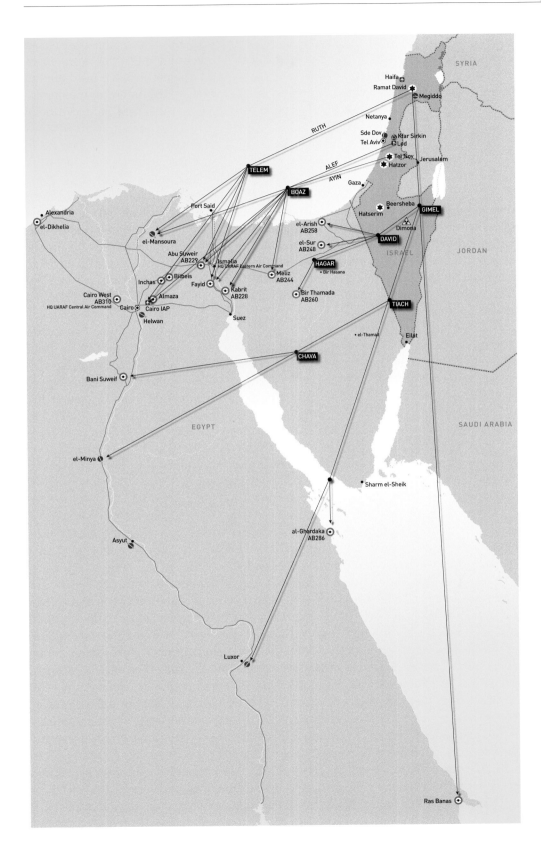

A map of the routes taken by Israeli fighter-bomber formations in order to reach various air bases and airfields in Egypt, especially during the first wave of attacks on the morning of 5 June 1967. As can be seen, some of the routes led over the Mediterranean Sea, but not as far west as usually reported. Furthermore, most of the attacks on three major UARAF air bases in the Sinai were launched directly out of Israel. (James Lawrence)

To ensure operational and tactical surprise, the first few waves were required to approach their targets along carefully pre-selected routes and at very low level. However, most subsequent operations were undertaken by aircraft flying at medium altitudes, while many formations returned to Israel at high altitude in order to conserve fuel: by then, of course, the Israelis had already achieved surprise and no longer found concealment necessary.

Some of the ingress routes selected for the first wave were over the Mediterranean Sea, but many others were well inland. Except for the opening wave, the Israelis do not appear to have found it difficult to reach their targets deep inside Egypt while flying at very low altitude. For their part, knowing that Egypt's low-altitude radar coverage was very poor, the UARAF pilots expected the Israelis to come in at low level – and take them by surprise. However, some formations tasked with targeting very distant bases within Egypt were scheduled to take off well after the initial attack in order to be able to save fuel and reach their targets flying at high altitudes. Even if it was to be expected that such formations would be detected by the UARAF relatively early, the IDF/AF could still count on the inertia and chaos that by then reigned in the Egyptian chain of command.

The weapons deployed by the Israelis were also simple: 30mm cannon ammunition was used against enemy aircraft on the ground, while runways were targeted with general-purpose (GP) bombs of 50kg, 70kg, 100kg, 250kg, 400kg and 500kg. Most of these were equipped with detonators set at 0.1 seconds, but some had delay detonators and were intended to explode long after the actual attack, in order to hamper any runway repair efforts. Unguided rockets of 80mm calibre were deployed only by the slower fighter-bombers in Israeli service. Stories concerning the use of 'infrared homing' rockets and/or missiles to target Arab aircraft on the ground belong to the realm of fantasy. Indeed, even the stories concerning the use of runway-penetration (so-called 'dibber') bombs are much exaggerated. In cooperation with France, the Israelis developed two types of runway-penetration weapons, but these were not only in short supply but also proved relatively unreliable. Less than 150 such weapons were deployed on 5 June. In contrast, the majority of Israeli fighter-bombers sent to attack the Arab air bases which were capable of supporting heavier aircraft and had particularly hardened runways, were armed with GP bombs equipped with hardened penetration cones.

Most of the Israeli formations consisted of four aircraft. However, technical malfunctions, combat damage and losses regularly reduced these to three or even two aircraft. Even so, it was impressed upon the pilots that they had to reach their targets and accomplish their mission regardless of the price. Every formation was authorised to fly a single bombing run, followed by as many strafing passes as the formation leader found necessary – while keeping in mind the allocated time-over-target, which was usually limited to between 10 and 15 minutes. By that time, the IDF/AF had developed two different schools of thought regarding tactics for airfield attacks. While some squadron commanders insisted on their aircraft operating in pairs that would approach their targets from opposite directions, other commanders ordered their formation-members to separate before reaching the target and each aircraft to attack from a different direction. There is little doubt that these slight tactical differences added much to the confusion seen at Arab air bases on that morning.

Operation Moked was actually launched on the evening of 4 June, when IDF/AF pilots were briefed about the forthcoming attack. Ground crews were only informed

The tactics for attacking Arab air bases as developed by the IDF/AF usually envisaged either pairs or single fighter-bombers making strafing runs from different directions. The first attack usually came along the runway axis and was followed by a series of 270° turns: no two strafing runs were to be flown from the same direction, while different fighter-bombers (or pairs of fighter-bombers) would converge on the target from different directions.
(James Lawrence)

on the morning of 5 June, because there was no necessity for them to know earlier: all the available fighter-bombers were already refuelled, armed and ready for combat. The first to launch on the morning of 5 June was a Boeing KC-97, equipped as an ELINT/SIGINT-gatherer, which took off at 03.25. This lumbering four-engined aircraft was followed some hours later by a number of Pipers that flew reconnaissance along the Israeli frontiers, and then by a group of six Fouga CM.170 Magisters that flew a deception sortie over the Mediterranean Sea, using the call signs of formation leaders from other units and imitating the flight pattern of normal Israeli training sorties.

The first wave of fighter-bombers launched between 07.14 and 08.28 Israeli time (08.14 and 09.28 Egyptian time). It included a total of 45 formations with 170 fighters – several of these flying post-strike reconnaissance and at least one with stand-off jamming equipment. These aircraft hit 10 air bases in Egypt. While achieving nearly complete surprise, this wave suffered a number of aborts due to technical difficulties and then faced stiff opposition, losing at least eight aircraft and five pilots to Egyptian defences.

The second wave launched between 09.33 and 11.55 Israeli time (10.33 and 12.55 Egyptian time). It included 31 formations and 115 aircraft that hit 14 air bases in Egypt. This wave fared much better – in part because it faced almost no resistance in the air – and suffered no losses: two aircraft aborted due to technical difficulties while one formation of four aircraft failed to find its target.

The third wave launched between 12.15 and 14.10 (13.15 and 15:10 Egyptian, Jordanian and Syrian time). It already included a series of attacks on Jordanian and Syrian air bases – in reaction to Iraqi, Jordanian and Syrian attacks on Israel – in addition to follow-up raids on Egyptian air bases. This wave consisted of a total of 25 formations with 95 aircraft, of which one formation was diverted from its original task in order to attack a radar station in Jordan. This wave is known to have suffered the loss of seven aircraft and four pilots (including one fighter shot down over Egypt, three over Jordan and three over Syria).

The fourth wave launched between 14.15 and 15.40 Israeli time (15.15 and 16.40 Egyptian, Iraqi, Jordanian and Syrian time). With air superiority largely achieved and due to the necessity of supporting ground operations, this wave included only 10 formations with a total of 33 aircraft that hit targets in Iraq, Jordan and Syria. It is known to have suffered a total of three losses, all over Syria.

The fifth wave launched between 16.36 and 18.00 Israeli time (17.36 and 19.00 Egyptian and Syrian time), and largely consisted of follow-up attacks on Egyptian and Syrian air bases, in order to maintain pressure upon local air forces. It included a total of 18 formations with 63 aircraft that hit 11 different air bases without suffering a single loss in the process.

In total, the Israelis report flying 470 to 474 sorties to attack Arab air bases on 5 June. In the course of these, their pilots claimed the destruction of 374 enemy aircraft on the ground and in air combat, including 286 in Egypt, 52 in Syria, 27 in Jordan and nine in Iraq.[4]

Blitz Before Snap

Around 04.00 on the morning of 5 June 1967, the first reports from Egyptian Army reconnaissance units deployed along the Israeli border in eastern Sinai began arriving at General Headquarters (GHQ) in Cairo, indicating concerted Israeli reconnaissance activity in the area of Abu Aweigla. This activity increased to an outright attack on nearby Egyptian units, which were forced to withdraw around 08.15, as subsequently concluded by Gabr Ali Gabr:

'Israeli penetration of Egyptian border and occupation of advanced post at Umm Bisis, at 07.30 local time on morning of 5 June, should have been taken as warning of impeding attack. It could have given our air force and air defence 75 minutes' warning before the first Israeli strike. But commanders failed to recognise this.'

Another report that arrived at GHQ around 08.25 was even more concerning. This was a telegram from Lt Gen Riyadh, C-in-C UAC, at the United Arab Command HQ in Amman, forwarding a warning from the Royal Jordanian Air Force (RJAF) Decca radar station, a system of British origin on the 1,350m (4,429ft) Mount Ajloun, near Jerash, in northwest Jordan. This radar provided excellent coverage of the airspace over Israel. Immediately after recording the flight of *'virtually the entire Israeli Air Force towards Egypt'*, the officer on duty in Ajloun aired the prearranged code for war – 'Inab' ('Grape') – to Lt Gen Riyadh's HQ in Amman. In turn, Riyadh relayed the information to Defence Minister Shams Badran in Cairo, his telegram not only warning that dozens of IDF/AF aircraft were taking off from their bases and departing in a westerly direction, but explicitly including the warning that this was the start of the war:[5]

'50 Israeli aircraft will attack Egypt between 08.35 and 08.45. Inab, inab, inab.'[6]

However, because the Egyptian military had changed its encryption code the previous midnight but nobody had thought to inform Amman of this fact, the Jordanian message arrived encrypted in the old code. As a result it was initially ignored, after which it took the Egyptians some time to decrypt it. In fact, it only became available to the UARAF High Command around 08.45.

The sad reality is that even if anybody had tried to warn key commanders within the military hierarchy in Cairo of the incoming Israeli strike, it would already have been far too late. These commanders were, in fact, already on board two Ilyushin Il-14s of No. 11 Squadron that took off from Almaza around 08.15 and flew towards Sinai. The first of these aircraft carried FM Amer, AM Sidki Mahmoud, and many other top-

By sheer chance, a formation of six Tu-16s led by Hosni Moubarak launched from Cairo West between 08.40 and 08.45 local time on the morning of 5 June 1967. Prepared for a training sortie, none of the aircraft was armed. This pre-war photograph was taken during a military parade in Cairo and shows examples with the serial numbers 35 (foreground), 05 or 65 (centre) and 55 (background).
(Nour Bardai Collection)

A formation of Il-28s from No. 8 or No. 28 Squadron as photographed prior to the war. Led by 1st Lt Mohammed Abdel Wahab Keraidy, six of these bombers took off from Abu Suweir to attack targets in Yemen early in the morning of 5 June 1967. They thus escaped destruction by the attacking Israelis and were to fly a number of combat sorties later in the conflict.
(David Nicolle Collection)

ranking Egyptian commanders, plus the Soviet Air Force liaison officer in Egypt and a number of other dignitaries. They were heading for Bir Thamada, where they were to inspect Egyptian troops stationed in Sinai. The second Il-14 carried the Egyptian Vice-President, Hussein el-Shafei, and an Iraqi delegation led by Iraq's Prime Minister Yahya el-Tahir. At the same time, all the 28 top Egyptian military commanders who were not actually on those two aircraft were waiting at Bir Thamada, ready to salute Amer.[7]

Because these aircraft were in the air there was an order for all AAA regiments and their batteries protecting Meliz, el-Sur and Bir Thamada airfields in Sinai, as well as AAA units protecting Fayid, Kabrit and Abu Suweir, not to open fire on any aircraft under any circumstances between 08.00 and 09.00. In fact, the newly established AAA unit allocated to protect Kabrit airfield was not yet in place, and the Antonov An-12 transport delivering its equipment was only due to arrive later that day. Air defence units protecting Beni Suweif and Cairo West had received similar orders due to train-ing and other activities that were to take place that morning.

A number of other UARAF aircraft were, however, airborne at dawn, primarily interceptors. Assuming that any Israeli attack would begin at first light – as was tradi-tional – these fighters flew a number of CAPs over all the major airfields. For example, at Abu Suweir the morning CAP – consisting of four Mikoyan i Gurevich MiG-21s from No. 26 Squadron – took off at 06.22 and returned at 07.13. While those MiGs were air-borne, a formation of six Ilyushin Il-28s led by 1st Lt Mohammed Abdel Wahab Keraidy also took off from Abu Suweir to attack targets in Yemen, where the civil war still raged, and were thus flying away from the forthcoming war.

Around 08.05, an Il-14 of No. 11 Squadron equipped for ELINT/SIGINT-gathering purposes took off from Meliz in Sinai and flew a broad circuit around the peninsula, listening for radio activity in Israel. Not only did its instruments fail to capture any Israeli radio transmissions but its crew also failed to detect any of the numerous IDF/

At least three Il-14s were airborne over Sinai on the morning of 5 June 1967. Two carried VIP passengers for a visit to Meliz air base while the third example was under way on an ELINT/SIGINT mission. (Albert Grandolini Collection)

AF formations that would be under way deep within Egyptian airspace only a short time later.[8]

Finally, in addition to a pair of Mikoyan i Gurevich MiG-17s on a CAP over Sinai and three MiG-15s that had taken off from Cairo West for a training sortie, a formation of Tupolev Tu-16 bombers was also in the air. By sheer chance they initially escaped destruction when taking off from Beni Suweif at 08.40, as recalled by Kamal Darwish:

'We planned to take off for a training mission carrying only dummy bombs, in two flights of three. The first flight was commanded by Hosni Moubarak … the second by me. The other aircraft of our regiment were all on the ground, fully fuelled and bombed up, their crews on alert – 'ready to go' if necessary … We had just become airborne when we heard a radio message from Cairo West announcing the airfield was under attack and we should therefore fly to Luxor …'

In contrast to the confusion and uncertainty within the senior ranks of the UARAF, the Israelis acted decisively. Since 1963, the IDF/AF had planned and practiced a concentrated campaign to destroy the UARAF at the very onset of hostilities. Taking a great risk, it committed nearly all its combat aircraft for an overwhelming first blow, holding back only 12 interceptors for air defence purposes.[9]

By 08.35 that morning, no fewer than 183 Israeli combat aircraft were on their way to strike Egyptian air bases. Flying at 15m (49ft) or less over the Mediterranean Sea, some 30 Israeli fighters approached the Nile Delta from the north entirely undetected. Additional formations were under way at similarly low altitudes over the northern Sinai, but over virtually unpopulated areas. Ten minutes later, the first of these approached their targets.

At approximately 08.40, while crossing the Suez Canal, the crew of the Il-14 carrying FM Amer and AM Sidki Mahmoud sighted several formations of Israeli fighter-bombers passing by. Obedient to their orders, the Israelis did not attack the lumbering transport but continued in an easterly direction while, instead of transmitting a warning, the crew called FM Amer to have a look. While he and AM Sidki Mahmoud conferred about what to do, and without mentioning the Israeli appearance at low level deep over Sinai, the pilot then called the tower at Kabrit air base, requesting permission to land there. A few minutes later, contact with Kabrit was lost, and when the crew attempted to raise the tower at Abu Suweir, this responded with the news that the airfield was under attack. It was only then that FM Amer ordered the Ilyushin pilot to return towards Cairo.

Five minutes later, the radio erupted in a chaos of voices, all reporting that they were under attack. While the other Il-14 from the formation turned for Fayid and landed there by 08.45, the aircraft carrying the two top Egyptian military commanders was not so lucky. On an order from Amer, the pilot first attempted to land at Inchas, itself already under attack by the IDF/AF. Finding it on fire, he then continued towards Cairo West. This decision resulted in Amer and Sidki Mahmoud remaining airborne – and thus having no control over the situation – for at least 90 minutes longer than they might have.

The End of Meliz Air Base

One of the 10 UARAF bases to receive the first Israeli attack was Meliz – the most exposed Egyptian airfield to house MiG-21s. Here the pilots of No. 45 Squadron were in the process of enjoying their breakfast when the attack came. Gabr Ali Gabr explained:

'In the Air Force it was policy that all aircrew must have 'full English breakfasts', because they needed the energy. They had to have a proper breakfast every day when they were on duty. None of this light, 'cups of coffee and bread' continental breakfast stuff. This seems to have been an RAF tradition which the EAF continued.'[10]

The first Israeli formation to hit Meliz consisted of four Dassault Ouragans, old fighter jets of the first generation, with straight wings, but modified to carry unguided rockets and light bombs and armed with two internally mounted 30mm cannon. The Ouragans that attacked Meliz dropped their bombs on the runway at 08.45 local time precisely. Egyptian pilots ran to their parked MiG-21s, jumping into the cockpits while shouting to the maintenance crews to help them power up, as recalled by one such ground crew:

'2nd Lt Said Othman jumped into his MiG-21 and shouted to the technicians, 'Get this plane moving!' His voice competed with the sound of bombs, but we heard him and obeyed, and so he took off. He attacked the Israeli formation immediately after taking off …'[11]

Together with an unknown pilot, Othman came under attack from an Israeli Ouragan as he was getting airborne. The other MiG-21 was shot down in flames, but Othman

The UARAF deployed four Mi-6s of No. 7 Squadron to Meliz, and two of these were present as of the morning of 5 June 1967. Their primary role was transportation of troops and supplies. This photograph shows serial number 817 about to embark an infantry company, prior to the war.
(Albert Grandolini Collection)

Mi-6 serial number 823 as photographed over the Cairo Citadel, before the war (other known serial numbers of Egyptian Mi-6s as of 1967 include 801, 807 and 820). At the time, this was the largest and heaviest helicopter in service anywhere in the world. (Albert Grandolini Collection)

turned around to fight the Israelis. Two massive Mil Mi-6 helicopters were present at Meliz as well, and one of their navigators, Ahmed al-Atrabi, recalled:

'There was a big air battle between our MiG-21s and Ouragans ... then the Israelis hit the runway and several buildings and I was shocked beyond description. The entire base was in ruins ...'[12]

AVM Qadri el-Hamid recalled what happened next:[13]

'Two of our Readiness State I aircraft got into the air and one of them was shot down by an Ouragan. I saw it with my own eyes. I was in the tower by the radar and saw the whole scene. I heard the sound of many aircraft. I said to myself, 'must be the MiG-19s from Hurghada flying to Meliz and back', and I thought, 'not the MiG-19s again, they are a terrible nuisance'. The MiG-19 looks like an Ouragan because of the colour. It was grey and the Ouragan was brown and they looked the same in bright sunlight. I saw the bombs coming from four Ouragans. Two from each. Two [Dassault] Mirages then came and descended to 200m [656ft] and dropped parachute bombs. Then they started to strafe. Our Readiness State I fighters needed about two minutes to scramble. The Israelis attacked them with cannon. They hit two of these MiG-21s and set them on fire, but the other two were able to take off. But, one of the Ouragan pilots turned and attacked the MiG-21 that had just left the ground. It was a quarter attack: he hit it and the pilot ejected. He couldn't attack the second one, though: the other MiG took off and engaged in air combat with one of the Mirages. We don't know what happened but he never showed up again. He just vanished'.[14]

2nd Lt Said Othman managed to take off from Meliz while the Israelis were attacking the base. He engaged the Ouragans of the IDF/AF in an air battle but subsequently vanished. (David Nicolle Collection)

Sadly, 21-year-old Othman, who flew the MiG-21 that first engaged the Ouragans and then the Mirages before vanishing, was killed, as was another pilot of No. 45 Squadron, Lt Hassan el-Sokary, who scrambled with one of the MiG-21F-13s held at Readiness State II, and engaged the second formation of Israeli fighters that attacked Meliz.

El-Hamid completed his recollection of the tragedy that befell No. 45 Squadron at Meliz when the next two Israeli raids came in, around 08.55 and 09.10, respectively:

'One of the MiG-21s held at Readiness State III took off. He got into air combat as well but in the rush to get his aircraft airborne the ground crew had forgotten to take the safety pins out of the missiles and he couldn't fire. He was hit in the rudder during that combat but kept flying. He didn't know that his rudder had been damaged until he landed in Cairo West.

'We were finished: we had 14 MiG-21s on the ground and a MiG-15UTI. In the first wave they destroyed all our MiG-21s. I cried and became hysterical. I was watching from the tower. All that we had trained for was gone in three minutes. After they had left, four Mirages came again and bombed the runways from the left.

'Twenty minutes later another wave came, still Ouragans, and they started to attack the radar and the fuel tanks near the airfield and the anti-aircraft batteries that fought back in a limited way. We were hiding in uncovered trenches and it was very dangerous. The Ouragans could manoeuvre very well at slow speed and we could see one of the pilots looking at us. He came down and strafed us. Some soldiers were killed but most of the pilots escaped [without injuries; authors' note]. We got into a lorry and evacuated the airfield. That was some journey! Should we go the northern route through the Giddi Pass or the southern route through the Mitla Defile? We went the southern way. Once we got to the centre of Egypt we went in an Egyptian transport plane to Jeddah, in Saudi Arabia, and then on to Baghdad, to bring back two MiGs to Egypt. All of this on the same day, 5 June 1967.'

This MiG-21F-13 of No. 45 Squadron probably belonged to one of the Readiness State II or III aircraft that was caught by successive Israeli attack waves while still on the ground. (Courtesy *Flight International*)

These two No. 45 Squadron MiG-21F-13s were also destroyed by attacking Israelis before getting airborne. Their pilots escaped injury. (IDF)

Another MiG-21F-13 from No. 45 Squadron destroyed on the ground at Meliz. Sadly, the wreckage is burned almost beyond recognition, making identification of this aircraft impossible.
(IDF)

No fewer than 13 MiG-21F-13s operated by No. 45 Squadron were either lost in air combat or to fuel starvation, or were destroyed on the ground, and only single examples of the MiG-15UTI and MiG-21F-13 managed to escape. Taken by surprise, six pilots managed to man their aircraft and scramble. Two MiG-21s were hit on the ground, but their pilots escaped injury. Four other MiG-21F-13s got airborne and three were either shot down or lost for other reasons within minutes, together with their pilots. Whether they scored any kills in return, as claimed by official Egyptian sources, remains unclear.[15]

Although the first IDF/AF formation to attack Meliz is known to have lost two Ouragans shot down and one badly damaged (the jet made an emergency landing back

The IDF/AF was swift to fly post-strike reconnaissance sorties over Egyptian airfields in order to collect crucially important, up-to-date intelligence on the situation there and cross-examine the claims of its pilots. This photograph shows the shadow of a Vautour IIBR under way low over Meliz, together with the wreckage of two Il-14s and one Mi-6.
(IDF via Albert Grandolini)

The same scene as viewed from the ground after the Israelis captured Meliz, later during the June 1967 War.
(IDF via Albert Grandolini)

in Israel), together with one pilot killed and another taken PoW, Israeli sources usually stress that they were all hit by ground fire, despite repeated engagements with MiG-21s that scrambled during that attack. Until either side provides additional reliable documentation or eyewitness accounts, no serious conclusions are possible. All that can be said with certainty is that the UARAF also lost two Il-14 transports and two Mi-6 helicopters destroyed on the ground, and the crew of one of its AAA sites protecting Meliz, when one of Ouragans crashed on the top of them.[16] With its surviving pilots and ground personnel evacuated back to Egypt, No. 45 Squadron – as well as the entire Meliz air base – essentially ceased to exist and was out of the war virtually before it had begun.

In addition to almost the entire strength of No. 45 Squadron UARAF, Egypt also lost two Il-14 transports and two Mi-6s at Meliz on the morning of 5 June. This photograph shows the burnt-out hulks of two Mi-6s with their giant rotor blades.
(IDF)

Wreckage of the second Mi-6 destroyed at Meliz on the morning of 5 June remained intact enough to reveal at least some details of the camouflage pattern and markings applied on the upper surface of the left wing and the boom.
(IDF)

Struck in the Locker Room: Fayid

At Fayid, Tahsin Zaki initiated operations on that fateful morning:

'*On the morning of 5 June I ordered a training sortie by eight MiG-21s and six Su-7s for 08.00, but then delayed it until 09.00 because of fog. Then we heard that our Vice-President Hussein el-Shafei and the Iraqi Prime Minister would be arriving around 09.00 ...*'[17]

Mamdouh Heshmat was scheduled to fly one of the eight MiG-21s of No. 47 Squadron that morning:

'*Early in the morning we powered up the engines of our MiG-21s. The model we flew was the early F-13 and if engines were not powered up early every morning, it tended to develop technical problems. We powered up and did all the checks and everything was OK, but there was fog and we could not take off. So, we went back to the squadron ready room, to wait until the weather improved ... On sunrise, the fog only got worse. The tower informed us that the visibility was down to 200m [656ft] ... I asked back if any other flights except ours were scheduled, and they answered that four MiG-19s should appear later on to fly a training exercise ... Eventually we decided to use the time until the weather improved to study technical manuals ...*'[18]

Salah Danish was already in the squadron ready room, receiving theoretical lectures concerning the Sukhoi Su-7:

'*A large number of pilots were around, including el-Shennawy from No. 55 Squadron, Medhat, Sumari, Mohammed Khamis, Mamdouh Heshmat, Farid Harfush and Farouk Hamda, many of them waiting for an aircraft with our vice-president and an Iraqi delegation to arrive ...*'[19]

Heshmat continued:

'*Around 08.15, the visibility improved to 2,000m [6,562ft], which meant we could fly. I put on my g-suit again and then went to check my aircraft. While doing my walk around, I could see Samir Aziz Mikhail and Farid Harfush check their aircraft as well, some 100m [328ft] away. Minutes later I was surprised to see two aircraft appearing over the runway. They came in at low level, and then climbed and my first impression was that these were MiG-19s announced by the tower. Then I saw two others and heard a loud 'click' – when their shells began to hit our aircraft! Two of them exploded shortly after. Next I saw that Ilyushin transport with our vice-president on board attempting to land on the runway ...*'

Tahsin Zaki added:

'*We were still standing beside our aircraft, ready for the training sortie ... when the Il-14 carrying the VIP delegation was about to land. Suddenly we were completely surprised to see two [Dassault] Super Mystère B2s flying very low. They crossed the airfield from west to east, releasing their bombs on the main runway in the process, while other aircraft attacked the MiG-21s with cannon fire.*'[20]

Samir Aziz Mikhail recalled:

'*I was on duty at first light and the Squadron CO and I sat the Readiness State I. We finished our duty at 08.30 and went to shave. While I was shaving I heard the strafing. We couldn't imagine that the Israelis would attack us ... I saw the attack with my own eyes: an Ouragan [sic] strafed the four Readiness State I aircraft and set the first MiG in the row on fire. The plane went up in flames and then a rocket shot out of that fireball and hit one of Su-7s and this exploded as well. All the aircraft*

A fireball marks the end of one of No. 55 Squadron's Su-7BMKs at Fayid, on the morning of 5 June, as seen on this still from an Israeli gun-camera film. An entire series of such detonations caused shock and great confusion at Fayid in the moments that followed.
(Albert Grandolini Collection)

were full of fuel and they exploded one after the other, each time damaging the next aircraft in the row …'[21]

Alaa Barakat recalled the fiery end of No. 47 Squadron's MiG-21s:

'We ran out of the squadron ready room … the bullets from one of the strafing aircraft missed us by 1.5m [4.9ft], hitting the staircase next to the room. There was a MiG-21 squadron at Fayd, commanded by Maj Amosis Azer, a Copt, who was very fat. This unit had four aircraft on Readiness State I, four at Readiness State II and

Another gun-camera still records an attack on two Su-7BMKs at Fayid, at the moment the rear aircraft received a direct hit in the engine area.
(IDF via Albert Grandolini)

Samir Aziz Mikhail, an Egyptian Coptic Christian, would become one of Egypt's most experienced MiG-21 pilots by the end of 1967. On 5 June, he was not particularly lucky when most of his unit's MiG-21s were destroyed at Fayid before he could scramble, but Mikhail went on to avenge the shame of that day in subsequent encounters with the Israelis. (Group 73)

four at State III. Azer ran towards the State I aircraft but they had all already been hit. So, he ran to the State II aircraft but they were hit as he ran. He then headed for the State III aircraft and the same thing happened again …[22]

Mikhail could hardly believe his eyes at the scenes around him:

'*In shock, my eyes met those of another pilot, so we took our jeep over to the squadron ready room. We ran to get our helmets and flight gear, but we found the ready room smashed by a bomb. We found and extracted our gear from the rubble and ran to try and reach the Readiness State II alert aircraft that were near the middle of the runway. But, before we drove 200m [656ft], these aircraft all blew up and were on fire from the Israeli attacks. So, we turned back. Within a maximum of five minutes all our MiG-21s and Su-7s ready for flight were destroyed. They were on the tarmac, parked wing to wing, 2m [6.6ft] from each other, and so when one blew up it damaged the others. No one took off because they hit the runway with bombs and blew up all the alert planes. We ran to a MiG-15 dual-control trainer. It had a cannon. There was no starter and when we came back with one that MiG had been hit too … Meanwhile, an Il-14 landed with the vice-president of Egypt and the Iraqi prime minister – I saw them running out of the aircraft. After that the Il-14 was strafed and it caught fire. So we gathered in the mess. We saw that they even shot up the [North American] Harvard trainer parked at the base. It was such a disaster.*'

Stumbling out of the Il-14 that barely managed to land at Fayid before receiving multiple hits from Israeli fighter-bombers and catching fire, the Egyptian Prime Minister el-Shafei first tried to find shelter behind a small hummock, then watched what was happening:

Egyptian Vice-President, Hussein el-Shafei, and an Iraqi delegation led by Iraqi Prime Minister Yahya el-Tahir barely managed to jump clear of a burning Il-14 that landed at Fayid air base while this was under the first Israeli attack. The burnt-out hulk of this transport subsequently blocked the main runway, rendering this air base closed for crucial hours. (Albert Grandolini Collection)

'*It was an unforgettable sight. Our fighters were lined up in rows and the Israelis took them out with single bursts from their guns. They were an easy target ... The Israelis flew so low I could see their faces.*'[23]

Tahsin Zaki continued:

'*Another wave of Israeli fighters attacked our aircraft parked near the middle of the runway. Some of our pilots manned the ready aircraft and tried to take off but were unable because the main runway was now holed. They attempted to taxi towards the subsidiary runway but found it blocked by the Il-14 that had been hit after landing. These aircraft trying to take off were hit next. Lt Sayed Kamil was killed in the process – he never had a chance.*'

Farid Harfush confirmed that the situation worsened during the second attack:

'*Eight minutes later came the second Israeli attack. They repeated the exercise and first bombed the runway then strafed parked aircraft, which were hit one after the other.*'[24]

Mamdouh Heshmat recalled the shock of the first attack:

'*We became furious and frustrated, we screamed at the Jews that attacked us and destroyed the four aircraft held at Readiness State I and then the four held at Readiness State II. And that Ilyushin not only stopped in the middle of the runway, but it was hit and burned out and Israeli bombs damaged the runway so that only 500m [1,640ft] was left in between the craters ... We then hastened to help the people that escaped from the Ilyushin. We took a car, drove there to pick them up and bring our vice-president and the Iraqi prime minister to the Officers' Club ... They were in a state of complete shock ...*'

Salah Danish concluded his recollection of the first Israeli attacks on Fayid:

'*The Israelis hit the airfield causing terrible commotion, big fires and huge clouds of smoke. I remember the trauma and shock that impacted everyone. We could not believe what was happening and were astonished that the Israelis dared to wage a war. Immediately after the Israeli strike, we found that the entire row of MiG-21s was completely destroyed, together with a number of Su-7s. The plane carrying el-Shafei and the Iraqi Prime Minister al-Tahir landed safely but was then hit on the ground and burned out. Our technicians then moved a number of Su-7s and MiG-19s underneath the trees around the airfield before the second strike came in. We attempted to move four MiG-19s to the road outside the airfield, but realised they were not going to be able to take off from there.*'

After being brought to the squadron ready room, el-Shafei was faced by a group of furious pilots, who had watched their fighters being blown to pieces – as ordered by their superiors. The pilots had little doubt as who was to blame for this mess:

'They said, 'Look what you've done! Are you happy with this? Why didn't you let us strike first?''

Initially hoping that the Israeli attack would remain limited in nature, Tahsin Zaki concluded that despite the terrible shock, complete destruction of eight MiG-21s and four Su-7s held at Readiness State I and II, and despite the fact that the runways at Fayid were heavily cratered, a significant number of aircraft under his command had survived the Israeli onslaught:

'There were explosions everywhere, but we kept going … After the first attack the pilots and mechanics under my command started dragging undamaged and lightly damaged aircraft into hiding in an area where there were lots of eucalyptus and pine trees … Some of the men doing the pushing were killed. We also found that most of the planes which had been dispersed around the base were untouched and that we still had about 16 fighters.'

Helpless pilots and other ground personnel continued fighting, nevertheless, and when four Ouragans appeared at low level, around 09.10, they returned fire with hand-held weapons, as Tahsin Zaki continued:

'Another Israeli wave came in low and this time most of our anti-aircraft guns opened fire. I myself shot down an Ouragan with an anti-aircraft machine gun. The pilot tried an emergency landing on the Fayid-Ismailia road but crashed and was killed … He looked as if he was asleep. He was a handsome, elegant young man. I told the men to bury him immediately … It is strange how fighter pilots are always seeking to destroy their opponents but always hope that their enemy will survive by baling out or crash-land safely once the battle is joined …'

The Israeli pilot Mordechai Pinto was killed. The Egyptians collected his body and this was buried at the nearby military cemetery. However, this loss did not stop the onslaught and yet more IDF/AF fighters appeared to extend the damage, as Farid Harfush recalled:

'After the first 40 minutes of attacks, we were left without a single MiG-21 ready for flight. The only aircraft remaining were Su-7s, meanwhile well hidden between eucalyptus and citrus trees outside the base. We decided to drive the Vice-President el-Shafey and his delegation to Cairo, and then go to el-Mansourah, which we'd heard was not yet attacked and where we were to find operational MiG-21s …'

Samir Aziz Mikhail's experience of subsequent Israeli attacks on Fayid was even less positive and demonstrated that the IDF/AF pilots were not only intent on attacking UARAF aircraft that morning:

'My friend Aziz, a Su-7 pilot, and I ran to a bunker to escape and we found out it was actually a bomb depot. So, we ran away again. They then told us to go to Fayid village, which is about 2km [1.2 miles] from the airfield. I remember that four of us took a Russian-made Volga car and went there, and then we watched further attacks. I saw a Super Mystère that had its nose painted like a shark make an attack at the airport and come by very low. So, I pulled out my Beretta 9mm pistol, took a deflection and shot at him. I remember very clearly that he looked at me and I could see his eyes. I thought that I had hit him but that I did not hurt him. My companions yelled at me that the aeroplane was coming back. My back was to him and when I looked

back I didn't know what to do. I thought, if I run to the right or left he could correct and easily shoot me. So, I ran towards him, and towards a wall for cover. As I ran towards the wall I saw him shoot and the shells hit only a few inches to my right. I jumped and I hit the wall and hurt my head – but I was alive. I wanted to know this pilot. He came from Israel to find and to kill me – why?'

In summary, Air Group 1 lost a total of 12 MiG-21s, two MiG-19s and 10 Su-7s at Fayid on that morning, while both runways and the sole taxiway were either destroyed or blocked by the wreckage of the ill-fated Il-14, which landed at 08.46. Tahsin Zaki's efforts to operate the remaining aircraft from the nearby road proved unsuccessful. Nevertheless, thanks to their immense efforts, the ground crews managed to save more than a squadron's-worth of MiG-21s, MiG-19s and Su-7s, hiding them between the buildings of the base and the nearby village.

Prime Target: Abu Suweir

Housing no fewer than four squadrons of Il-28s as well as the elite No. 26 Squadron equipped with recently delivered MiG-21PFMs, Abu Suweir was a primary Israeli target. Therefore, the IDF/AF deployed no fewer than three sections of Mirage IIICJs (12 fighters in total) to attack this base within the first 20 minutes, followed by additional formations later on. Fuad Kamal recalled:

'The first I knew about the attack was a loud explosion. It was the runway being bombed. Seconds later two Israeli aircraft came over very low and there were more explosions. They had dropped their 'dibber' [runway-piercing; authors' note] bombs on the runway intersections. I jumped into a jeep and drove fast to the ops room, which was quite a long way away. I telephoned my squadron leader at Meliz and told him to scramble his aircraft to cover Abu Suweir, but he told me that exactly the same had happened where he was. So I called Inchas, and they said the same …'[25]

However, the Israeli plan had a significant flaw: the pilots of the first four Mirages were ordered to bomb the runway only, and not to strafe. Instead, they went on to fly a CAP over Sinai. This decision enabled a number of MiG-21 pilots of No. 26 Squadron to scramble in the following minutes, while most of the other aircraft were meanwhile hidden in various corners of the air base. Kamal continued:

'Two of the ready aircraft did take off on a sub-runway. One was shot down while retracting its undercarriage and the pilot killed. The other [flown by Capt Sami Marei; authors' note] flew cover, before safely landing on a sub-runway.'

The next to depart were to be Awad Hamdi and his wingman, Capt Asim Ghazi. As Hamdi recalled:

'We scrambled – without orders – after the first attack. The Israelis bombed the cross-section with anti-runway bombs. It was our first experience with these weapons. After inspecting the situation, I figured out that flying an aircraft without any drop tanks I could get airborne. Our main runway was 27, but I was scrambled from Runway 22, which crossed it. My base commander marked the place where I left the ground – I cleared the next crater by 6-8m [20-26ft].'[26]

The procedure Hamdi and Ghazi used in order to get airborne from barely 500m (1,640ft) of runway that remained intact was in fact strictly forbidden. Nevertheless, the pilots knew that taking off from such a short runway was next to impossible: there-

Capt Sami Marei, who was among the first pilots to scramble from Abu Suweir on 5 June 1967.
(David Nicolle Collection)

Capt Sami Marei in the cockpit of a MiG-21F-13, prior to the June 1967 War. He managed to return to base safely after a mission of which the exact details remain unknown. These photographs show the massive windshield and instrumentation in front of the pilot, which severely obstructed the view out of the cockpit and to the front of the early MiG-21.
(David Nicolle Collection)

fore, they kept their brakes on hard while pushing the throttles to full afterburner, waiting for their engines to spool up to full power before releasing the brakes. The two MiGs jumped off like rockets, their pilots pulling the sticks hard into their stomachs. Clearing the craters on the runway by only a few feet, Hamdi and Ghazi accelerated away towards the north, just in time to hear frantic calls for help from the Il-14 under way as an ELINT gatherer, and which was now being attacked by several Super Mystère B2s while attempting to land at Kabrit. Making a hard turn towards the south, the two Egyptians accelerated and headed in that direction, but arrived too late: the Il-14 was hit and forced to make an emergency landing in the sand dunes of Sinai.

Awad Hamdi was one of at least five UARAF MiG-21 pilots who scored confirmed kills on 5 June. His victim was one of two Super Mystère B2s of No. 105 Squadron IDF/AF which were withdrawing eastwards after attacking Kabrit, having downed an Egyptian Il-14 transport. (Awad Hamdi Collection)

Moments later Hamdi and Ghazi engaged several Super Mystères that attempted to withdraw eastwards:

'I achieved a single kill with one of my R-3S Atolls. We had no cannon in the MiG-21FL. I saw them [the Israelis] and made a rendezvous ... They made a break. I picked one and I was certain I was going to get him. Their finger four broke into four directions. My wingman tried one of his missiles but because we were at low altitude it just went into the ground. I aimed at the centre point of his [the Israeli's] exhaust while my speed was more than 1,200km/h [746mph]. I launched my missile. It hit close to the Mystère, so I engaged again. They did not stay and fight. They had a mission: attack and go.'

Fuad Kamal commented on the effects of the Israeli attacks on Abu Suweir, which continued almost undisturbed:

'Between Israeli attacks, the ground personnel pulled surviving aircraft, including some damaged ones, out of the exposed area. They put them under trees outside the airfield and in other sheltered areas. Meanwhile, the delayed-action bombs continued to go off ...'

At 09.20, Brig Gen Saad Rifat, Base CO of Abu Suweir, gave permission to four other pilots to take off in a similar fashion to Hamdi and Ghazi. Capt Hassan Shihata and Lt

The one that did not get away: this was the third UARAF Il-14 of No. 11 Squadron UARAF airborne on the morning of 5 June. It was caught by several Super Mystères following their attack on Kabrit. After being hit by cannon fire it had to make an emergency landing in the Sinai desert. (IDF)

Gallal Abdel Alim flew as a pair, followed by Capt Abdel Moneim Mursi and George Tossah. The latter two received a strict order to remain over the base while Shihata and Alim were told to provide cover for Fayid as the personnel in Abu Suweir's tower could see thick columns of smoke rising in the area.[27] Shortly afterwards, though at an unspecified time, Shihata and Alim engaged an Israeli fighter that was withdrawing eastwards, starting a long pursuit towards el-Arish, as recalled by Taher Zaki:

'*Shihata and Alim engaged several enemy formations, including one near el-Arish and there was an air combat. Shihata came away and flew back to Fayid but had to eject after running out of fuel, shortly before reaching the Canal. Alim's fighter was hit during the combat and started losing fuel. He also ejected shortly before reaching the Canal. Both managed to get back safely together with withdrawing Army units.*'[28]

Kamal also confirmed Zaki's recollection:

'*Gallal Abdel Alim took off and engaged several Israelis, firing both of his R-3S missiles in the process. He ran out of fuel and ejected over Sinai, but came back with the Army.*'

Capt Abdel Moneim Mursi was one of six pilots from No. 26 Squadron UARAF who managed to scramble from the ruined runways of Abu Suweir on the morning of 5 June. Egyptian sources credit him with two kills during the course of subsequent engagements. While attempting to land at Abu Suweir following an approach from the west and into the sun, Mursi failed to see a bomb crater and crashed. (David Nicolle Collection)

Taken after the first wave of IDF/AF attacks, this Israeli reconnaissance photograph of Abu Suweir shows that at least five of Air Group 61's Il-28s survived the initial onslaught. Nevertheless, apparently no attempt was made to fly these bombers to airfields beyond Israeli reach, and they were all subsequently knocked out. (IDF)

The first formation of Israeli Mirages to attack Abu Suweir did not strafe any Egyptian fighters on the ground, so enabling a number of MiG-21PFMs of No. 26 Squadron to scramble during the minutes that followed. This gun-camera still from an Israeli fighter shows two intact MiG-21PFMs with open cockpits. Minutes later, both MiGs were airborne. (IDF via Albert Grandolini)

Shortly before 10.00, Mursi was almost out of fuel and about to land, when a formation of Mystères was detected approaching Abu Suweir, as AVM Mohammad Okasha recalled:

'Mursi achieved a tangible success, bringing down two enemy aircraft. Sadly, he subsequently perished while attempting to land his aircraft on the damaged runway.'

Although disrupting the Israeli attack on Abu Suweir and firing his two R-3S missiles at two different opponents in the process, Mursi shot down only one Mystère IVA from No. 116 Squadron, flown by Dan Manor. The Israeli ejected safely and spent the rest of the day attempting to hide, before being captured by Egyptian ground forces the next morning.

Mursi's failed attempt to recover at Abu Suweir was witnessed by Maj Ali Zine el-Abidine and Lt Abdel Hamid Mustafa, two MiG-21F-13 pilots from No. 40 Squadron who arrived from Hurghada. Short of fuel, they decided to divert to el-Mansourah, landing safely around 10.20. However, el-Mansourah was only a secondary air base at that time, mainly used by transport aircraft. It therefore lacked facilities and ground personnel capable of servicing MiG-21s. Not surprisingly, it took a long time to prepare the two MiGs for another sortie and both were destroyed on the ground during the first Israeli attack on that airfield, around 11.30. Two other MiG-21s from Hurghada subsequently landed at Cairo West, where they were successfully hidden between the local buildings.

Despite repeated Israeli attacks and several losses, as well as heavily damaged runways, No. 26 Squadron's force of MiG-21PFMs at Abu Suweir remained largely intact and was to see more action around noon. Fikry el-Ashmawy, also at Abu Suweir on that morning, recalled why:

'The sandbagged revetments to shelter aircraft at Abu Suweir were constructed only four days before the Israeli attack. Although they were only 5-6ft [1.5-1.8m] high, they proved very effective and none of the aircraft inside these revetments was damaged – or even attacked – by the Israelis during their first strike. These aircraft were the ones we used to fight back during the following days, before the Algerian aircraft arrived. We flew them from an undamaged taxiway.'[29]

Taher Zaki, who had long argued for such additional defensive arrangements, came to a similar conclusion during the course of a telephone call to Mamdouh Taliba, the CO of Air Group 2 at Kabrit:

'I called Mamdouh to ask what was going on there. He answered; 'It's fantastic. They are attacking the dummy planes and the old runway'. The real planes that had been covered weren't attacked. None of them were hit during the first two attacks. But there were also about eight or nine open pens and these had one aircraft in each. They were the only ones attacked. We also had very big hangars at Kabrit, so we had put four MiGs in each, one in each corner of the hangar where they were less likely to be hit.'

Knock-out at Inchas, Cairo West and Beni Suweif

At 08.50 a very painful blow hit the UARAF MiG-21 units based at Inchas, when four Mirage IIICJs attacked. As well as scores of fighters destroyed on the ground, the two MiG-21F-13s that managed to scramble around 09.00, flown by Lt Ahmed Atef and Lt Hassan el-Qusri from No. 49 Squadron, were also lost. These losses occurred during a furious air combat in which Atef claimed one Mystère as shot down directly over the air base, before beginning a pursuit of the remaining Israeli formation that brought him far away from his base. Running out of fuel, the Egyptian pilot ejected safely and came down under his parachute in a field outside the village of Kirdasa, near the Suez Canal. Once on the ground, Atef found himself surrounded by threatening farmers who thought he was an Israeli, and was saved only through a last-minute intervention by the crew of a nearby SAM site. Atef returned to Inchas around an hour later, in a jeep supplied by the same air defence unit that had saved him. El-Qusri returned in similar fashion shortly later. His aircraft had run out of fuel while pursuing an Israeli fighter towards the Mediterranean coast and he was forced to eject.

In total, no fewer than 28 MiG-21s were lost at Inchas during the first hour of attacks, together with no fewer than 80 per cent of the base's technical equipment, all three runways and the sole taxiway. However, with Atef and el-Qusri disturbing at

This MiG-21FL of No. 43 Squadron survived the onslaught on Inchas on the morning of 5 June with relatively light damage and was photographed by an IDF/AF reconnaissance fighter shortly before noon. Notable are a pair of UB-16-57 rocket pods, as well as identification stripes on the wingtips and around the rear fuselage.
(Albert Grandolini Collection)

As seen in this photograph taken at Cairo West in the mid-1960s, parking MiG-21s and MiG-17s (background) in long rows was the everyday norm within the UARAF, and resulted in the massive losses suffered by both types on the morning of 5 June.
(David Nicolle Collection)

least one of the Israeli formations, Egyptian pilots and technicians managed to save at least eight MiG-21s and a subsequent inspection revealed that around 900m (2,953ft) of runway could still be used. Inchas thus become operational once again around noon.[30]

No such scenes occurred at Cairo West. The tremendous detonation of two Tu-16s hit on the ground right at the start of the attack (both aircraft were loaded with a total of around 25,000 litres/5,500 Imp gal of fuel, 2,300 rounds of 23mm ammunition and four KSR-2 air-to-surface missiles) forced most of the base personnel into their trenches. As a consequence, none of the MiG-21s operated by the locally based Fighter Training Unit managed to scramble. Furthermore, both runways and one taxiway, the nearby radar station and the SAM site were all knocked out. Subsequently, the Israelis concentrated their efforts on destroying the remaining six bombers of No. 95 Squadron, along with two MiG-15UTIs and 12 MiG-17s, as well as four partially assembled Su-7s on the ground.

Beni Suweif fared only slightly better – and then mainly because five Tu-16s took off only minutes before the attack began, and were given timely warning by the tower to distance themselves towards the south. The 12 remaining Tu-16s were destroyed on the ground, together with the main and secondary runways, and much of the ground support equipment.[31]

The scene at Beni Suweif as photographed by an Israeli reconnaissance fighter, following the first wave of IDF/AF attacks. A Tu-16 bomber is burning fiercely in the foreground, and several others in the background, while one example (centre) appears to remain intact.
(IDF)

Gridlock at GHQ

At the time of the first Israeli strike, almost the entire Egyptian military leadership was either on board two Il-14 transports under way to Bir Thamada, or was waiting for their arrival at that air base. Unlike the aircraft carrying the Egyptian vice-president and the Iraqi prime minister, which landed at Fayid, the Il-14 carrying FM Amer and his entourage remained airborne throughout the first wave of Israeli attacks – its pilot searching for a safe landing place for more than 1.5 hours. Eventually, this Il-14 landed at Cairo International some time between 10.30 and 10.45. Characteristically, at Cairo International, Col Muhammad Ayyub – Amer's air force liaison officer – was waiting with a drawn pistol, convinced that a coup had been staged against his superior. Ayyub shouted, *'You want to murder him, you dogs!'* as the other officers present pulled out their guns as well, but Sidki Mahmmoud stepped in between them, averting a firefight: *'Fools, put your guns away! Israel is attacking us!'*

FM Amer then suffered the additional humiliation of having to use a taxi to get to Supreme Headquarters. Arriving there some 20 minutes later, he and AM Sidki Mahmoud were informed of the full extent of the Israeli onslaught. Although receiving incorrect information that only between 37 and 40 Egyptian fighters had survived the first wave of attacks, Amer was elated when the same reports claimed the downing of 86 enemy aircraft. Bypassing Lt Gen Riyadh in Amman, he called Damascus and Baghdad and requested the Syrian and Iraqi air arms to execute Operation Rashid immediately.[32] Only then, minutes later, did he wire the C-in-C UAC, Lt Gen Riyadh, in Amman, telling him that the Israelis had lost 75 per cent of their air power and that the Egyptian Army was mounting an offensive into the Negev Desert. This was an obvious lie, but it seems that from around this time Amer began to suffer from such shock and confusion that he was entirely incapable of rational thinking and even less of taking aggressive action that could still have altered the outcome of the battle. Reacting in his usual fashion, he then continued bypassing his subordinates to telephone various base commanders on *open lines* – delivering even more intelligence straight into Israeli hands. Around 10.45, Tahsin Zaki received such a telephone call:

'Next I got a telephone call from our Supreme Commander, Abdel Hakeem Amer, who asked about the situation at our base, so I told him how much had survived the attack. All the MiG-21s were destroyed. Twelve Sukhois and three MiG-19s had been saved. 'Very well', Amer said, 'execute Operation Puma', but I told him that this was impossible because our runways were damaged. I promised to try and use the Fayid-Ismailia road as a runway and that I would report back in two hours. Unfortunately it is a very narrow road and it was impossible for the large Su-7 to use it …[33]

The former C-in-C EAF, AM Abd el-Latif Boghdadi explained the situation that developed in the minutes that followed:

'Amer kept asking Sidki Mahmoud how many planes he had shot down so far. He'd answer with a figure which Abdul Hakim [Amer] would repeat loudly so we could hear it. Then he would say, 'so why are you upset then?' Then Sidki would call again, repeating that wave after wave of attacks were coming in on our airfields. Sidki said that the Americans and the British must be helping the Israelis. They [the Israelis; authors' note] just did not have that many planes on their own. Abdul Hakim asked him to get proof of what he was saying.'

Before long, Amer stopped questioning Sidki Mahmoud's statements regarding US and British involvement and became paralysed by indecision. Boghdadi attempted to talk with Amer:

'Then I said I would come back later if the Field Marshal was too busy to brief me. Amer insisted I take a seat … Then I noticed that AM Sidki Mahmoud kept tele-phoning … as far as I could see, he was crying. Amer told him more than once to pull himself together.'[34]

Soon Amer himself was also stricken by panic. His state of shock ensured that he failed to do anything to change the situation, and worse still, the leading Egyptian mili-tary officer had developed a picture of the situation that was far more pessimistic than the reality. Anwar el-Sadat arrived at the GHQ around 11.00, to find Amer standing in the middle of his office:

'He looked around with wandering eyes. I said, 'Good morning', but he didn't seem to hear me. I said 'Good morning' again, but it took him about a minute to return my greeting. I immediately realised that something had gone wrong. I asked the others in the room and they told me that our air force was completely destroyed on the ground.'[35]

The sheer incompetence of the top Egyptian military commander then paved the way for the complete destruction of the Egyptian military. Indeed, a situation mani-fested itself in which Amer began reacting precisely in a manner that was favourable to the Israelis. Instead of realising that the UARAF had already received the major blow and that the Israelis were now mainly causing additional damage to runways and installations, Amer failed to issue any kind of coherent orders, as explained by Daghedi:

'A rumour had reached the GHQ that all the Egyptian aircraft had been destroyed by the very first Israeli air strike. Our top military commanders never commis-sioned the Air Force to engage in any kind of operations because they seemingly believed that rumour … Actually, the planes were ready, but we received no author-ity to impose air protection. The C-in-C never issued any orders to engage the 212 aircraft under his command and waiting for his orders.'[36]

Clearly, most of the top UARAF officers followed Amer's example: nobody decided to take the initiative and began issuing orders independently.

Amer next began desperately clutching at Sidki Mahmoud's suggestion that the major powers were involved, eventually losing himself in fantasy. Nasser arrived at the GHQ shortly after and, in contrast to Amer, not only failed to recognise the true extent of the disaster, but also ignored it. Still, he was not ready to believe Amer's claim of US involvement. He replied:

'I am not prepared to believe this nor to issue an official communiqué that Amer-ica was the aggressor – not unless you can produce the wing of a single aircraft with American markings on it!'[37]

One of President Nasser's closest confidants, Hassanein Heikal, later explained that despite his presence at the GHQ, the president was unaware of the true extent of the destruction of the UARAF. Whether this is true, it is certain that, instead of exercis-ing his responsibility through intervening and dismissing FM Amer on the spot and thus averting the catastrophe which would befall the entire military the next morning, Nasser left the military to its own devices. While it is quite obvious that – for what-

ever reasons, whether through his own decision or differences with Amer – Nasser attempted not to meddle in military issues, it is clear that as the leading political decision-maker, the President of Egypt was personally responsible for the control of the military leadership. In this capacity, he failed to act. Instead, he left for his villa and did not re-emerge for the next two days.

It is therefore of lesser importance that Nasser – despite calling GHQ on regular basis – should not have discovered the true extent of the Air Force's losses until that afternoon, between 14.00 and 16.00. The first realisation should have come during a visit by Vice-President Shafei, who informed Nasser of his own experience at Fayid, and secondly during the course of a telephone conversation with FM Fawzy. However, if this was really the case and if Nasser shared no blame for the catastrophe which befell the UARAF, why did he make a call to Lt Gen Riyadh and King Hussein in Amman, around 13.45, telling them not only that the Air Force was hitting back at Israel but also inflicting heavy losses on the IDF/AF? He even claimed that an Egyptian division was advancing into Israel – in turn leading to a number of entirely incorrect decisions on the part of the HQ Eastern Front UAC.

While a satisfactory answer might never become available, it is certain that later on, upon realising the extent of the disaster, Nasser decided to issue his first statement about US and British involvement, instead of bringing the situation at GHQ under control. He sent a message to the Soviet Premier Kosygin informing him that '… *the United States is backing Israel to its full extent and there is definite evidence that the US Sixth Fleet and US bases in the area participated in this operation*'. Eventually, Nasser became convinced that US pressure was designed to prepare the international theatre for the coming events and to give Israel time to get ready and take advantage by launching the first strike.[38]

Sidki Mahmoud's conclusion about US involvement, all too easily accepted by Amer and subsequently followed by Nasser, might appear surprising – considering that an opening Israeli air attack had been expected for days. The crucial question is therefore, if such an attack had been expected, as Nasser and his top commanders announced to

A dramatic photograph of Cairo West, taken by an Israeli reconnaissance fighter after the first wave of IDF/AF attacks. It shows not only thick smoke rising from several destroyed Tu-16KS bombers, but also at least one burning An-12. The destruction of the bulk of the UARAF bomber fleet came as a rude surprise for the top Egyptian commanders, though elsewhere losses were not as heavy as they had initially assessed.
(IDF)

all their subordinates and even to King Hussein of Jordan on a number of occasions, and if AM Sidki Mahmoud knew that the Air Force would suffer losses in that strike, why did the attack cause such a shock?

It is obvious that the reports of losses – and the successes in downing large numbers of Israeli fighters – that Amer and Sidki Mahmoud received from various commanders proved highly influential. As Tahsin Zaki explained, however, the reports in question were actually nowhere near as inflated as the figures accepted by GHQ. Much more importantly, neither of the top two Egyptian commanders ever realised that, in order to counter its lack of strategic depth, Israel had developed highly mobile, mechanised ground forces backed up by air power and designed to fight on Arab territory. The Israeli forces relied on detailed intelligence about their enemy's capabilities and intentions, as well as surprise and aggressive operations. Correspondingly, the Egyptians considered it inconceivable that Israel could achieve such surprise and such a tremendous sortie rate without additional support from aircraft and pilots provided by external sources. They could also not believe that the IDF/AF would take the risk of leaving its strategic air defence depleted in order to launch a mass strike against Egypt. Obviously, not even AM Sidki Mahmoud realised that by minimising the turnaround times required to re-arm and refuel their aircraft – in the manner in which the UARAF expected to operate as well – Israel managed to fly so intensively that its air force appeared much more powerful than it actually was. Instead, the Egyptians let themselves be influenced by the number of US and British interventions launched with the help of aircraft carriers in previous years. Prematurely assuming that the UARAF was completely destroyed, and dumbfounded by Israel's capability to launch massive air strikes, Amer and Sidki Mahmoud simply gave up the fight. They panicked and concluded that the Israelis were being helped by the US and UK.[39]

The assumptions of Amer and Sidki Mahmoud provided the basis of the subsequent accusation that American and British aircraft had assisted the Israelis, but they also formed the foundation of the Egyptian defeat. Because of the nature of their training and because of the way the Egyptian military was organised at that time, this meant that none of their subordinates was free to act independently. Instead of taking the initiative and ordering their aircraft into the air, the Egyptian base commanders were limited to awaiting orders or trying to hide surviving jets, as summarised by Daghedi:

'... the Air Force fell into a state of confusion which rendered it impossible to provide any air protection ... No air protection was ordered from the C-in-C of the Armed Forces nor requested from the commander on the front ...'

Search for Aircraft

With senior commanders paralysed through shock, chaos, heavy losses, and their own incompetence, as well as a debilitating chain of command, UARAF officers, pilots, NCOs and other personnel found themselves left on their own to search for serviceable aircraft which they could operate in order to defend against continued Israeli attacks. As usual, Tahsin Zaki was at the forefront:

'We learned that the Su-7s dispersed at Cairo West had not been destroyed, so I ordered half the surviving Su-7 pilots from my base to move to Cairo West at the first opportunity. We still had 16 pilots available and wanted to hit back.'

During the early afternoon of 5 June, MiG-21 units at Abu Suweir and Inchas managed to scramble a number of jets. Most of these became involved in air battles with Israeli fighters, in the course of which their pilots scored several confirmed kills. This pre-war photograph shows two MiG-21s taking off from Inchas.
(Nour Bardai Collection)

Several MiG-21 pilots from Fayid jumped into a car and travelled to el-Mansourah, as Samir Aziz Mikhail recalled:

'… I took my squadron leader, the second in command and several others and drove a car at high speed to el-Mansourah AB, where they said there were safe aircraft. But, we found nothing at all there – no planes. So, we went to Inchas and found that air base also badly hit, with many fires.'

Farid Harfush was with Mikhail's group:

'Sufficient to say we found no aircraft at el-Mansourah. It wasn't really much of an air base back then: just some barbed wire and a runway. Next we met Col el-Abidine, who led two MiG-21s based at Hurghada and landed there. Local villagers provided us all with some cheese and olives so we made a short break before continuing our voyage to Inchas …'

Meanwhile, working frenetically under repeated Israeli air attack, the ground crews at Abu Suweir managed to prepare no fewer than 11 MiG-21s for operations. Awad Hamdi was one of the first pilots to get airborne:

'On my second sortie I took another aircraft and I started it using the ground battery … It was a disaster: the Il-28s were in flames and the Israelis were bombing and strafing. They kept strafing and bombing our airfield until the last light. On my second sortie our air defences shot me down over the centre of our airfield. I ejected and was in a very bad shape.'

Awad Hamdi landed safely, but suffered spinal injuries. He continued a successful career with the UARAF, but was out of the business of flying supersonic fighters.

The MiG-21 units at Inchas were not entirely finished either. On the contrary, by 13.00, the ground crews had managed to prepare four MiG-21s for take-off, and Taher Zaki recalled their subsequent action:

'Brig Gen Sami Fuad attempted to scramble with his MiG-21 but was hit by the Israeli fire while still on the ground and killed. Capt Nabil Shuwakri followed. He managed to get into the air and attack the enemy. He shot down an Israeli fighter but was forced to land at Zagazig because of a shortage of fuel. After refuelling, he returned to his base.'

Other Egyptian sources indicate that Sami Fuad had actually managed to take off and become involved in an air combat with four Israeli jets. Together with his wingman, the Egyptian brigadier general might have claimed one of them as shot down. The Egyptian pilots then disrupted attacks by the other Israeli fighters to such an extent

The flying career of one of the most courageous Egyptian MiG-21 pilots, Awad Hamdi, ended after he sustained spinal injuries resulting from an ejection over Abu Suweir, after Egyptian air defences shot down his aircraft on the early afternoon of 5 June 1967.
(Awad Hamdi Collection)

Brig Gen Sami Fuad was the CO Air Group 9 at Inchas. He managed to take off and engage several Israeli fighters in the early afternoon of 5 June, and was credited with at least damaging an IDF/AF fighter-bomber before his aircraft was shot down in error by Egyptian air defences.
(David Nicolle Collection)

that they jettisoned their bombs well away from the air base. In fact, the bombs hit the nearby barracks of the Egyptian Commandos, killing 58 men.[40]

Minutes later, Fuad's MiG-21 was hit by an Egyptian SA-2 SAM, or by 37mm AAA – as Nabil Shuwakri, who scrambled around 13.30, related:

'We were storing some MiG-21FLs and two or three MiG-21F-13s at a place outside the base, but all the other aircraft on the ground at Inchas were destroyed. They [the Israelis; authors' note] bombed the runways and Inchas was paralysed. Eventually, we found a stretch of taxiway next to Runway 22 that was around 900m [2,953ft] long. I know since I measured it in a car. I was the first one to take off and the Brigadier General [Sami Fuad; authors' note] also took off, and after that two captains took off. I did a CAP over Bilbeis, which is very close to Inchas. After a short time Inshawi, one of the captains, joined me over Bilbeis. I was at about 15,000ft [4,572m] when they told me that the Israelis were now attacking again. I dove down but did not see any. Then I climbed again and did some hard manoeuvres and my wingman got lost in the process. Then they called me again and said there were Mirages over Inchas. So, I flew over and saw two Mirages flying to the left. I came behind them until I saw the flying helmet of the wingman. I was just looking because I couldn't shoot because of the limitations of my missiles. If they kept in formation I would be behind them. They tried to get behind me using horizontal manoeuvres but they didn't succeed. All the time I was hoping that they would turn back towards home. Then they dove and ran and I got a chance. I followed them and fired an Atoll at the leader. The first missile hit and there was heavy smoke. I looked at the wingman but didn't see him so I decided to launch a second missile at the same target. The Mirage exploded completely and pitched up in a stall turn and then the nose went right down. At the same time the brigadier general of the MiG-21F-13s was going after another Mirage but he was shot down by our 37mm flak and ejected. The MiG-21FL was limited. If I had a cannon I could have shot down the two turning Mirages so easily. But, I had to wait to get a missile shot.'

Another pilot who managed to scramble from Inchas in the early afternoon was Lt Hassan el-Qusri from No. 49 Squadron, who had ejected from his MiG-21 after it ran out of fuel over the Mediterranean Sea earlier the same morning. There are no reports of el-Qusri engaging any enemy fighters during his second sortie.[41]

The Secret of Israel's Success

Most accounts of the June 1967 War published in Israel and the West contain plenty of praise for the excellent training and preparations, as well as the execution of combat operations, by the IDF/AF. The same accounts frequently point to the fact that it was very precise intelligence about Arab air forces that permitted this success.

Indeed, some of the most recent Israeli publications on this topic indicate a surprisingly timely collection of information of such quality, that it appears IDF commanders had a better – and above all a more detailed – insight into the deployment and condition of various UARAF units than did top Egyptian commanders at the time.[42] Corresponding accounts have caused a great deal of unrest, mistrust and accusations of treason by various officers, particularly so in Egypt over the last 40 years. However, hardly any accounts – regardless of whether they were published in the West or

in Arabic – provide sufficient explanation of the manner in which Israel was able to gather such precise intelligence.

Many sources point to the activity of Israeli intelligence agents who penetrated particularly high circles in Egypt and Syria during the mid-1960s. In particular, affairs such as the 'Champagne Spy' in Egypt and Elli Cohen in Syria, or the defection of Munir Redfa became well known. The 'Champagne Spy' was Wolfgang Lotz, a German-born Jew who managed to penetrate some of the highest Egyptian defence circles. However, Lotz's activity concentrated on obtaining intelligence about the stillborn Egyptian surface-to-surface missile project. Presenting himself as an ex-Wehrmacht officer who had served in North Africa during World War II and as a businessman, Lotz put together a list of German scientists working on Egyptian rocket projects and sent letter bombs to some of them, threatening them to cease their work.[43] But Lotz could not provide an almost minute-by-minute update on the deployment of UARAF units and aircraft around various air bases on 5 June 1967 – he had been arrested in 1965 and sentenced to life imprisonment.

Even some of the UARAF commanders accused of treason following the 1967 War could not be held responsible for providing detailed intelligence about the status of their units, aircraft and personnel, for the simple reason that the commander of any particular air base had only a limited ability to learn what was going on at the other airfields on that fateful morning.

Similarly, the Alexandria-born Jew Eli Cohen – who entered Syria in 1961, presented himself as the son of a rich Damascene family under the fake name Kamal Amil Taabs, gained the confidence of many Syrian military and government officials, even toured the Syrian fortifications on the Golan Heights, and regularly sent intelligence to Israel by radio – had been captured in January 1965. He was then publicly hanged in Damascus in May of the same year. Therefore, the IDF lost at least two major sources of intelligence in Egypt and Syria long before it could launch Operation Moked.

Furthermore, even though bringing a flying manual for the MiG-21F-13, delivering his aircraft intact and in flyable condition to Israel, 'defector' Munir Redfa was certainly in no position to provide precise information about the deployment of the Egyptian, Jordanian and Syrian air arms, nor the numbers of aircraft these operated. Finally, the IDF/AF clearly flew dozens of reconnaissance sorties over Egypt, Jordan and Syria in the 1960s. Even though these provided the quality of information necessary to disable most Egyptian airfields, even operations such as these could not provide the information necessary for what the Israelis pulled off on the morning of 5 June 1967.

Nevertheless, from available publications it is perfectly clear that the IDF/AF collected very precise information throughout 1966 and 1967, and continued to do so while Operation Moked was under way.

The question that remains open, therefore, concerns the means of collecting information that enabled Israel to effectively track the movement of specific UARAF formations, as we will see in the next sub-chapter.

Obviously, Israeli military intelligence is extremely unlikely to ever openly reveal its methods of collecting intelligence. This topic is extremely sensitive, for the simple reason that intelligence is the only reliable source of information to the military. Nevertheless, over time a significant amount of circumstantial evidence has been published, pointing in a very specific direction: the laying of taps on telephone and telegraph cables connecting major Arab air bases with air force headquarters.

As early as 1954, the Syrian Army caught a team of five soldiers from the 1st Golani Infantry Brigade IDF while they were moving near an unspecified Syrian post on the Golan Heights. Given that even official Israeli military reports confirm that the task of this team was to replace the batteries that powered a tap on a telephone cable used by the Syrian Army, it is obvious that the tap in question had already been in service for some time.[44] This was very unlikely to have been the only such case and it is therefore not surprising that, as early as the start of the Suez War of 1956 – which began with North American P-51 Mustangs of the IDF/AF sweeping low over Sinai to cut the telephone cables connecting various Egyptian air bases – the Israelis clearly understood the importance to the Egyptians of this method of communication.

During the 1960s the IDF/AF undertook a number of operations which included the nocturnal insertion and recovery of small groups of special forces in Sinai, such as Operations Pioneer (in August 1963), and Bee-eater (in March 1964), both of which were reportedly motivated by the success of the Egyptian Army's deployment in Sinai in 1960, which had gone entirely unnoticed by Israeli intelligence. One of the largest enterprises of this kind was apparently Operation Kachal (Coraciidae), launched in the night of 1–2 December 1965, when three Sikorsky S-58 helicopters led by Maj Eliezer Cohen again flew three parties of Sayeret Matkal (a special forces unit assigned directly to GHQ IDF) deep into Sinai.[45] The last known operation of this kind launched before June 1967 was probably Operation Yargezi (Parus), undertaken in the night of 20-21 February 1967, when Aérospatiale SA.321 Super Frelon helicopters (introduced to Israeli service barely a year before) inserted another party of Sayeret Matkal into Sinai. Although none of the available reports specifically mention tapping Egyptian telephone cables, they do state that all of the involved helicopters carried 'special equipment' in addition to the special forces. A classic type of contemporary 'special equipment' likely to be deployed on such opportunities were sealed containers of various sizes, containing tapping devices, recording and transmitting equipment and a power supply.

Considering how much praise and decorations the involved Israeli soldiers received from their superiors after the June 1967 War, as well as a number of specific reports from high-level Arab sources about the use of open telephone lines and the obvious repercussions of such actions, it is almost certain that most of these Israeli operations were related to the planting of listening devices on various Egyptian, Iraqi, Jordanian and Syrian communication cables. Indeed, it is obvious that, particularly during the days before the war but especially so on the morning of 5 June, various Arab commanders made extensive use of telephone communications, conferring on various issues at length. This is the only logical source for the extremely precise intelligence the IDF continued collecting throughout the morning of 5 June 1967.[46]

Correspondingly, irrespective of complaints about the failures of various subordinates and extensive studies of so many failures from the first half of the 1960s, if anybody 'betrayed' the Arab air forces, it was most likely their own top officers through their own lack of caution on the telephone, as much as through their lack of knowledge, understanding and respect for their main enemy, and a misconduct of operations in general. Nowhere can this be so starkly seen as in the following description of what was going on in Egypt during the afternoon of 5 June 1967.

Bonanza in Hurghada

On the morning of 5 June 1967, the CO Air Group 15 at Hurghada airfield, Brig Gen Abd al-Aziz Badr, had a total of 12 MiG-19s and six MiG-21s under his command. Immediately after receiving reports about attacks on air bases in the north of the country, Badr scrambled two MiG-19s and two MiG-21s. Nevertheless, he declined a request from the CO No. 20 Squadron, Maj Sayd Shalash, for permission to raid the Israeli port of Eilat, citing a lack of corresponding orders. Instead, other than deploying two MiG-21s on a CAP over Abu Suweir at 09.30, and deploying two MiG-21s to Cairo West around 10.00, the crews of Air Group 15 spent most of that morning doing nothing at all, or flying lazy circles in their MiGs a few kilometres north of their own air base.[47]

As already described, the landing of two No. 40 Squadron MiG-21s at el-Mansourah had been reported *on open telephone lines* to various other UARAF air bases, which in turn resulted in an Israeli air raid against this airfield, at around 11.30.[48] It is certain that something similar happened at Helwan airfield, which was not a regular UARAF air base – and thus not included in the plan for Operation Moked – but rather an installation used for testing aircraft manufactured by the nearby Factory 36, where Kapil Bhargava still served as the chief test pilot for the Helwan HA-300 fighter project. Once again a *telephone call* from this airfield prompted an Israeli attack, as Bhargava recalled:

'No flights were planned for 5 June. I had started to carry my transistor radio to work to listen to the morning news from the BBC. I was not too surprised when just after 09.00, it reported the outbreak of hostilities. Around 09.15, I heard jet aircraft overhead. Looking out of the window, I saw three MiG-17s coming in to land. After parking them on the tarmac with orders to refuel and arm them, Zohair Shalabi walked into my office. His account of the sortie showed how the Egyptians had been caught completely off guard.

'Zohair had taken off from Cairo West AB with two pilots under training for operations for battle formation practice. Near the end of the sortie, when they arrived over Cairo West, he could see puffs on the ground and several aircraft, including Tu-16 bombers, on fire. He at once realised that the Israeli Air Force was 'visiting' the base. He asked the tower for instructions, and he [the tower] told him to get out, and away. Since he had been flying from Helwan until his recall to the Air Force, he diverted to our airfield. I advised him to leave Helwan and go somewhere far away such as el-Minya, well to the south. He phoned the headquarters for orders and was apparently told that there was nowhere left to run.

'Factory 36 had been working on clearance for an underwing rocket launcher on a MiG-19. The aircraft was serviceable for flight. Zohair promptly issued orders for it to be brought out, made ready for flight, and armed. To the right of the MiG-17s, this aircraft became the first of four MiGs in the line. Factory mechanics soon reported that the three MiG-17s were in fact already armed – a fact unknown to their pilots. To the left of these, two HA-200 Saeta trainers were being serviced. Thus, the line was a total of six aircraft. There were perhaps 50 other HA-200 trainers on our airfield, dumped back at the factory by the Egyptian Air Force as they wanted to clear Bilbeis, their training base, for operations. I had dispersed them, often inside some World War II brick pens, left over from RAF days. These were all covered with sand-coloured tarpaulins …

A row of HA-200Bs photographed at Helwan before the 1967 War. While up to 50 of these aircraft were present at this airfield on the morning of 5 June, only two were destroyed when lined in a row together with three MiG-17s and one MiG-19.
(Tom Cooper Collection)

'At 11.10, I heard the scream of low-flying jets. Running to the window, I saw four Mirage IIIC aircraft in a low run over our single runway. As they pulled up and turned left, two [Sud Aviation SO.4050] Vautours did a low pass on the runway and dropped 1,000lb bombs. Two loud explosions followed after a short delay ... Some Egyptian friends tried to pull me away from the window to go down with them to the ground floor, which was presumed to be safer if bombs fell over us. I refused to move and told them that the Israelis had come to destroy airplanes and would not waste ammo on people. I was proved right. The four Mirages came into classic front gun attacks at the aircraft lined up on the tarmac ... the leader went for the MiG-19. The others took the three MiG-17s. Seconds later, these four aircraft were on fire. The Vautours did not do a second run, but the Mirages came in for their second attack, as if they were on range practice. The leader and his number two took out*

A gun-camera sequence records the attack on the An-12B used as a test-bed for the E-300 engine at Helwan airfield on the morning of 5 June 1967. Although hit by several 30mm rounds that punctured fuel tanks and caused a large spill on the tarmac, the aircraft remained intact. In the background can be seen the towers of Factory 135's engine-testing facilities, run by Dr Ferdinand Brandner. See also the photo on p30.
(IDF)

the two HA-200s. The third pilot chose to fire at an An-12, which was the test bed for the E-300 engine. While the HA-200s caught fire, the An-12 leaked tons of fuel, which miraculously never ignited. The fourth pilot had no target left. He wasted a few rounds at the cement wall of the engine test-bed facility, making harmless pock-marks on it. One of the shells ricocheted and landed inches from an officer visiting from HAL … Soon after the Israelis had left, the air raid siren went of and several anti-aircraft guns opened fire!'

Inspecting the damage on the tarmac, Bhargava concluded that all six aircraft were destroyed, even though the An-12 test-bed remained intact. The only casualty was a young mechanic who was working on the MiG-19 and had chosen to hide under its wing when the attack came.[49]

Although Israel thus gradually expanded its list of targets to include airfields not regularly used by the UARAF, as far as Air Group 15 was concerned the situation at Hurghada remained calm. This changed dramatically around 13.05.

It began when two MiG-19s returning from a CAP due north of the airfield, and led by Abd el-Moneim el-Tawil, reported several Israeli fighters some 30km (18.6 miles) to the north and approaching. Badr immediately ordered two MiG-19s to scramble and provide cover, since el-Tawil and his wingman were now short of fuel. Barely a minute later, four Mirages attacked the air base, but both MiG-19s landed safely. One of them was destroyed on the ground shortly afterwards, while the other suffered consider-able damage. Superior Israeli fighters swiftly overwhelmed the two MiG-19s that had scrambled in an attempt to provide protection, though each of the MiG pilots claimed one Mirage as shot down using ORO-57K rocket pods. The leader of the pair was shot down while his wingman's aircraft crashed while attempting to land on the damaged runway, killing the pilot. Two other MiG-19s, one Il-14, and two helicopters (a Mil Mi-4 and a Mi-6) were destroyed during the course of subsequent attacks by Israeli fighters.[50]

According to Israeli sources, none of the attacking Mirages was shot down, but Israeli pilots certainly exaggerated their claims as well: two of them were credited with a total of three kills, even though they shot down only one MiG-19 in air combat.[51]

Previously believed to have been taken in Syria, this photograph was actually shot at Hurghada prior to the 1967 War, and shows at least three ex-Iraqi MiG-19S fighters of No. 20 Squadron after their return from deployment in Yemen. (Tom Cooper Collection)

Hurghada and Air Group 15 were subsequently 'finished' – but as the result of an instruction from above. Around 15.00, Brig Gen Badr was ordered to evacuate all the remaining aircraft. Still, this order was not completely followed, because only three MiG-19s, as well as the two remaining MiG-21F-13s of No. 40 Squadron, were successfully flown to Cairo IAP. The support equipment was taken to Cairo West by train during the following night, but four MiG-19s remained at Hurghada.[52]

Dial M For Kill

The next target dealt with by the IDF/AF was Luxor airfield, and this was again clearly based on intelligence obtained from listening to Egyptian telephone conversations. As mentioned before, a formation of six Tu-16s led by Lt Col Hosni Moubarak had taken off from Beni Suweif barely five minutes before the first Israeli attack, and reached Luxor around two hours later. As Kamal Darwish, one of the pilots involved, recalled:

'We followed the order from Cairo West and flew to Luxor on the spur of the moment … I contacted the tower and was told to make my approach and land on runway 02. As I came in, short of a touchdown, I saw another Tu-16 heading directly towards me, approaching to land on the same runway but from the opposite direction. I used some very bad language, the only part of which can be cited as, 'who is that damned donkey that is landing straight in towards me?' The pilot of the other Tupolev then applied full power and pulled away and to the right to avoid a head-on collision …'[53]

Once on the ground, Moubarak realised that Luxor was not protected by a single AAA piece and thus not only completely exposed to air attacks, but was also overcrowded, with no fewer than nine Il-14s, five An-12s, and three civilian Douglas DC-6s parked around it in addition to the six newly arrived Tu-16s. He ordered his crews to swiftly refuel the aircraft while making a *telephone call* to Cairo, demanding permission to launch again. Unknown to the Egyptian Air Brigade commander, his call alerted the Israelis. Always keen to neutralise the UARAF's bomber component, the IDF/AF swiftly dispatched a formation of three Vautours to Luxor. The unavoidable catastrophe occurred around 13.30, when the Israelis attacked in spite of the Egyptian belief that this airfield was outside the range of IDF/AF fighter-bombers. All six of Moubarak's Tu-16s, as well as several transports were destroyed within few minutes.

Another airfield hit as a result of intelligence reports was Cairo International, which came under attack around 18.00 local time. This is hardly surprising, as this airfield had become a sanctuary for the formation of six Il-28s, led by el-Keraidy, that had bombed targets in Yemen early that morning. After completing their mission, these bombers landed at Ras Banas airfield, in southern Egypt, in the early afternoon. They were refuelled and took off with the intention of returning to Abu Suweir, but while under way received the order to divert to Cairo IAP, where they landed safely around 17.00. Obviously, somebody then made a telephone call to GHQ, for barely one hour later this airfield was attacked by four Mirages. However, the Israelis only bombed the runway, and did not strafe, in turn enabling el-Keraidy's Il-28s to survive undamaged.[54]

Cheating Fate

5 June 1967 was clearly an ignominious day for the UARAF. It ended with the loss of around 130 fighters, 57 bombers, 27 transports and 13 helicopters, representing around 60 per cent of Air Force assets available that morning – as well as heavy damage to 15 of the most important air bases and airfields, and considerable ground equipment losses. The six units flying MiG-21s had suffered losses of around 66 aircraft, of which 13 were sustained in the course of 28-30 sorties flown. In response, their pilots claimed five enemy aircraft, comprising one Mirage IIICJ, three Super Mystère B2s and one Mystère IVA, while losing only three in air combat (one of these was actually due to fuel starvation caused by combat damage), and suffering another damaged. However, such a positive exchange rate is not surprising bearing in mind that the MiG-21 was a lightweight, point-defence interceptor which was operating relatively close to its bases on that day. Far more serious was the fact that five pilots had been killed, two MiG-21s had been shot down by their own ground defences, while eight pilots ran out of fuel and had been forced to eject after engaging different Israeli formations – obviously due to overexcitement caused by the lack of realistic training and combat experience.

The sole squadron flying MiG-19s performed relatively well, flying a total of nine sorties and claiming two (unconfirmed) kills, but had one of its aircraft shot down and another destroyed and its pilot killed while landing on a damaged runway, and four further aircraft destroyed on the ground. Additionally, a MiG-19 used for test purposes was destroyed at Helwan airfield. In comparison, the only operational Su-7 unit lost 12 of its mounts on the ground, and did not fly a single sortie. Unsurprisingly, in the light of heavy losses on the ground, the achievements of the Egyptian pilots went completely unnoticed by the public, while the emboldened Israelis vastly exaggerated the success of their own pilots.[55]

Hit – but really 'shot down'? An Israeli gun-camera photograph showing a UARAF MiG-21 'going down in flames'. Considering the number of Israeli claims and the actual number of UARAF MiG-21s confirmed as shot down on 5 June, it appears the IDF/AF credited its pilots with far more kills than they actually scored. As countless examples have demonstrated, even a badly damaged MiG-21 did not automatically translate into a lost MiG-21.
(IDF via Albert Grandolini)

The day ended with various types of activity on the part of UARAF pilots and ground crew. A furious Samir Aziz Mikhail returned to Fayid in the afternoon, only to witness one of the closing Israeli attacks:

'We drove from Fayid village back to the air base and I went to the command centre. I found two flaks on the roof and no one was firing them when the next Israeli wave came. So, I jumped up and tried to make them work. I moved one around with the wheel and saw a Mystère diving towards me. So, I left the gun and jumped again and two rockets came and blew up the gun.'

Other pilots from Fayid remained at Inchas and subsequently withdrew to a location nearby, as recalled by Farid Harfush:

'There was an old palace of King Farouk nearby, and many pilots gathered there. There I heard that Nabil Shuwakri shot down an enemy aircraft directly over Inchas but was (himself) shot down and injured. A military truck passed by, carrying the body of the dead Jewish pilot …'

Undaunted, Nabil Shuwakri was meanwhile busy manning another MiG-21, but sadly, the exact scene of his next mission remains unknown:

'On my second sortie I changed to two pods of those [S-5 rockets; authors' note] and attacked some tanks in the northern Sinai.'

Fuad Kamal recalled the remarkable work of the technicians at Abu Suweir:

'After sunset the maintenance crews started to assemble aircraft during the night, combining undamaged parts from damaged aircraft – wings, tail units and so on …'

Tahsin Zaki remained busy as well, doing whatever was possible to get Fayid airfield back to operational condition:

'During the evening of 5 June, 2nd Lt Ahmed el-Simary and me, with the help of workers from the construction company that had built our runway, removed the wreckage of the ill-fated Il-14 and cleared the subsidiary runway. Fayid was thus ready for action by first light on 6 June.'

Still in high spirits, Salah Danish helped Zaki and el-Simary in their efforts:

'Despite the destruction of the runways and many of our aircraft, we had no doubt that the victory in this war would be on our side. Morale was very high and we rushed to help our technicians to repair the damage. During the night we restored the secondary runway with help of rapidly-hardening cement and this became a viable runway by the morning.'

Concentrated at the abandoned palace near Inchas, Harfush and the other pilots were to all intents and purposes 'out of business'. Instead, they prepared themselves for a rather unpleasant night in a house that had no electricity or water supply:

'Shortly after midnight, Maj Amozis came to the palace and called the members of his squadrons. I stood up, Samir Aziz Mikhail and another captain too, and we drove in a minibus to Cairo International. There the CO of the Transport Brigade found accommodation for us in the local military ambulance. We slept the rest of the night on stretchers …'

1   For an example of Egyptian pilots being court-martialled by their superiors for discussing the capabilities of the fighters flown by the Israeli Air Force see *Volume 2*, p215.

2   Usually available Israeli accounts of Operation Moked – as the integrated plan for attacks on Arab air bases on 5 June 1967 was codenamed – indicate that on the morning of that day the IDF/AF was in possession of the following combat aircraft:

65 Dassault Mirage IIICJ/BJ and CJ/R (64 serviceable)

1 MiG-21F-13 (ex-Iraqi example)

35 Dassault Super Mystère B2 (all serviceable)

19 SNACSO SO.4050 Vautour IIA/N/BR (18 serviceable)

35 Dassault Mystère IVA (32 serviceable)

51 Dassault Ouragan (48 serviceable)

This is a total of 206 available fighter-bombers. The number was further increased through the decision to put all 44 Fouga CM.170 Magisters (all were serviceable) into service as light fighter-bombers, for close air support tasks. However, the Magisters were too slow and vulnerable to any kind of threat that could be expected over major Arab air bases, and therefore relatively few became involved in Operation Moked: 16 were involved in attacks on Egyptian radar stations in Sinai, while six others flew deception sorties over the Mediterranean.

3   Countless reports in the West detailing Israeli pilots flying up to seven or eight combat sorties every day during the June 1967 War all proved unrealistic. More recent Israeli publications indicate that the majority of the 277 available jet fighter pilots (this figure includes 42 Magister pilots) flew three or four sorties on 5 June, with only a handful of exceptions – i.e. pilots that flew five or six sorties (the last of which took place in the night from 5 June to 6 June and concerned operations other than attacks on Arab air bases). The operational tempo was relaxed the following day, with most pilots flying three sorties or fewer. Additionally, it should be kept in mind that the availability of IDF/AF fighter-bombers decreased due to losses and combat damage. Despite the hard work of the Israeli ground crews, a number of aircraft damaged in the course of attacks on Egyptian and other air bases on 5 June could not be returned to service before the end of war. These figures also make it clear that the usual reports of the IDF/AF having 'at least three trained pilots for each front-line aircraft' are entirely unrealistic (see Dunstan, *The Six Day War 1967: Sinai*, Osprey, 2009). Actually, the rate of pilots per aircraft was nearly the same as in Egypt (for comparison see figures provided in *Volume 2*, p221).

4   Data based on Shalom, *Like a Bolt Out of the Blue*, and Aloni, *The June 1967 Six-Day War*.

5   Mutawi, *Jordan in the 1967 War*, p122.

6   'Grapes' repeated three times meant that war was about to start.

7   Uda and Imam, 'A Lesson we Should have Learned', *al-Ahli*.

8   Sources differ as to the actual task of this aircraft. Some Egyptian sources stress its purpose was ELINT/SIGINT reconnaissance. On the other hand, Israeli sources say that this Il-14 was occupied by the bodyguards, paratroopers and a number of journalists that were to escort FM Amer and other dignitaries on their trip to Meliz air base. However, if this was the case, the aircraft would not have taken off from Meliz, but from Almaza and it would have been a different example equipped for VIP transport purposes, albeit operated by the same No. 11 Squadron.

9   While some sources appear to suggest that these 12 interceptors represented the entire air defence of Israel on that morning, the fact is that in addition the IDF/AF also operated five battalions of MIM-23 HAWK SAMs as well as a total of 54 AAA batteries equipped with 20mm, 30mm and 40mm anti-aircraft guns. The HAWK sites – the equipment for which was delivered to Israel by West Germany in April 1965 (though with full agreement of the US) – were deployed as follows: one for protection of the nuclear complex in Dimona; one at Mount Ataka; one near Zmorot (for protection of Hatzor and Tel Nov); one at Sde Dov; and one at an unknown location. Israeli airspace was thus anything but 'defenceless' on the morning of 5 June 1967. On the contrary, the Israelis concluded that they were unlikely to need more assets for their own protection.

10 Gabr Ali Gabr, interview, April 2005; this and most of subsequent quotations from Gabr Ali Gabr are based on transcriptions of the same interview.

11 Al-Moneim, *Wolf in the Sun's Disc*, Chapter 1.

12 Ibid. and AVM Ahmed Himmat al-Atrabi, interview with Group 73, August 2010; clearly, Egyptian recollections concerning what happened over Meliz on that morning are quite different to those of the Israelis. While most of the latter recall that the 'other' MiG-21 which took off during the first attack 'left the scene without trying to defend its base', the Egyptians recall that the aircraft flown by Said Othman enthusiastically engaged the Ouragans in air combat and shot down one before being hit by another Israeli fighter.

13 For details of AVM el-Hamid's role within the UARAF see *Volume 2* pp205–224.

14 Qadri Abd el-Hamid, interview, December 2011; this and all subsequent quotations from el-Hamid are based on transcriptions of same interview.

15 Okasha, in *Conflict in the Sky*, Chapter 3, cites that 2nd Lt Said Othman rammed one of the attacking Ouragans with his aircraft.

16 Ibid., Chapter 5; Okasha cited the destruction of two MiG-19s on the ground at Meliz as well, but no other UARAF documents or other sources confirm the presence of MiG-19s at that air base or any such losses. Note that the downed Ouragan pilot ejected over the sea near the Gaza Strip. He was captured and interrogated by Maj Ibrahim el-Dakhany of the Egyptian Military Intelligence. The Israeli stated that the IDF/AF was in the process of destroying Egypt's airfields and every aircraft on them. El-Dakhany subsequently put the Israeli pilot into a car and sent him to Cairo for more questioning (Bowen, *Six Days*, p110).

17 Tahsin Zaki, interview, February 1999; this and all subsequent quotations from Zaki are based on a transcription of the same interview.

18 Mamdouh Heshmat, interview with Group 73, November 2009; this and all subsequent quotations from Heshmat are based on a transcription of the same interview.

19 Salah Danish, interview with Group 73, 2010, and Alaa Barakat, interview, 2003; this and all subsequent quotations from Danish are based on transcriptions of the same interviews.

20 Ibid., Chapter 5; Okasha implied that the visit by the Iraqi Prime Minister to Fayid, on the morning of 5 June, was connected to the basing of 'Iraqi aircraft' at that air base. Actually, the MiG-19s in question were operated by No. 20 Squadron UARAF, being flown by Egyptian pilots and two Jordanians who had defected to Egypt earlier and then joined the UARAF. However, some of these MiG-19s were donated to Egypt in 1964 as a gesture of goodwill (see *Volume 2* for details).

21 Samir Aziz Mikhail, interview with Lon Nordeen, March 1989 and with Group 73, November 2009; this and all subsequent quotations from Mikhail are based on transcriptions of the same interview.

22 Alaa Barakat, interview, March 2003; this and all subsequent quotations from Barakat are based on transcriptions of the same interview.

23 Bowen, *Six Days*, pp135–137.

24 Farid Harfush, interview with Group 73, November 2009; this and all subsequent quotations from Harfush are based on transcriptions of the same interview.

25 Fuad Kamal, interview, February 1999; this and all subsequent quotations from Fuad Kamal are based on transcriptions of the same interview.

26 Awad Hamdi, interview with Lon Nordeen, March 1989; this and all subsequent quotations from Hamdi are based on transcriptions of the same interview.

27 Okasha, *Conflict in the Sky*, Chapter 5 and al-Moneim, *Wolf in the Sun's Disc*, p46.

28 Taher Zaki, interview, February 1999; this and all subsequent quotations from Taher Zaki are based on transcriptions of the same interview.

29 El-Ashmawy, interview, July 2005. Born in 1946, in Cairo, el-Ashmawy grew up in Alexandria and joined the UARAF at the age of 16, in 1962. After three years at the Academy in Bilbeis, where he flew Gomhourias and Yak-11s, he graduated in 1965 and was immediately selected for fighter squadrons. After converting to

MiG-15s and MiG-17s with the FCU at Kabrit, in 1966 he completed the Advanced Fighter Training Course and joined No. 43 Squadron flying MiG-21F-13s from Cairo West. By June 1967 he had completed advanced training with this unit and was reassigned to No. 26 Squadron at Abu Suweir.

30 Gabr Ali Gabr, interview, April 2005; Al-Moneim, *Wolf in the Sun's Disc*, pp52–53; Okasha, *Conflict in the Sky*, Chapter 5 and Shalom, *Like a Bolt Out of the Blue*; the Israeli book indicates the loss of one Super Mystère B2 over Inchas, flown by Lt Dan Angel who was KIA, but credits 'anti-aircraft artillery' for his loss.

31 Gabr Ali Gabr, interview, April 2005; Okasha, *Conflict in the Sky*, Chapters 3 and 5, and al-Moneim, *Wolf in the Sun's Disc*, Chapter 1.

32 For details about Operation Rashid, see *Volume 1*, pp176–178.

33 For details about Operation Puma, see *Volume 1*, pp160–162.

34 Bowen, *Six Days*, pp138–139.

35 Sadat, *In Search of Identity*, p152.

36 Uda and Imam, 'A Lesson We Should Have Learned', *al-Ahali*, 29 June 1983 (this and all subsequent quotations from Abdul Hamid Abdul Salem el-Daghedi are based on transcriptions of the same interview).

37 Sadat, *In Search of Identity*, p152.

38 Gabr Ali Gabr recalled that Nasser had felt US pressure since 27 May. He also recalled that it was only three days after the opening attacks on 5 June that an authoritative report of the sighting of US Navy fighters flying within Egyptian airspace appeared. According to Gabr, although the Egyptian and Syrian media were meanwhile full of claims that the US actively supported the Israeli attack, and despite Nasser's joint statement with King Hussein citing US and British involvement, the Egyptian President still had his doubts about the truth of this, until the above-mentioned report of the clear sighting of US national markings arrived. This report was subsequently confirmed by US President Johnson, who informed Nasser that the aircraft in question had been sent from the US Navy's Sixth Fleet to help the reconnaissance ship USS *Liberty*, after this had been attacked and heavily damaged by Israel, while sailing off the coast of el-Arish on 8 June.

39 Despite all the evidence that has become available over the last 40 years, such opinions remain quite widespread in the Arab world even today, some Arab sources maintaining that the maps captured together with downed Israeli pilots and excellent low-level photographs of various Arab airfields mentioned by captured Israelis while under interrogation, pointed at direct US involvement. This is particularly odd, considering the fact that the Egyptians ought to have known how many reconnaissance sorties Israeli aircraft had flown over their bases since 1956 (and also that their own air force had attempted to do the same over Israeli air bases between 1958 and 1961). After all, as early as 1963 AM Sidki Mahmoud demanded Sukhoi Su-9 interceptors from Soviet Union precisely because he believed that such aircraft might help his pilots prevent these Israeli incursions.

40 Okasha, *Conflict in the Sky*, Chapter 5.

41 Shuwakri, interview with Lon Nordeen, March 1989, and interview with Group 73, August 2010. An explanation that Sami Fuad's MiG-21 was shot down by an Egyptian SA-2 after he engaged in air combat with several Israeli fighters, and that he shot down one of the Israelis, can be found in al-Moneim's *Wolf in the Sun's Disc*, pp51–52.

42 For examples revealing the precision of Israeli intelligence in regards to the deployment of various UARAF units, see Aloni, *The June 1967 Six-Day War*, and Bowen, *Six Days*, p104. Bowen cited that while searching for the downed Israeli pilots, the Jordanians found that each man had a small book in his flying overalls. This not only contained precise diagrams of each air base in Egypt, Iraq, Jordan, Lebanon and Syria, but also showed the best place to crater the runways, as well as the dispositions of air defences.

43 Wolfgang Lotz, *The Champagne Spy – Israel's Master Spy Tells His Story* (New York: St Martin's Press, 1972).

44 Tali Yahalom, 'Timeline: Israeli Prisoner Exchanges', *Financial Times*, 16 July 2008, and Moshe Rom, 'Uri Ilan – Message Notes', *Haaretz* (online article in Hebrew, retrieved from www.haaretz.co.il in July 2008).

45 Offer Drori, Operation Kachal (retrieved from www.global-report.com in September 2009), and Cohen, *Israel's Best Defence*, p166.

46 Iraqi Brig Gen Ahmad Sadik (ret.) stated in a March 2005 interview with the authors that it is very likely that IDF Intelligence intercepted FM Amer's call to AM Sidki Mahmoud, on 4 June, when the former ordered the UARAF to prepare two Il-14s to take him and his entourage on an inspection of defences in the Sinai Peninsula, the following morning. As well as Sadik, many other Arab sources stress the major advantage provided to Israel by the fact that Egyptian air defences were more concerned in *not* opening fire on FM Amer's aircraft than offering protection to crucially important airfields. Whether the Israelis set up the timing of their attack accordingly remains unknown, but they obviously took the flight of these two Il-14s into account. Furthermore, Sadik stressed that similar Israeli tapping operations were undertaken at later dates as well, for example in preparation for the IDF/AF attack on the Iraqi nuclear complex in Tuwaitha, near Baghdad, in June 1981. According to Sadik, in the course of subsequent investigation, the IrAF Intelligence Department detected and unearthed a tapping device installed by the Israelis on the communications cable connecting H-3 air base with the IrAF HQ in Baghdad.

47 None of the available Egyptian sources can confirm the story propagated by the Israelis shortly after the June 1967 War, in which the CO Hurghada ordered a total of 20 of his fighters to take off and protect airfields over the Nile Delta, and that these 20 fighters were all either shot down by Israeli interceptors or ran out of fuel and crashed since their pilots could not find any intact runway. This rumour, apparently based on an interview with Ezer Weizmann, was first published shortly after the war by Randolf and Winston Churchill in their book *The Six Day War* (London: William Heinemann, 1967), and has been re-reported by numerous other authors ever since – obviously without the necessary cross-examination of Egyptian sources.

48 Sure enough, the IDF/AF did launch a four-ship flight of Super Mystère B2s from No. 105 Squadron to raid el-Mansourah earlier that morning. The formation in question took off at around 10.35, but failed to find their target. Nevertheless, shortly after 11.00 another formation of four Super Mystères was launched to attack el-Mansourah specifically in reaction to an intelligence report that cited the landing of two MiG-21s there. See Aloni, *The June 1967 Six-Day War*, pp118–119.

49 Bhargava, interview, October 2009, and Bhargava, 'Eyewitness to the Six-Day War', extracted from *Bharat-Rakshak.com* website with kind permission from author.

50 Okasha, *Conflict in the Sky*, Chapter 5.

51 Ibid. and Aloni, *The June 1967 Six-Day War*, p131.

52 Okasha, *Conflict in the Sky*, Chapter 5.

53 Darwish, interview, April 2005.

54 Okasha, *Conflict in the Sky*, Chapter 5, Aloni, *The June 1967 Six-Day War*, p131, and Ahmad Keraidy, interview, June 2010.

55 In comparison, the IDF/AF originally claimed up to 19 kills over Egypt for no losses on their own side. While this total was later reduced to eight MiG-21s, three MiG-19s and one Il-14 in exchange for two of its own losses, it was only decades later that some Israeli publications available in the West admitted the possibility of between three and four of their own losses in air combat, while two further losses to Egyptian MiG-21s instead remain associated with Egyptian ground-based air defences. Notably, except for the losses they suffered in air combats with the UARAF pilots, the Israelis also lost at least three Magisters involved in attacks on Egyptian ground forces in Sinai – all to ground fire, and including one example shot down over el-Arish and one over Umm Katef.

Chapter 2

FIGHTING THE LOST BATTLE

If the war began very badly for the Egyptian military, the situation became even worse during the night to 6 June 1967, as all the failures regarding generalship, tactical leadership and information management began to result in the collapse of unit cohesion and the morale of the entire Army and Air Force.

Amer in Panic

On the early morning of 6 June, after succumbing to his own panic over the reported 'destruction' of the UARAF, and following exaggerated reports concerning Israeli advances in Sinai, FM Amer issued two orders that proved crucial for the outcome of the war and critical to the subsequent history of the entire Middle East. According to those who sympathise with Nasser, this he did without consulting other members of the General Staff or President Nasser himself. In contrast, Amer and Badran later testified that Nasser personally approved the order.[1]

The first order was for all Egyptian Army units in eastern Sinai to withdraw to the Second Zone of Defence, roughly along the line Nakhel – Hashanah – Jebel Libni. The order was issued during the early hours, but, long before any of the units in question could reach their new positions, at around 05.00 the same day, FM Amer ordered a general withdrawal of all forces to the western side of the Suez Canal – thus evacuating Sinai altogether.

Suffice to say, these two orders resulted in a catastrophe for the Egyptian Army in Sinai – most units being either still entirely untouched by the fighting or holding their positions in the face of determined Israeli attacks – followed by the Israeli occupation of the peninsula. Furthermore, over the following 48 hours, these orders provided the Israelis, who were left with the equivalent of two much-weakened divisions after the first day of hard-fought attempts to break through the first line of Egyptian defences, with the freedom to exploit the opportunity and successfully conquer all Sinai. The order also led to the collapse of the entire Egyptian military structure, a tremendous loss of Egyptian prestige, and six years of bitter and extremely expensive warfare that practically bankrupted the country. At the same time, the Israelis were left to redeploy some of their units to the West Bank and the Golan Heights – a move that also had significant strategic consequences.

Acting on Amer's orders, the C-in-C UARAF ordered an evacuation of all remaining assets from Sinai – while those units based west of Suez were thrown into providing

FM Hakim Amer addresses Egyptian pilots during his inspection of Abu Suweir air base on 20 May 1967. (Courtesy UP)

support for the Army in a haphazard and inefficient manner. Gabr Ali Gabr was already under way when Amer's orders for withdrawal came through:

'I was told to move only during the hours of darkness and take my unit through the Giddi Pass. In fact, nobody was to move until during darkness, the idea being that the withdrawal should be completed by dawn the following day. To me this appeared quite impossible, since not everybody could go along the few available roads and through the passes at the same time and by night. So, in the only instance during my entire career when I disobeyed an order, I had my unit set out to start during the last hour of daylight, and we came back to Egypt through the Mitla Pass, rather than the Giddi.'

Behind Gabr, el-Arish air base was overrun by Israeli troops on the morning of 6 June. The group that Gabr led through the Mitla Pass eventually grew quite large, resulting in a convoy extending for around 5km (3.1 miles) along the road:

'We got back to Ismailia without any problems, and lost no people or vehicles, but subsequently all the passes in the western Sinai became completely choked with vehicles that turned into sitting ducks for the Israeli Air Force. By that time no air cooperation with the Army was possible, so my group and me had no work to do. Instead we had been told to return to the Air Force HQ in Cairo and wait there.'

Air Group 1 Hits Back

The pilots of Tahsin Zaki's Air Group 1 at Fayid air base had been the first to react to Sidki Mahmoud's order to support the Army, on the morning of 6 June. After only a few hours' sleep, the first four MiG-19 pilots launched at 05.30, as recalled by Barakat:

'Our mechanics made the six MiG-19s in the hangar serviceable. At first light on 6 June I led a mission of four MiG-19s to protect an Army unit reportedly attacked by Israeli aircraft. We did not see any of the enemy, so we continued to fly the CAP over the area until we ran out of fuel. Then we returned to the base without combat.'

Half an hour later, two Su-7BMKs flown by Tahsin Zaki and Lt Zakaria Abu Sa'ada were launched with the same objective. Before reaching el-Arish air base, they detected an Israeli camp with several Centurion tanks in the process of being refuelled from drums that had obviously been flown in by an Israeli helicopter that had landed nearby. Zaki and Sa'ada turned to attack, firing all their 57mm rockets in the process:

'We attacked Israeli Centurion tanks with Soviet-made 57mm 'anti-armour rockets', but these could not penetrate even the weak armour on the top and the side of the enemy tanks. On the other hand, our Egyptian-made 78mm rockets, as used by the MiG-17Fs, proved more effective by a wide margin …'

Short of fuel, and saving their cannon ammunition for possible air combat with Israeli fighters, the two pilots only made one attack pass each. Sa'ada's Su-7BMK was hit by ground fire, but both pilots managed to return safely to Fayid.

At 06.45, two other Su-7s were scrambled from Fayid, supposedly to fly a CAP over the eastern Sinai. Clearly, the type was completely unsuitable for that purpose but, lacking sufficient numbers of MiG-21s, the CO Air Group 1 had no other choice.[2] Zaki's own recollection of this sortie, however, does not indicate any intention to fly a CAP, but to fly what he described as an 'armed reconnaissance mission':

'Flown by the late Capt Ahmed Hassan el-Samary and Lt Medhat al-Meligy, these two Su-7s penetrated ever deeper over Sinai without encountering any kind of oppo-

sition. Eventually, they crossed the border and reached the Beersheba railway. It was only then that they found a small airfield nearby and attacked several helicopters parked there. On their return they had to increase their altitude in order to conserve fuel and as a result were intercepted by Israeli Mirages while only 30km [18.6 miles] away from Fayid AB. El-Samary's Su-7BMK was hit and al-Meligy urged him to eject immediately. El-Samary remained with his aircraft and managed to land on the taxiway at Fayid AB. The aircraft was subsequently repaired and was back in operation four days later … Al-Meligy meanwhile attempted to reach Abu Suweir AB, but ran out of fuel and attempted to land on a stretch of straight road near Ismailia instead. He almost collided with a civilian car in the process … While swerving to the side, his aircraft rolled into the soft sand while at high speed, cartwheeled and exploded, killing the pilot.[3]

Salah Danish similarly recalled that mission:

'At first light Medhat al-Meligy and Ahmed el-Samary took off in two Su-7s to fly a pre-planned mission against the Israelis, but both encountered Mirages. Samary returned with his Su-7 in flames, trailing a thick trail of smoke, but landed successfully and jumped out of the cockpit safely. His aircraft did not explode. However, we later learned that Medhat al-Meligy was not as lucky while attempting to land in Abu Suweir.'

Fikry el-Gindy recalled the fate of al-Meligy:

'Medhat was a real patriotic hero and he died while trying to save his Su-7. He attempted to land on a road but the aircraft turned over and caught fire.'[4]

Israeli and Western reports indicate that one of the IDF/AF S-58 helicopters encountered by el-Samary and al-Meligy carried Gen Yehu Gavish, commander of the Israeli Southern Command in the Sinai. The crew was first warned of the approach by a flight of MiG-17 fighter-bombers, and then attacked by two Su-7s. While calling for fighter support, the Israeli pilot managed to escape the fire of his pursuers. However, Israeli reports that both Sukhois were shot down are clearly unrealistic.[5]

Meanwhile, Danish was himself airborne with three other MiG-19 pilots, on a CAP over the northern Sinai:

'I took off together with el-Derayni, Alaa Barakat and Heshmat Sidki to fly a CAP. We wanted the Jews to see us on their radars and to know that this airfield was still operational. Our aircraft were armed with cannon and unguided rockets, and carried two fuel tanks. As we climbed to a flight level of around 4,000m [13,123ft] we began to realise that our planes had been assembled in a rush following their return from Yemen, and were not in the best technical condition. Alaa Barakat's aircraft was burning fuel much faster than necessary and the plane flown by Heshmat Sidki would not take fuel from the drop tanks. Eventually, el-Derayni ordered them to return and we continued to patrol alone. When the time came for us to land, the sun was coming from the direction of runway 27, right into our eyes. I approached el-Derayni's aircraft keeping slightly above him as he entered the landing pattern at a level that appeared very low to me.

'There was a traffic controller we called 'Jordan', a pan-Arabist and a political refugee from Jordan who escaped from King Hussein, and he guided us back down. Jordan informed el-Derayni that there were two aircraft behind him, or between him and his number two. Anyway, el-Derayni understood that the planes in question were Israelis and began to fly a series of evasive manoeuvres, and I tried to

follow him. The MiG-19 is not equipped with a periscope mounted on the top of the cockpit for the pilot to see what is going on behind him, like the periscope mounted on the MiG-15 or MiG-17 before. So, he continued manoeuvring for some time, and I continued manoeuvring behind him, until el-Derayni decided to land. We came in at a high speed and swiftly rolled off the runway, stopping only underneath the nearby trees. We jumped out of our cockpits and met again in a ditch nearby. Later, we laughed a lot about this situation.'

Around 11.20, four MiG-19s led by Majs Saad Zaghloul and Heshmat Sidki took off from Fayid with orders to attack Israeli tanks advancing along a road in northern Sinai, as Barakat recalled:

'A lot has been said in the West about the UARAF flying 'Soviet tactics' … Sufficient to say that during this period the Egyptian pilots flew a mix of the British tactical system with some Egyptian modifications that allowed greater freedom and initiative to the pilots. Our basic formation was 'fluid four', rather than any Soviet formations like 'finger four' or various 'trails' … This formation was intercepted by eight Mirages and lost two MiG-19s. Both pilots ejected safely. Heshmat Sidki landed near the Canal and was OK. Zaghloul landed deeper over Sinai and teamed up with some retreating soldiers. They walked for a long way and were captured by Israeli soldiers only 1.5km [0.9 miles] from the Canal. One of the Israelis opened fire on them but the magazine of his machine gun ran empty before reaching Zaghloul, so they let him go …'

At 12.40, two Su-7s led by Capt Zakaria Abu Sa'ada launched with orders to attack the same column of Israeli armour. The two Sukhois hit several Israeli tanks with unguided rockets, but without any visible effects, and were then intercepted by a pair of Mirages, as recalled by Tahsin Zaki:

'Abu Sa'ada landed safely at Inchas, completely out of fuel, but the other pilot was shot down during the air combat and killed.'

An entry in the logbook of Abdel Moneim el-Shennawy shows that he flew one combat sortie on the morning of 6 June as well, but no other details are available.

Despite considerable losses, the MiG-19S aircraft of No. 20 Squadron continued flying combat sorties over Sinai for the rest of the 1967 War. This pre-war photograph shows three MiG-19s taking off from Fayid. Note that on this occasion they appear not to carry any of the usual ORO-57K rocket pods under their inboard underwing pylons.
(Nour Bardai Collection)

During the afternoon, two MiG-19s were scrambled with orders to provide top cover for four MiG-17s flying an attack on the Israeli armoured column advancing into the northern Sinai. The MiG-19s clashed with four Mirages and claimed one of them as shot down, but both were lost in the process. The two pilots ejected safely, one returning to Egypt together with withdrawing Army units, while the other was almost overrun by the advancing Israelis and spent the next seven days evading capture while making his way towards the Canal. He later reported that one of the Israeli Mirages opened fire upon him while he was hanging beneath his parachute.[6]

Drama at Cairo West

Cairo West became the scene of a major drama that began to unfold in the early morning of 6 June, as recalled by Farid Harfush:

'Early in the morning I woke up to the sound of furious screams of Maj Amozis ... The Operations Officer at Cairo West ordered him to fly an attack with aircraft armed with unguided rockets against a target that was too far away for the range of our MiG-21s ... We attempted to explain, but the officer was uncompromising ...'

The Operations Officer at Cairo West had indeed issued such an order at around 22.00 on 5 June, requesting that the most experienced pilots take four of the newly assembled Su-7BMKs and fly these to Fayid by night so that they would be able to launch at first light the following morning, to attack an airfield in Israel. However, not only were there hardly any pilots qualified to fly Su-7s at Cairo West, but also none of them had ever done so by night. Furthermore, simple calculations made by several pilots showed that the Su-7 lacked the range to reach any major Israeli airfield even if taking off from Fayid, which was much closer to Israel than Cairo West. Furthermore, it turned out that there were no unguided rockets for the Su-7s available at that air base.

After many heated discussions this plan was abandoned, but the Operations Officer then ordered the same attack to be flown by four MiG-21 pilots. In fact, the idea was only dropped after additional protests by Maj Amozis, who had to prove that his MiG-21s were unable to reach any important Israeli airfields while carrying UB-16-57 unguided rocket pods. Undaunted, the Operations Officer finally ordered four MiG-19 pilots who had recently returned from a Su-7 conversion course to take off at first light and fly a CAP over the Port Said area, supposedly to protect other fighters involved in attacks on Israeli ground forces. The pilots chosen to fly this mission, including Maj Galal Abd al-Alim, Capt Muhammad Ali Khamis and Capt Shehata, did not even receive information about the identity of the other fighters they were supposed to cover. Nor were they informed of the radio frequencies on which they could communicate with these aircraft, nor any advice about what to expect from the enemy or indeed from their own forces. After the fourth member of the formation aborted due to mechanical problems, they took off early in the morning and reached Port Said without any problems. Once there, they were vectored by ground control to attack Israeli ground units in the el-Arish area, as recalled by Barakat:

'While in the air they were informed that el-Arish was under attack and that the Egyptian forces had not yet been overwhelmed, so they were ordered to go and help. They did not have enough fuel to get there and return but were told to 'obey the orders'.'

The three Sukhois were still 30km (18.6 miles) away from el-Arish, when a light on their fuel gauges informed the pilots that they were running out of fuel. AVM Mohammad Okasha summarised:

'The leader, al-Alim, acknowledged the order but informed the GCI that their fuel was insufficient to reach such a distant target: the officer on the ground answered that it was a direct order from the C-in-C UARAF and there was not to be any discussion about its execution. Obviously, flying a combat sortie under such circumstances made absolutely no sense and this was just one more out of dozens of grave mistakes resulting in entirely ineffective operations on that day.'

With grim determination, all three pilots kept pressing on towards the east, and Alaa Barakat and Taher Zaki completed the story of this mission:

'Over el-Arish they engaged some Mirages despite the fact that the Su-7 was a fighter-bomber and had poor manoeuvrability. Capt Muhammad Ali Khamis outmanoeuvred one Mirage and shot it down. Then Mohammad Shehata was shot down and another Mirage attacked Khamis' aircraft, hitting it in the cockpit first: the round split his helmet open like a melon, and he was shot down. Both ejected safely, but Shehata fractured his leg on landing and could never fly jet fighters again. They were hidden by the local people for three weeks full of adventures before they [the local people] managed to smuggle them out on a camel to Lake Bardavil, then on a boat to Port Said. The third Su-7 escaped.'[7]

Fuad Kamal clearly remembered Shehata:

'He was half-Egyptian, half-Sudanese, and flew MiG-19s before converting to the Su-7. Shehata survived the downing near el-Arish, in 1967, and later opened a cropdusting company in Egypt.'

Of Egyptian-Sudanese origin, Capt Shehata flew MiG-19s and Su-7s before the June 1967 War. This still from a film taken on 22 May 1967 shows him moments before he took off in a Su-7BMK for a demonstration flight in front of President Nasser. Shehata was shot down during the course of an air combat near el-Arish on 6 June. (Tarek el-Shennawy Collection)

The formation leader, Maj Galal Abd al-Alim managed to evade the Mirages, but ran out of fuel over the Ramadah area. He ejected safely and got back to Cairo West the same evening, together with one of the retreating Army units.

To summarise, on 6 June the two UARAF fighter-bomber units experienced their bloodiest day of the war. The MiG-19s of No. 20 Squadron flew a total of 14 sorties, suffered a loss of four fighters, one pilot killed and another injured, claiming one Mirage as shot down in return. No. 55 Squadron flew 10 sorties but lost five aircraft, of which three were in air combats, one on landing and one to fuel starvation, together with two pilots killed, claiming just one Mirage as shot down in return.

The MiG-21PFM pilots of No. 26 Squadron at Abu Suweir began combat operations at 05.30 in the morning, some of them in conjunction with a number of MiG-17s that had been redeployed from Cairo West. Fuad Kamal was also angered by some of the orders he received that morning:

'Some orders from the High Command were so stupid that I simply didn't carry them out. In fact, I was rude to some of the senior officers. One example of an impossible or stupid order was, 'Take four aircraft and attack Israel!' I told him, 'You come and do it!' I simply ignored that order …'

Nevertheless, Kamal proceeded to prepare his surviving MiG-21s for operations and launched four of them early that morning:

'Our four surviving MiG-21s took off at first light from a sub-runway. One was shot down by one of our own SAMs shortly after. The missile caused an automatic ejection. I saw it, and there were flames coming from the seat, but still the parachute opened. The pilot had serious burns and was sent to England for hospital treatment.'

The remaining three MiG-21s, followed by four MiG-17s, made attacks on Israeli ground units advancing along the coastal road in the northern Sinai, using UB-16-57 pods containing unguided rockets. In the course of his attack, Maj Adil Nasr sighted an Israeli Super Mystère B2 that was attacking Egyptian ground units nearby and diverted to attack, shooting his opponent down with a salvo of S-5 unguided 57mm rockets.[8]

Two other MiG-21s jumped an S-58 helicopter of No. 124 Squadron IDF/AF under way at low level over the central Sinai. Unable to get their R-3S missiles to lock on to the low-flying helicopter, which then landed among the palms, the frustrated pilots flew off back to base.[9] Fuad Kamal's deputy, Lt Col Farouk el-Ghazawy himself led two missions that day:

'I flew two air-to-ground missions with 57mm rocket pods against Israeli targets east of Mitla Defile. These were hit-and-run types of attacks, because we had a very small number of aircraft left, and we did not have the time to evaluate what happened.'[10]

Although many of their weapons hit their targets, the S-5 rockets again proved as useless as the S-3s deployed by the Su-7s. Correspondingly, these attacks were not only insufficient in number but were also largely ineffective. Taher Zaki recalled the end of another mission flown by MiG-21s:

'Capt Nabil Shuwakri and Lt Hassan el-Qusri attacked Israeli ground units but were intercepted by Mirages and there was an air combat. El-Qusri was killed, but Shuwakri managed to land his damaged MiG-21 at Fayid.'

In fact, el-Qusri's MiG-21 was damaged during that air combat, and began losing fuel. The pilot, who also claimed one of the Israelis as shot down, nursed his aircraft back across the Suez Canal, but crashed while attempting to land on a roadway.[11]

Lt Hassan el-Qusri of No. 49 Squadron was one of only two UARAF pilots who managed to scramble from Inchas on the morning of 5 June. He continued flying the next day, but was killed while attempting to land his damaged MiG-21 on a road near the Suez Canal, following an air combat with Israeli Mirages. The UARAF credited him with two kills during the June 1967 War. (David Nicolle Collection)

To summarise, No. 26 Squadron – which was the only UARAF MiG-21 unit active on 6 June – launched a total of 12 combat sorties during that day, losing two fighters and suffering one damaged in air combats (as well as one shot down by Egyptian SAMs in a so-called 'friendly fire' incident), for only one unconfirmed claim in return.

Two MiG-17s that took off from Abu Suweir around 16.00 flew the final Egyptian mission of the day, but the experience of their pilots reveals the problems the UARAF began to face while attempting to cooperate with ground forces. It also clearly demonstrated how pilots were sent into combat without even the most basic information about enemy dispositions. Under way deep over the northern Sinai, the two Egyptians sighted a long column of buses full of troops. Lacking any means of identification or communication with the Army, they decided not to attack and instead returned to their base. Only after landing back in Abu Suweir did they learn that the buses in question belonged to the IDF.

7 June: Reorganisation

The UARAF spent much of the third day of the war reorganising its remaining assets and expecting the arrival of replacement aircraft from Algeria (see the following sub-chapter). Early that morning, the remaining seven Su-7s of Air Group 1 were transferred from Fayid to Inchas, and the three remaining MiG-19s were similarly ordered to Cairo IAP. The three MiG-17s that were still operational at Abu Suweir were evacuated to Almaza air base.

The purpose of this redeployment was to concentrate remaining assets and also to remove them from air bases in the Canal Zone, which was expected to come within range of Israeli artillery. During the course of this process, all surviving MiG-21s were concentrated at Cairo West, as Fuad Kamal explained:

'Meanwhile, eight or 10 more of our aircraft were repaired. Surviving MiG-21s from other bases also arrived, and they were all later concentrated at Cairo West. From this a new wing or 'big squadron' was formed. We had enough aircraft for two squadrons, and I was put in command of this new unit.'

In a similar fashion, all the remaining Su-7s were concentrated at Inchas, while the remaining Il-28s operated from both Cairo West and Cairo IAP. Furthermore, AM Sidki Mahmoud ordered all ground personnel from air bases in the Canal Zone to be evacuated to air bases in the Cairo area, in order to bolster the efforts to repair a significant number of damaged aircraft that had assembled there.[12]

In addition to the order for evacuation, Air Group 1 at Fayid was tasked with launching four MiG-19s for an attack against an Israeli armoured column near el-Arish. The pilots involved were Taysir Hashish, Saad Zaghloul, Samir Salah Idris, and Salah Danish. Their aircraft were armed with ORO-57K pods and carried two drop tanks each, but because of the distance to their target, a decision was taken to reach the target zone flying at a level above 5,000m (16,404ft) to conserve fuel, and only egress the combat zone at low altitude. Barakat recalled:

'During this mission the formation engaged eight Mirages already over the Bitter Lake and fought with them for 20 minutes. The front pair evaded the Israelis but the rear was in trouble: the number 3 did a split-S but was shot down and killed. His wingman was also shot down and bailed out.'

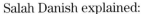

Salah Danish explained:

'Of course, we were detected almost immediately after we reached our cruising altitude. Our ground control called to tell us there were Israeli aircraft vectored to intercept and we must fly back immediately. Normally, we would have MiG-21s for protection, but not in this case. Shortly after I saw a Mirage approaching so I engaged the afterburner to accelerate my aircraft to maximum speed, and we slowly started distancing from the enemy planes. I calculated that if I continued this way for another three seconds, we would be safely out of their range. Then I saw the aircraft flown by Samir Idris lagging behind us. It was obvious he did not engage afterburner and then I saw an Israeli aircraft behind him and opening fire. Set ablaze, Samir Idris' aircraft crashed to the ground without ejection.

'I was angered and wanted to shoot down the aircraft that killed Samir. I manoeuvred around and behind the enemy and opened fire in short bursts as we had trained before the war. My shells missed but I continued my attack until I was close enough to see the white helmet of the enemy pilot. I fired again but the Israeli manoeuvred and thus my shells missed again. It was wrong on my part to focus all my attention at getting the Mirage that killed Samir. I failed to see the planes that manoeuvred behind me. Right in the moment I was about to continue my attack using rockets, I felt two shells strike my plane and it shook violently, then began to spiral towards the ground. I was still able to control the rotation but the plane was falling and it was clear that the tail would never raise the nose of my aircraft again. I lost almost 4,000m [13,123ft] of height in that way, and could all the time hear the sound of other aircraft and their shots, and I fired again, once or twice, but then decided to eject.'

Salah Danish landed on the ground near the still-burning wreckage of his aircraft. Acting as he had been trained, he collected the canopy of his parachute and sat on top of it, to make himself easier to spot by rescue teams. The area where he came down was in the mountainous part of central Sinai, some 80km (50 miles) away from the Suez Canal. After waiting for two hours, and having neither a radio nor water and food with him, he concluded that there were no signs of anybody looking for him:

'I decided to walk towards the Canal, using the direction of the sun for orientation. After a while, I reached a mountain and saw a small hut near its summit, so decided to climb on its top for orientation. That was the wrong decision. The climb consumed all my strength and the hut was empty: actually, it was a small shrine with some skeletons of various animals around it ... Going back down, I was surprised to see a woman some distance from me. When I approached her and asked for water, she pointed me back towards that hut. When I came back there, I concluded it was a bad idea to drink water surrounded by dead animals. So, I decided to continue walking towards the west. Then I saw two other MiG-19s, flying at low altitude towards the east. Of course, at their speed of 800–900km/h [497–559mph], the pilots inside could never distinguish a man on the ground, so they never saw me. A few minutes later I saw a jeep approaching from the direction of Egypt in the distance and fired several shots to attract the driver's attention ... When the jeep came closer, I saw it was carrying Border Guards. They took me to the al-Taqati coal mine.

'This mine had 700 employees, including several engineers and technicians and others who were curious to hear news about the war. They told me there was another plane that fell to the ground close to mine and I was surprised to find another pilot from *my formation there, Saad Zaghloul. His aircraft came down quite close to mine but the miners rescued him quite quickly … Despite the loss of our two aircraft, we were still full of confidence and feelings of a certain victory filled all of us … We spent a quiet evening listening to radio reports that claimed we had shot down 90 enemy aircraft.'*

The mission thus ended in disaster, with all four MiG-19s being shot down and two pilots – including Samir Salah Idris – being killed. Two others ejected safely but landed deep over Sinai and there was no hope of their recovery before the fighting ended.

In the afternoon, Alaa Barakat led four MiG-19s to attack Israeli tanks near Bir el-Abd, midway between el-Arish and Ismailia. They attacked their targets undisrupted, only to find out that the rockets launched from the ORO-57K pod could not penetrate even the top armour of the IDF tanks. The formation subsequently returned to Fayid without suffering any losses.

The MiG-21s of the 'big squadron' flew a total of 18 combat sorties on 7 June, mainly in attempts to provide cover for Army units withdrawing from Sinai. Reda el-Iraqi, who graduated from the Air Force Academy in 1965 and was assigned to No. 43 Squadron when the war broke out, recalled a sortie flown on the morning of 7 June:

'Early that morning another group of our pilots left for Algeria on board an Antonov aircraft. The air traffic at Cairo IAP was very 'one-sided': the aircraft would take off in the direction of Sinai but not return … A group of us sat next to a number of MiG-17, MiG-19 and helicopter pilots in the squadron ready room when Maj Samir Abdullah appeared. To our surprise, he pointed at my wingman, Ehab, and me and called us to come with him … Outside the room, he told us about the enemy armoured advance along the coastal road, that there were orders to disrupt this advance before it could reach the Suez Canal, and that I was to lead that attack. I was surprised by his decision: I had only 20 hours on the MiG-21, and knew next to nothing about the responsibilities of a formation leader … Ehab and me launched from Cairo IAP and turned in the direction of our target, in complete radio silence … although on an attack sortie, we were ordered to fly as high as possible, supposedly in order to remain 'above' the radar detection envelope … Climbing over Abu Suweir AB we crossed the Suez and then reached our target zone. We found no Israelis at the expected place so made a turn over the sea and came back towards the coastal road in an attempt to find an alternative target. That's when we sighted a column of armoured vehicles, some 20km [12 miles] away. We dove to attack and agreed to launch all of our rockets at once. As I fired, horror struck me: I saw all the rockets hitting the first tank with excellent accuracy. This was not thanks to my efficiency or cleverness… But I put all my focus on that attack and the rockets hit precisely, as did those fired by Ehab, which knocked out another Israeli tank. I would say that attack disrupted their advance for a while …

'We were returning towards Cairo IAP via Abu Suweir at maximum speed. All was quiet until we entered the landing pattern: that's when our own anti-aircraft gunners opened fire at us! Ehab's jet was hit almost immediately and he was forced to eject … I managed to land safely and I was almost the only pilot that day who took off from Cairo IAP and returned to the airport with his plane … nobody cared about me returning: during that period between 6 and 8 June, we saw so many fighters departing Cairo IAP but not returning. We nearly never knew what had happened and simply had to conclude that they and their pilots were destroyed. Nobody knew what was going on outside the airport and the general atmosphere was gloomy …'[30]

When not armed with R–3S missiles for air combat, UARAF MiG-21s flew ground-attack sorties against Israeli Army units in Sinai armed with UB-16-57 rocket pods, as seen in this pre-war photo. Their success was limited, however. Despite countless Soviet assurances and attempts to blame Egyptian pilots, the S–5 rockets launched from these pods were remarkably ineffective. It took the Egyptians years of tense discussions with various Soviet advisers and much hard work to improve these weapons. (Nour Bardai Collection)

Farouk el-Ghazawy flew no fewer than three of these sorties that day, including one that protected two MiG-17s that attacked the Israelis near Bir Gifgafa at around 15.30:

'My last mission on 7 June was in the mid-afternoon. I was on a CAP at 8,000m [26,247ft] with my wingman, and another section was at 6,000m [19,685ft]. We orbited in reverse directions; on a north-south axis … The Russians told us the MiG-21 was a high-speed, high-altitude fighter. I had this in my mind then … All of a sudden, in a typical Israeli fashion, they attacked us from below … Their tactics were to show themselves and then descend in order to get us to the best altitude for the manoeuvrability of the Mirage, but also the worst for the MiG-21, because of our poorer manoeuvrability and higher fuel consumption at lower levels … Also, by descending to low altitudes our radars could not track them so we did not receive any GCI support any more. The other section was directed against the enemy and we accelerated as well … Shortly afterwards the other section was hit and they killed my friend who flew as number 2. Dibbs was his name. Number 1 then panicked and yelled on the radio, 'I got hit!' and asked me to come down and save him. But I was too far away. So, I told him to pull up and bale out. He ejected and came back, but got a spinal compression from that ejection …'

Once again, Mirages were quickly on the scene, but not before the MiG-17Fs caused some casualties on the ground: after damaging one of the Israeli jets, the Egyptians disengaged successfully.[13]

MiG-21s from Abu Suweir similarly provided top cover for four MiG-17s that hit Israeli Army units in the Romani area, leaving a number of vehicles destroyed.[14] A four-ship formation of MiG-17s from Almaza, supported by four MiG-21s, then hit an Israeli unit in the process of refuelling while advancing in the direction of Kantara, causing additional losses in vehicles and men. On this occasion the Egyptian formation reached its target undisturbed but on its way back to base it was intercepted by two Mirages. The MiG-21s were only partially successful in distracting the attention of the Israeli pilots from the vulnerable fighter-bombers: one MiG-17 was shot down and its pilot killed, while one of the MiG-21s returned to Fayid in a damaged condition. As described in *Volume 1*, a pair of MiG-17Fs led by Maj Mamdouh Taliba shot down another Israeli Super Mystère that morning. A pair of MiG-17s then intercepted the Piper of No. 103 Squadron IDF/AF sent to recover the downed Israeli pilot, before the Piper was rescued by two other Super Mystères, which forced the Egyptians to evade.

While indicative of what would have been possible if the UARAF had not received the blow that stunned its commanders to such a degree on the morning of 5 June, these efforts by Egyptian pilots remained insufficient in number and impact to alter the overall situation. The Army continued its increasingly chaotic withdrawal from

Tahsin Fuad Hussein Saima, an ex-RJAF Hunter pilot who defected to Egypt in 1962, served with No. 20 Squadron UARAF during the 1967 War and claimed one Israeli Noratlas as shot down on 7 June. Thereafter, Saima continued his highly successful career in Egypt, reaching the rank of air commodore/brigadier general (as seen in this photograph). (Group 73)

Sinai, which, under continuous Israeli air and ground attacks, slowly but surely turned into a rout.

Elsewhere that day, four MiG-19s of No. 20 Squadron were about to redeploy from Hurghada to Cairo International when the ground controller diverted them to intercept a formation of Israeli aircraft on course for Sharm el-Sheikh. Led by Maj Said Shalash with Capt Mustafa Darwish as wingman, the formation was completed by Capt Tahsin Fuad Hussein Saima (the ex-RJAF Hunter pilot who had defected to Egypt in 1962) and Lt Abdul Rahman Sidki. They succeeded in assuming a favourable attack position unobserved by the Israelis. As Alaa Barakat recalled:

'Shalash and Darwish sighted four Mirages. The formation leader ordered, 'Drop auxiliary tanks' – and went after the Mirages. Shalash and Darwish engaged the Mirages in a dogfight and both were shot down. Both ejected safely. Saima and Sidki attacked [Nord] Noratlases and claimed two as shot down … Sidki's tanks failed to separate and after they hit the Noratlases they attempted to continue their voyage to Cairo International. Saima did not have enough fuel for this and he landed at Fayid … Sidki had lost sight of Saima during the combat and flew to Cairo International, 'chased by a pack of wolves'. Because his tanks hadn't separated he was able to reach that airfield and land safely. Sidki was the most junior pilot in the squadron and immediately after landing he ran up to me in great excitement, shouting, 'We shot down two Noratlases!' He also said that he saw Shalash's aircraft 'in a ball of flames' and did not realise that he had ejected until later. The MiG-19 pilots who bailed out in this combat were picked up by the Egyptian Frontier Corps forces in Sinai and brought back without trouble.'

As well as Sidki, Tahsin Fuad Hussein Saima also returned safely.

The claim for two Noratlas and one Mirage IIICJ shot down by UARAF MiG-19s on 7 June is probably the most controversial of this entire war. None of the Israeli publications available in the West even mention any such clash, while several Israeli researchers fiercely deny that any air combat of this kind took place or the IDF/AF suffered such losses. The IDF/AF Historical Branch cited only one Noratlas loss during the entire war, and the aircraft in question was destroyed on the ground, during an attack on Kfar Sirkin airfield in central Israel, on 5 June. A few other Israeli publications mention only one Noratlas ever being intercepted by any Arab MiGs, though over western Iraq and southwest Syria, during the evening of 7 June (see Chapters 5 and 6). In contrast, not only do a number of former UARAF pilots recall this air combat but also most of them – as well as at least two former IrAF pilots – recall reading reports about heavy losses sustained by Israeli paratroopers, caused by the downing of two Noratlas transports, as published in contemporary Israeli newspapers. They further recall that the reports in question expressed the great sadness of their families. Despite their best efforts the authors have so far been unable to identify these newspapers.[15]

Also active on the afternoon of 7 June were three of the six Il-28s that had survived the Israeli onslaught of 5 June. The formation led by Maj Hanfy Mahgoub reached its target undisturbed and attacked Israeli units under way along the coastal road in northern Sinai. Although flying subsonic bombers without protection from UARAF interceptors, these pilots pressed home their attacks, hitting a number of vehicles and other targets with 250kg bombs and 23mm cannon. Due to a series of mistakes, the Israeli GCI misdirected its interceptors and all the Il-28s returned safely to their base.

Apart from the Egyptian Army units withdrawing from Sinai, it was above all the Egyptian SA-2 sites of the still to be properly established Air Defence Command that came under attack on 7 June. Scattered along the Suez Canal or protecting various air bases, and lacking proper support from the UARAF's radar network which had itself suffered considerably under Israeli attacks, only a few of these sites were protected by AAA. The IDF/AF was thus free to deploy Mirage IIICJs to attack them with 30mm cannon. The Israelis rapidly learned that a few hits to the big 'Fan Song' fire-control radars usually rendered the entire site non-operational. On the other hand, although several SAM sites were knocked out during these attacks, their crews shot down two Mirages in return on 7 June.

A UARAF Il-28 releases a stick of FAB-250M-45 bombs upon Israeli positions on 7 June 1967. (Nour Bardai Collection)

The Algerian Mystery

While some UARAF pilots flew numerous combat sorties on 6 and 7 June, others were assigned different tasks at Cairo West, as recalled by Farid Harfush:

'During the morning of 6 June, after quarrelling about the orders, many commanding officers and most of the MiG-21 pilots gathered at one of the local squadron ready rooms. Around 06.00 we arranged a meeting and began discussing a possible attack on Israeli airfields ... Instead of that, they told us that transport aircraft would carry some pilots to Algeria and others to Iraq. I was selected to go to Algeria, together with Maj Amozis and 12 other pilots, among them Zidane, Samir Farid, Ezz al-Din Abu el-Dahab, Fawzy Salama, Samir Aziz Mikhail, Sakr and Samir Abdullah ... So, we boarded the Antonov and flew to Algeria.'

The decision to send Harfush and his comrades to Algeria resulted from a telephone call President Nasser made to the Algerian President Houari Boumediene. According to unofficial Algerian sources, Nasser described the situation of the UARAF as *'catastrophic'* and provided some details about the number of aircraft lost. Wasting no time, he asked Boumediene to send to Egypt all the fighter-bombers the Algerian Air Force (al-Quwwat al-Jawwiya al-Jaza'eriya – QJJ) could put into the air. The reaction was almost immediate, and in accordance with corresponding orders, the QJJ signalled back to Algiers that it had 47 fighters ready for transfer, including all its currently operational MiG-17Fs, a complete unit of 12 MiG-21F-13s and six MiG-21FLs. That same evening, 5 June, the first group of Egyptian pilots arrived in Boufarik aboard an An-12, followed by another aircraft that landed in Algiers. The first group of Egyptians, including Capt Tameem Fahmy Abdullah, managed to get 12 MiG-21F-13s ready during the night and promptly departed in the direction of Egypt on the morning of 6 June. Led by an Algerian An-12 that carried spares and weapons, they arrived in Egypt the same evening, after making stops in Tripolis and Benghazi.[16]

An attempt to reach a similar agreement with Baghdad failed: indeed, although a number of UARAF pilots, including Qadri Abd el-Hamid, reached Rashid air base near Baghdad on the morning of 6 June, with orders to take responsibility for several IrAF MiG-21s and return with them via Saudi Arabia, nothing of this kind happened.

El-Hamid recalled the Iraqi reaction:

'The Iraqis treated us very badly. We had lost everything and they knew it. They said, 'big-mouthed Egyptians: where is your air power now?' They made fun of us. They had plenty of MiGs hidden under the trees at Rashid AB near Baghdad.

They put us in what was virtually a jail without even bed sheets. We came back on 9 June, via Jiddah to Aswan and then Cairo – and without any aircraft. But, if we had flown any MiGs to Meliz, they would only have been captured. We meanwhile realised on our own that it was a complete defeat. Then I met AM Sidki Mahmud and he was crying. He told us to go home to our families because there were no more planes. It was a political game now, and Nasser had to stop the war … Our generation cannot forget the sights and scenes of the 1967 War. Those scenes will never be out of my mind.'

In Algeria, Farid Harfush and Samir Aziz Mikhail were much luckier, even though their dreams of returning to Egypt to continue the fight in new aircraft evaporated as soon as they landed, as Mikhail recalled:

'We found that they only had six MiG-21FL aircraft ready. I was very sad that I was not chosen to fly one of them back to Egypt.'

Obviously, by the time Harfush and Mikhail arrived in Algiers, the first six Algerian MiG-21FLs had already been prepared for a trip to Egypt, and were dispatched shortly afterwards. However, what exactly happened to these six aircraft following their arrival in Egypt remains unclear. No Egyptian sources concerning their deployment are available. Instead, ever since the end of the 1967 War there have been a number of reports claiming that six Algerian MiG-21s were captured after landing at el-Arish, which was by then under Israeli control. Supposedly, they were directed to this air base as a result of chaos within the UARAF chain of command, the pilots not having been informed that el-Arish had been occupied by the Israelis during the night of 5-6 June. One of the first such reports of six Algerian MiG-21s being captured at el-Arish was published in *Flight International* magazine, as early as 22 June 1967, citing an unnamed source in Tel Aviv.[17] This report was subsequently neither confirmed nor denied by official sources. There was also a rumour that the story was censored from official press releases. Although repeated in a number of accounts published since that date, no tangible evidence concerning the capture of six intact MiG-21s of any variant ever appeared again.

In 1995 a person presenting himself as Khalid al-Qadi, a former Algerian MiG-21 pilot living in the US since 1968, contacted the authors. Al-Qadi explained that he was one of six Algerian pilots who flew these MiG-21s to el-Arish. While the authors still have doubts about the authenticity of this story, we offer it here for readers to judge it upon its own merits:

'I was the last to land. Only a few seconds after I stopped the plane and shut my engine down, I opened the cockpit and noticed several soldiers approaching my aircraft. That's when I realised that el-Arish was under Israeli control. Already outside my aircraft, I pulled my sidearm and began firing at my MiG-21, trying to set it on fire. I think I caused quite some damage, but was then hit by one of the Israelis, injured and captured … The Israelis interrogated me for weeks, before deciding to send all of us home. Concerned that I might be seen as a traitor upon returning to Algeria, I then requested political asylum in the US, where I have lived since 1968 … From what I know, all six of our MiG-21s were soon to follow …'[18]

Khalid al-Qadi passed away a few years later. All attempts to verify his story remain unsuccessful. Furthermore, no pilot with his name is ever known to have served with the QJJ, and the authors are therefore unable to confirm or deny his narrative. Nevertheless, Fuad Kamal, the CO of Air Group 7, who had been put in command of the 'big squadron', which included all UARAF MiG-21s that survived the first days of the war, categorically stated:

'We knew nothing about Algerian MiG-21s coming to Egypt. Only about MiG-17s, which arrived later.'

Put another way, is it possible that the arrival of six MiG-21FLs from Algeria went unnoticed by the UARAF officers who would have been responsible for them once they were in Egypt? Judging by the entirely misguided orders issued by some top UARAF officers during the early morning of 6 June, such as the previously described order by the Operations Officer at Cairo West for MiG-21s and Su-7s to attack airfields in Israel, or AM Sidki Mahmoud's order for three Su-7s on a CAP to attack targets in the el-Arish area despite their lack of fuel, it does seem possible that someone could have come up with the idea of rushing six MiG-21s to el-Arish, even though this base had never previously been used by the type.

As already described by Salah Danish, even the deployment of MiG-19s to el-Arish had previously been considered 'unsafe' by various squadron leaders. Also outlined above is the fact that the High Command of the UARAF already knew that el-Arish was overrun by the Israelis and had issued orders for all air bases in Sinai to be evacuated. However, it remains unknown whether such information was provided to the Alger-

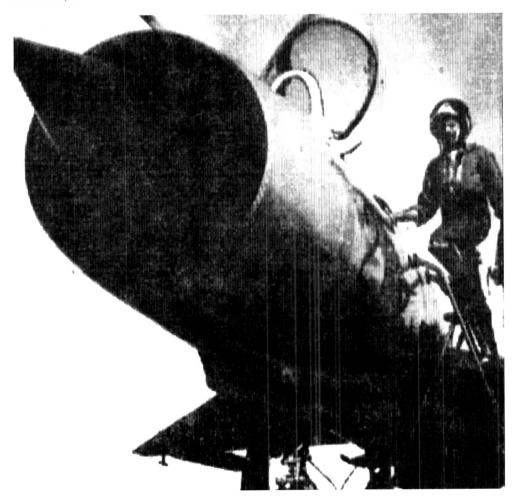

An Algerian pilot about to enter the cockpit of MiG-21FL serial number 21. Despite many reports, it remains unclear exactly how many Algerian MiG-21s, and of what variant, were sent to Egypt during the June 1967 War, although it appears that six MiG-21FLs were the first to leave. (Tom Cooper Collection)

Assisted by his aircraft captain, an Algerian pilot takes his place in the cockpit of a MiG-21F-13. Whether any QJJ MiG-21s actually ended up in Israeli hands, as often reported over the last 40 years, remains unclear. Most reliable reports indicate that the first batch of MiG-21s flown to Algeria consisted of more advanced FLs, and that they entered service with the UARAF at the close of the June 1967 War.
(Tom Cooper Collection)

ians, and therefore there is a distant possibility that, for one reason or another, somebody in Egypt rushed the first six MiG-21s arriving from Algeria to el-Arish – perhaps still flown by the pilots who had brought them, and without the knowledge of other relevant officers in Egypt. Nevertheless, tangible evidence for this, and for six intact MiG-21s from Algeria ending up in Israeli hands during the June 1967 War remains unavailable.

Meanwhile, according to most available Algerian and Egyptian sources, the first confirmed transfer of 12 Algerian MiG-21F-13s only occurred on 6 June. These were flown by a number of Algerian pilots, plus five Egyptians, including Capt Tameem Fahmy and Lt Abdel Hamid Mustafa. Led by an An-12 that carried baggage and some spare parts, they took off early in the morning from Boufarik air base, and flew via Tripolis and Benghazi to Marsa Matruh, arriving there on the morning of 8 June.[19]

According to unofficial Algerian sources, once in Egypt, the Algerian MiG-21s were divided into two groups, one based at Marsa Matruh and the other at Inchas, with the latter becoming involved in the fighting only hours after its arrival, flying a remarkably effective attack upon an Israeli column advancing along the coastal road in northern Sinai. Flown on the morning of 9 June, primarily by Egyptian but also by a few Algerian pilots, this mission apparently proved a success.

The MiGs swooped down on the Israelis while they were replenishing near Romani, following a nocturnal clash with a number of Egyptian T-55 tanks, and caused a number of losses.[20] However, Egyptian sources indicate that this mission was actually flown on the afternoon of 8 June and was intercepted by at least two Mirages, resulting in the loss of one of the escorting MiG-21s and the death of its Egyptian pilot, Lt Abdel Hamid Mustafa.[21]

Although additional groups of UARAF pilots were sent to Algeria on 7 and 8 June, it took the Algerians and Egyptians several more days to ready the second batch of QJJ aircraft for transfer to Egypt. This then mainly consisted of MiG-17Fs, most of which first had to be assembled. Another problem was that most of the Egyptian pilots sent to Algeria were not qualified to fly that particular type. Once again, the Egyptian pilots proved far more capable of improvisation than their commanders, as Farid Harfush explained:

'Our Algerian brothers received us with great enthusiasm. Sadly, we found only very few MiG-21s there, but plenty of MiG-17s. The problem was, Mikhail and I had never flown the MiG-17 before. Samir Abdullah thus had to brief us on the type and explain all the details about flying it. My first flight on the type lasted 30 minutes … As next, we were transferred to another airfield in southern Algeria. This was really a primitive place, full of scorpions and with very poor accommodation. We had to build ourselves a small table from palm leaves. On 8 June we were transferred again, this time to Boufarik and there I heard the speech by President Nasser and his announcement that we had lost the war and he was resigning … we were shocked, and if this was not enough, the Algerians then put us all under armed escort and took us to Blida airport … on the next day, Nasser withdrew his decision. This improved the mood of our Algerian friends, who praised Nasser and his decision to fight for the liberation of our country …'

Samir Aziz Mikhail summed up his trip to Algeria:

'On the next morning [after Nasser's withdrawal of his resignation; authors' note], we were finally given permission to fly back to Egypt … We made a stop at Tripoli and Benghazi in Libya. The Libyans treated us well … Finally, we reached Cairo … Our feelings on return were very bad and we could not look the others in their eyes because of shame.'

According to official Egyptian sources, the last transfer of QJJ aircraft to Egypt took place on 9 June, but the pilots involved were ordered to return their MiGs to Algeria after reaching Libya – apparently on orders from President Boumediene after he learned that Egypt had accepted a ceasefire. Nevertheless, Farid Harfush recalled:

'On 11 June, 12 of us – 11 Egyptians and one Algerian named Jeballah – took off in MiG-17s for the long journey home. After making a number of refuelling stops in Algeria, Tunis and Libya, and at Marsa Matruh in Egypt, we arrived at Cairo International only on the evening of 12 June. The day of my return to Egypt was the worst day of my life … After my landing, I saw destroyed passenger aircraft and then I finally realised the extent of losses and destruction and how many officers were killed … I was in agony.'

Furthermore, according to unofficial Algerian sources, six MiG-21FLs were sent to Egypt as late as 13 June, flown via Libya to Marsa Matruh by several QJJ pilots and a third group of UARAF pilots who had been sent to Algeria. Subsequently, all the Algerian pilots were withdrawn from Egypt and returned home in a civilian airliner. The same source noted that the QJJ eventually transferred a total of 47 fighters to Egypt, including 12 MiG-21F-13s and six or eight MiG-21FLs, but that these aircraft were not as lucky as their Algerian pilots: only six were eventually returned by Egypt, in early 1968.[22]

In comparison, official Egyptian documentation reveals that Algeria donated a total of 21 MiG-21s, 20 MiG-17s and 12 Il-28s to Egypt by late July 1967.[23]

8 June: Textbook Operations

During the fourth day of the war, the UARAF finally began launching well-coordinated operations, carefully deploying its remaining assets to attack specific targets. The primary target of most of the Egyptian fighter-bombers that took off early in the morning was an Israeli mechanised column advancing along the coastal road towards el-Kantara. For this purpose, almost all the remaining MiG-17s had been concentrated at Abu Suweir, and all the MiG-19s at Cairo IAP. While their aircraft were refuelled, pilots received the first proper briefing they had been given during the course of the conflict. At 06.00, six MiG-17Fs and four MiG-19s took off with the aim of attacking targets in the Bir el-Abd area. At 07.30 two additional MiG-17Fs were sent against the same target, followed by four MiG-19s that again attacked the same area around 08.30, shortly after the Israeli column ran headlong into an Egyptian blocking position. The result was a battle that continued for the rest of the day. The IDF/AF was initially slow to react to these hard-hitting Egyptian air attacks and only the latter formation was intercepted by Mirages. One MiG-19 was shot down and its pilot killed. Another loss occurred when the remaining three MiG-19s were returning to their base. Passing close to Inchas shortly after this airfield had come under Israeli air attack, the MiGs themselves came under fire from Egyptian ground-based air defences. One of the MiG-19s was hit and the pilot forced to eject.

There were nevertheless still some exceptions to this rule of flying well-coordinated operations, for example when Tahsin Zaki took part in a separate mission from Fayid against Israeli units advancing towards Bir Thamada:

'On the afternoon of 7 June we moved from Fayid to Inchas air base. The next morning, AM el-Kadi told me over the telephone that all our troops were now west of the Mitla Defile, and that all forces east of there were Israelis and could therefore be attacked at will. He also told me that Israeli commandos had parachuted near the Mitla Defile and ordered my Su-7 squadron to attack them at once.

'At first light I took off accompanied by Lt Zakaria Abu Sa'ada. We headed for the Mitla Defile but found no trace of the enemy, so we kept flying east along the road until we reached the area of Nakhel, east of the Mitla Defile. There we saw Egyp-

MiG-19S serial number 3024 served with No. 20 Squadron UARAF during the June 1967 War. The aircraft survived that conflict and at least two subsequent wars and is now on display at the EAF Museum at Almaza. Unfortunately, this museum is not yet open to the public.
(Tarek el-Shennawy)

tian forces still retreating along the road towards Nakhel. Shortly after, I noticed 12 Israeli Centurion tanks, plus the rest of their vehicles, near Bir Thamada, some 30km [18.6 miles] away. I flew low and saw that these Centurions were firing on our retreating vehicles and so I ordered Abu Sa'ada to attack. We made three passes, firing between two and four 57mm rockets at each tank we targeted. Not a single Israeli tank was knocked out, which showed just how ineffective those Soviet 57mm rockets really were. Some of the rockets just dropped to the ground within 10m [33ft] of our wings!

'*On our way back I saw some tanks coming from Bir Thamada heading south, and so I decided to fly low to have a look. They turned out to be Egyptian tanks. As soon as I got home I informed AM el-Kadi about the position of our forces still to the east of the Sinai passes.*

'*Ten minutes later the telephone rang again and my base commander informed me that we had attacked Egyptian tanks by mistake. I denied this accusation strongly, as the tanks we attacked had been firing on our own vehicles. These tanks also had white 'Xs' marked on them, which we did not use, plus white rings around their barrels!*'

It turned out that Zaki's attack on the Israelis assisted the efforts of local Egyptian Army units to prevent – or at least to delay – the enemy from capturing Bir Thamada, in turn keeping open the escape route for units withdrawing from the Nakhel area.

Around noon, MiG-17s from Abu Suweir again became active, four fighters attacking targets in the Romani area around 11.50, followed by two other jets around 14.00. As had been the case earlier in the morning, most of these ground-attack missions were protected by MiG-21s, which flew a total of eight escort sorties on 8 June. Two of these fighters reportedly engaged a formation of Mirages and Lt el-Ashmawy shot down the Israeli interceptor that crashed near Tel el-Kebir, on the Suez Canal.

Around the same time, and after their mission had been cancelled no fewer than three times, Maj Hanfy Mahgoub took off as a leader of three Il-28s – including one flown by Capt Abdel Wahab el-Keraidy – with the aim of attacking Israeli troops advancing in northern Sinai. Under way at very low level, the bombers again evaded enemy interceptors and hit an Israeli armoured column encamped between Bir el-Abd and Romani. Israeli Mirages only appeared as the Il-28s were making their way back towards the Suez Canal. In their first attack, one Il-28 was damaged by 30mm cannon fire, but the pilot managed to land the burning jet safely at Cairo West on a single engine.

Minutes later, two other Mirages attacked the Il-28 flown by Mahgoub and managed to shoot his bomber down, forcing the crew to bail out. The crew of the remaining Il-28 saw Mahgoub ejecting, but he was never heard of again. Until today, there are persistent rumours in Egypt that Mahgoub was either shot by the Israelis during or after ejection, or was captured on the ground and that he spent the rest of his life in Israeli prisons.[24]

By chance, a pair of MiG-21PFMs was flying in the same area. Their appearance clearly drew the pair of Israeli interceptors away from the slow and vulnerable Il-28s, as recalled by Nabil Shuwakri, who flew two combat sorties on that day:

'*We were at low level and our only armament were two pods of S-5K rockets which had hollow-charge warheads. After we passed the Canal we saw two Mirages approaching from the left. I told my leader, 'Two Mirages attacking from the left!'* –

Tahsin Zaki's sortie from Fayid on the afternoon of 8 June 1967 was his last ever combat mission. Unfairly, he was severely punished and forced to leave the UARAF following the June 1967 War. These photographs came into being during the 1980s, when he served in agricultural aviation. (David Nicolle Collection)

The Il-28 of Maj Mahgoub or Lt el-Keraidy during the attack on an Israeli camp between Bir el-Abd and Romani on 8 June. Flying such missions over an area effectively under the control of IDF/AF Mirages was practically hopeless, yet the crews of the Egyptian Il-28s accomplished such tasks remarkably well.
(Albert Grandolini Collection)

Capt Hanfy Mahgoub (centre) photographed at Hodeida airfield in Yemen in 1964. Mahgoub was leader of the Il-28 formation that bombed and strafed Israeli troops in northern Sinai on 8 June 1967. Mahgoub was posthumously decorated with the Medal of Honour, one of Egypt's highest military medals. On the right of this photograph is Lt Abdel Moaty Darwish, one of the first Egyptian bombardier-navigators, who later trained several generations of navigators before retiring with the rank of air vice-marshal.
(Ahmed Keraidy Collection)

but he did not see them. So, I put my afterburner on, jettisoned my drop tank and saw that the Mirages were already attacking. While turning around, I put the seat fully back and turned to see where my leader and the two Mirages were. Then, while turning left, I saw a Mirage behind me. That Mirage left the combat and disappeared. I warned my leader, 'There is a Mirage behind you!' and he reversed. At that moment his MiG-21 exploded from cannon fire. After he shot my leader, the Israeli did a right turn and headed towards el-Arish. I put the nose down with maximum afterburner, but I had those two rocket pods under the wings of my aircraft that created lots of drag. I came to the same level as the Mirage, within a range of 1 mile

[1.6km], *but had no way to close because he was accelerating. I started firing one rocket from each pod at him, but I didn't succeed. If I had a cannon I could have jettisoned those pods and run after him, but I couldn't do anything.'*

Tahsin Zaki recalled Shuwakri's efforts:

'I would like to commend the dedication and bravery of Nabil Shuwakri, who kept flying one sortie after the other in his MiG-21 despite fatigue, which showed so clearly!'

While returning towards Cairo, el-Keraidy diverted his Il-28 to attack the Firdan Bridge near Ismailia, where Egyptian ground troops were holding on in order to get as many of their tanks as possible across to the west bank. The bridge was hit but not disabled and the Army continued using it to withdraw additional units until the morning of 9 June. Eventually, el-Keraidy returned to Cairo IAP undisturbed. Subsequently, all the remaining Il-28s were ordered to fly to Sana'a in Yemen, to be kept safe from possible Israeli follow-up attacks.[25]

The final two attack missions by MiG-17Fs on this day were launched against targets in the el-Kantara area again, around 16.30, being flown simultaneously with two Su-7s flown by Maj el-Shennawy (Su-7BMK serial number 7185) and 1st Lt Mohammed Naguib. They attacked Israeli ground units in the Bir Thamada area, as recalled by Tahsin Zaki:

'Arriving over Bir Thamada they engaged Israeli Mirages that were attacking those Egyptian tanks that I saw in the morning, moving towards the west from Bir Thamada. It was then that we lost the Su-7 flown by Mohammed Naguib … when the fighting stopped, our Su-7s [those flown by No. 55 Squadron; authors' note] had flown 32 combat sorties.'

Meanwhile, Salah Danish and Saad Zaghloul were still in the camp at the al-Taqati coal mine:

'We took a great deal of sleep and rest after two hard days and woke up at the sound of workers. Outside, we met a tank commander, Ahmed, talking with the miners. His face and clothes were mired in oil and his long beard indicated he had been under continuous stress for days. Ahmed told us the Israeli forces destroyed his tank unit just half an hour's drive away, and were heading for us and we should evacuate our place or expect to become prisoners within the shortest period of time. We went to the manager of the mine and explained the situation. He explained he had only three buses and these could not take more than 150 men at a time, while there were 700 employees around … So we began a march towards the Canal. Our column extended for 4km [2.5miles]. All the time I did not stop wondering how the Israeli forces could reach this far into central Sinai, and that's when I began to realise that the claims on the radio were different from reality … Later on we met several soldiers from the Army. One of them had a small radio and that way we learned that President Nasser had stepped down. That was how we learned about the extent of the tragedy and disaster that befell Egypt. From that moment on, everything became equal: clinging to our own life was the only goal for all of us. We dispersed into several groups, each one going in a different direction.'

However, 8 June 1967 was a day on which the leadership in Cairo continued to make wrong decisions. Around noon, Nasser suddenly entered the Supreme Headquarters and announced that he had conducted telephone conversations

An Egyptian MiG-21FL (or PFM) as photographed by the Israelis during an attack on one of their columns in Sinai. The aircraft was apparently armed with UB-16-57 pods for unguided rockets, as was Nabil Shuwakri's MiG-21 on 8 June 1967. (IDF via Albert Grandolini)

Lt Abdel Wahab el-Keraidy was the pilot of the only Il-28 of three within Mahgoub's formation that got back to Cairo International undamaged. El-Keraidy was subsequently ordered to evacuate his bomber to Yemen. He later continued a very successful career with the Egyptian Air Force. (Ahmed Keraidy Collection)

with Soviet and Algerian leaders, and that 200 new MiGs were on their way. He explained that the Egyptian forces would regroup, hold the passes in Sinai, and then rally for a massive attack. Although Moscow demanded Egypt accept the ceasefire, the Egyptian President was determined to fight until the Israelis were driven from his country's territory. This stance changed only during a conference between Nasser and Amer, later during the day, when the former finally realised that his military was in no condition to continue fighting. That evening, the Egyptian representative to the UN conveyed the decision to accept the ceasefire on the condition that Israel would also cease combat operations, but without demanding an Israeli withdrawal from Sinai.[26]

The Setback

Negotiations regarding a ceasefire between the Arabs and Israel were launched only a few hours after the Israeli attack. As of the evening of 5 June, the Soviet leadership had concluded that the Arabs should accept an immediate ceasefire, even though their position was not yet catastrophic. However, Nasser did not accept this line of reasoning. Furthermore, in the course of consultations at the UN, Moscow refused to accept the simple ceasefire resolution and instead urged adoption of a resolution combining a ceasefire with the call for withdrawal of troops to pre-war positions. Israel refused to accept this condition, while the UAR refused to accept a ceasefire without it. Therefore, the Security Council unanimously passed a simple ceasefire resolution.

After two days spent persuading Nasser that the UAR accept a simple ceasefire, Moscow finally acted on its own. On 7 June it requested an immediate meeting of the Security Council and tabled a second ceasefire resolution, simply calling on the governments concerned to cease firing at 20.00 GMT that night. This was unanimously adopted, but Egypt again rejected it. It was only on 8 June that Nasser realised the hopelessness of Egypt's military position and finally decided to accept. Correspondingly, another resolution was presented by Moscow on 9 June, demanding fulfilment of the two previous resolutions and calling for a ceasefire to become effective from 02.30 local time on the morning of 9 June. This was unanimously passed and Israel and Syria had both accepted it just two hours after passage.

Although the Israelis agreed to the ceasefire in principle, they were determined to reach the Suez Canal first, and therefore ignored the armistice. By 02.30 on 9 June the first Israeli ground units were in Ras al-Sudr, on the eastern bank of the Gulf of Suez, and approaching the Great Bitter Lake, but were still kilometres away from the Suez Canal. In between and behind them, tens of thousands of disorganised Egyptian troops were limping back towards the west. Certainly, the eastern bank of the strategic waterway was already in the process of being abandoned by the Egyptians, who scuttled ships in order to block it, and the only area where the Egyptian Army was still offering organised resistance was Port Fuad, on the northern terminus. However, the Israelis – supposedly without a clear idea where to stop their advance – were still to complete their conquering of Sinai. Because of this, the last day of the war on Sinai was characterised by the frenetic advance of IDF ground units towards the west, and last-ditch attempts by several Egyptian, one Kuwaiti and one Sudanese Army units that remained more or less intact to fight back against heavy odds. Several battles on the ground continued to rage until around 20.00.[27]

The UARAF hardly flew this day. On the morning of 9 June, AM Sidki Mahmmoud issued an order for the final evacuation of all unnecessary pilots and ground personnel from air bases along the Suez Canal to Cairo IAP. Correspondingly, all the remaining MiG-17s were withdrawn from Abu Suweir, leaving only guards there, as well as at Fayid and Kabrit.

The available Egyptian accounts indicate that only two missions were launched on this day. One mission included three MiG-15s from Almaza air base, with the purpose of providing protection for the few Army units still active in the Ismailia area. Once there, however, this formation was intercepted by Mirages and one of its aircraft was shot down. The pilot ejected safely, but was killed by civilians on the ground who thought that he was an Israeli. The other formation consisted of four MiG-17s that launched from Cairo West, led by Zohair Shalabi. After providing close support for the remaining Army formations withdrawing through the Mitla Defile, the Egyptians were intercepted by two Mirages and lost three aircraft in the process – including the MiG-17F flown by Zohair Shalabi, who was killed.[28] In a recent interview, Wg Cdr Kapil Bhargava, who worked with Zohair Shalabi on the HA-300 project, corrected our previous reconstruction of this clash,[29] recalling:

Subject to persistent Israeli air attacks, the road through Mitla Defile became an Egyptian 'highway of death'. This Israeli photograph taken following the June 1967 War shows it still littered with the burnt-out hulks of hundreds of trucks, artillery pieces and tanks abandoned after they ran out of fuel. (IDF)

'I checked with Sobhy el-Tawil, who gave me some details about talking to the sole survivor of Shalabi's formation. Zohair Shalabi flew several missions for close air support in the MiG-17, which was no match for the Mirage IIIC. On 9 June he led a formation of four MiG-17s in support of the Army over Mitla Pass. On its way back, two Mirage aircraft bounced the formation. Three MiG-17s, including Zohair's aircraft, were shot down. The number 4 escaped to tell the sorry tale. There was no dogfight. It was simply a run back home that did not work out for Zohair. A MiG-17 could not possibly run away from two Mirage III aircraft. I obtained the name of the Israeli pilots who had reported exactly the same conditions, on the same day and over the same area. Asher Snir claimed two MiG-17s. Avi Lanir downed the third one. One of these two pilots must have got Zohair's aircraft. Zohair had shown great courage in fighting for his country. He was posthumously awarded the Order of the Nile (Egypt's equivalent of the Victoria Cross). I lost a dear friend and Egypt a very good human being.'

Collecting Pieces

Salah Danish, MiG-19 pilot of the No. 20 or 'Araba' Squadron, was shot down in an air combat over Sinai, on 7 June. His evasion attempts failed and three days later he became the only Arab pilot captured by the Israelis during that war. (Salah Danish Collection)

The June 1967 War was far from over for tens of thousands of Egyptian soldiers and civilians in Sinai, who were still desperately attempting to reach the Suez Canal. As of 10 June, Salah Danish was still heading in that direction. After two days of hard march, his group was out of water:

'Everybody began to store urine in our field bottles to drink it later ... During the night of our fifth day under way, a Bedouin with a camel came across our way ... The Bedouin told us he was going to bring some water and it was better for us not to walk by night, since we did not know the terrain around. After waiting for him for some time, we became hysterical and decided to move without waiting for him. During the walk I heard that Saad Zaghloul, under way with another group nearby, was meanwhile arrested and then killed by the Israelis (later on I learned that Saad was actually wearing worker's clothes, so when the Israelis ambushed his group and killed everybody else, Saad and another man managed to escape and walk back to Suez). I was drained, physically and psychologically, and felt that death was near now ... Later that evening, we found an abandoned tank and decided to stay there for that night ... A while later, we heard a helicopter above us and then saw it spiralling down. A quarter of an hour later, some armoured cars approached us and soldiers disembarked. I was hiding under a tank pretending to be dead, together with several others. The Israelis set the tank afire before leaving, so we – only eight of us were left – had to eventually move into the open. Minutes later, the Israelis returned, arrested us and began searching for 'a pilot' in broken Arabic and English. It was obvious now that they had learned about me. Out of intensive thirst and despair, I handed myself to them.'

Danish thus ended up as the only Arab pilot to become a 'prisoner of war' during this conflict. He was taken via Bir Thamada to Israel for interrogation. In order to force him to collaborate, the Israelis explained to him that nobody in Egypt would know that he was still alive and therefore his life was not worth much. Shut inside a solitary cell measuring 2m by 3m (6.6ft by 9.8ft), with a blackened out window, without a toilet and barely fed, Danish began to provide some answers, talking about pilots known to have died before the war in various accidents, carefully memorising them by night in order not to offer any kind of contradictions. For over a month he was questioned repeatedly about navigation, engines, about photographs of various pilots, coordination between UARAF and ground-based air defences, and frequently caused much anger on the part of the interrogators when refusing to answer. It was August 1967 by the time Danish was granted permission to write a letter for the first time to his young wife, which was forwarded via the Red Cross. After more than two months of solitary imprisonment, Danish was eventually released into a PoW camp near Netanya, where he was later joined by the pilot Morteza Rifai, who had been shot down during the first post-war skirmishes, on 14 and 15 July 1967. Danish was eventually exchanged in January 1968, together with Rifai and hundreds of other Egyptian PoWs, for the German-born 'Champagne Spy' and a group of Israeli combat divers who had been captured in Alexandria during the June 1967 War.

Saad Zaghloul was actually far more fortunate than the account heard by Danish had suggested. He remained unharmed and reached the bank of the Suez Canal on 17 June, together with a group of around 50 coalminers – many other miners having been killed in successive attacks by Israeli fighter-bombers flown on the days *after* the ceasefire. Zaghloul, together with those miners who were still able to do so, then swam over the Canal to safety.

Thus ended the story of the UARAF's participation in the June 1967 War with Israel – a story marked by catastrophes and countless tragedies and one that still casts a shadow over the entire Middle East; a story that began with, and was decided by, a major failure of the Egyptian Air Force. Regardless how often it has been ignored, or even denied, the courage and skill of the Egyptian pilots – and particularly their dedication to continue fighting regardless of the odds – cannot be overlooked. Outsmarted by their opponent, practically abandoned by their superiors, and let down by their equipment, they continued flying and fighting to the end, despite clear threats to their personal safety. Taher Zaki provides the following conclusion:

'I would like to say that the Egyptian pilots were heroes and carried out their duties to the full. In fact they did more than could be expected. For them the defeat was very painful. They did everything they could, and did not spare their own lives. Many people say that there is no point in talking about the defeat of 1967 but I think it is our right and our duty to say what happened, for the sake of those people who died.'

1   Fawzy, *The Three-Years War*, Chapter 8; Sadat, *In Search of Identity*, p176; *Al-Hawadith*, interview with Shams Badran, 2 September 1977; Oren, *Six Days of War*, pp214–215.

2   Okasha, *Conflict in the Sky*, Chapter 6.

3   Zaki, *Testament*; Okasha, *Conflict in the Sky*, Chapter 6 and Al-Moneim, *Wolf in the Sun's Disc*; Chapter 1 also mentions this mission; al-Moneim described Ramat David as the target of this formation; in fact, positioned in northern Israel, Ramat David was hopelessly beyond the range of Su-7s based in the Canal Zone. Okasha concluded that both Su-7BMKs returned safely to their air base.

4   El-Gindy, interview, February 1999; this and all subsequent quotations from el-Gindy are based on transcriptions of the same interview.

5   For corresponding Israeli claims see Aloni, *Israeli Mirage and Nesher Aces*, p36; Warren C. Wetmore, 'Israelis Relied on Helicopters for Movement of Troops, Logistical Support and Pilot Rescue', *AW&ST*, 7 August 1967,

p95; Norman Polmar and Floyd D. Kennedy Jr, *Military Helicopters of the World, Military Rotary Wing Aircraft Since 1917*, Naval Institute Press, 1981, p9 and p14; R. L. Shoemaker, 'The Arab-Israeli War', *Military Review*, August 1968, pp60–61; Thomas J. Marshall, 'Israeli Helicopter Forces: Organization and Tactics', *Military Review*, July 1972, p96.

6   Okasha, *Conflict in the Sky*, Chapter 6.

7   According to another version of this remarkable adventure, only one of the downed pilots was hidden by the local population, during which he pretended to be a donkey driver.

8   Adil Nasr, interview with Lon Nordeen, November 1987, and Shuwakri, interview with Lon Nordeen, March 1989. The IDF/AF confirmed the loss of two Super Mystère B2s from No. 105 Squadron over Sinai on 6 June 1967 but credited both of these to ground fire. The Super Mystère flown by Lt Eli Zohar was reportedly shot down by SA-2s; the pilot ejected safely and was recovered by Israeli ground troops. The Super Mystère flown by Lt Yair Barak was reportedly hit by AAA; the pilot ejected safely but was taken PoW.

9   Warren C. Wetmore, 'Israelis Relied on Helicopters for Movement of Troops, Logistical Support and Pilot Rescue', *AW&ST*, 7 August 1967, p95; Norman Polmar and Floyd D. Kennedy Jr, *Military Helicopters of the World, Military Rotary Wing Aircraft Since 1917*, Naval Institute Press, 1981, p9 and p14; R. L. Shoemaker, 'The Arab-Israeli War', *Military Review*, August 1968, pp60–61; Thomas J. Marshall, 'Israeli Helicopter Forces: Organization and Tactics', *Military Review*, July 1972, p97.

10   El-Ghazawy, interview with Lon Nordeen, February 1989; this and all subsequent quotations from el-Ghazawy are based on transcriptions of the same interview.

11   Al-Moneim, *Wolf in the Sun's Disc*, p51; in comparison, the Israelis claimed two MiG-21 kills in two different air combats, see Aloni, *Israeli Mirage and Nesher Aces*, p38.

12   Okasha, *Conflict in the Sky*, Chapter 6.

13   O'Ballance, *The Third Arab-Israeli War*, p145.

14   Eshel, 'The Six Day War', *Born in Battle* magazine, Volume 6, pp43–44. O'Ballance in *The Third Arab-Israeli War* also cites 'a few daring and surprising sorties by Egyptian aircraft which caused Israeli casualties, especially at refuelling points' (p155).

15   Tahsin Zaki, letter from his son forwarded to Nicolle, May 1991; Barakat, interview, March 2003; Okasha, interview with Group 73, October 2009. Probably the most detailed Israeli publication on the Noratlas in IDF/AF service was published by Ilan Warshai and Noam Hartoch: 'Nord 2501 Noratlas in IAF Service', *Kne-Mida* ('In Scale', IPMS Israel Magazine), No. 47, December 2007.

16   This account is based on an interview with Tameem Fahmy, though it is notable that nearly all the interviewed Egyptian sources provided entirely different accounts in regards to when these 12 MiG-21F-13s arrived in Egypt. Fahmy recalled the evening of 6 June, while others recalled different times during 7 June.

17   'The Bomb That Won a War', *Flight International*, 22 June 1967.

18   Al-Qadi, interview, April 2002.

19   Cooper and Nicolle, *Arab MiGs Volume 1*, p182, and Okasha, interview with Group 73, June 2010.

20   M. A. (retired MiG-21 pilot of the QJJ), interview provided on condition of anonymity, 2003.

21   The fact that these aircraft were based at Marsa Matruh and Inchas might account for Fuad Kamal not knowing about their activities.

22   M. A.; according to the same source, the Algerians subsequently replaced their air force contingent in Egypt with the 4th Mechanised Brigade, under the command of Commandante Abdelrezak Bouhara, who remained in charge of all Algerian forces deployed in Egypt until some time in 1970.

23   M. A. and EFM, Document No. 44.

24   El-Keraidy, interview, June 2010, and Fuad Kamal, interview, February 2003. Maj Mahgoub was posthumously decorated with the Medal of Honour, one of the highest Egyptian military decorations. As far as is known, the IDF captured only one UARAF pilot during this war (see the rest of this chapter for details). Although a number of other downed Egyptian fliers managed to escape, many of them recalled that in the light of reports

about mass arrests and summary executions of Egyptian PoWs and male civilians alike by Israeli troops in the Gaza Strip, as time went by the local population became much too concerned for its own safety to provide help to Egyptian military 'evaders'.

25 El-Keraidy, interview, June 2010. Note that according to FM Fawzy, over 100 other – still crated – aircraft were evacuated to Yemen by UARAF transports on this and the following day (see Fawzy, *The Three-Years War*, Chapter 8). However, figures from Document No. 44 indicate that no such a large number of crated aircraft was available at the time.

26 Riyadh, *The Struggle for Peace in the Middle East*, p30, and 'Cease-Fire Orders in the Egyptian, Jordanian, and Syrian Sectors', p26, Supreme Headquarters communiqué in BBC, Daily Report, Middle East, Africa, and Western Europe, B1.

27 Irrespective of its involvement in this epic battle, the participation of a small Sudanese contingent (one infantry battalion) in the fighting on Sinai Peninsula is beyond the scope of this book.

28 Okasha, *Conflict in the Sky*, Chapter 6, and Barghava, interview, October 2009.

29 See *Volume 1*, p183.

30 Reda el-Iraqi, interview with Group 73, Cairo, November 2010.

Chapter 3

HESITANT JORDANIANS, WAITING IRAQIS

If the Egyptian military – and thus the UARAF – was ill-prepared to fight a major war against Israel in June 1967, and was thrown into complete disorder by a series of chaotic and countermanding orders from its leadership, then the armed forces of Iraq, Jordan and Syria were soon to find themselves in a similar position. This was largely because these forces were insufficient to accomplish even the task of defending their respective homelands.

Matters were compounded (in the case of Jordan), when they were put under Egyptian command following hasty negotiations in the days before the Israeli attack. Jordan's military therefore depended upon orders from top military officers in Cairo who not only lacked the capability to command forces of this size in battle, but also were not in possession of sufficient knowledge about their enemy, their own forces, and the peculiarities of the local terrain.

In the case of Syria, the activities of which are described in a separate chapter, differences between its military leadership clearly resulted in the decision to remain on the defensive and 'wait and see' what would happen in event of war.

Meanwhile, Iraq, where the military was expecting to deploy significant contingents to Jordan or even Syria, was at first requested to do nothing. Subsequently, Iraq had to rapidly deploy as many assets as possible within the last few days before the war began. Saudi Arabia was to deploy a brigade of ground forces to Jordan, but this failed to arrive in time, while Lebanon spent the war doing little more than monitoring the situation.

The King's Late Decision

Although nearly all available Jordanian sources stress that King Hussein was convinced that Jordan would become a primary target in the coming war, it was only on 28 May 1967 that he did something about the vulnerable military position of his country. On that day he sent his Chief of Staff, Gen Amer Khammash, to Cairo for a briefing on Egyptian war plans.

Returning to Amman on the same evening, Khammash had no more to report than the fact that the Unified Military Command did not really exist. After a short conference with the Egyptian Ambassador in Amman, only hours later King Hussein received an invitation from President Nasser to travel to Cairo. Hussein arrived in Egypt on the morning of 30 May 1967. The result of his negotiations with the Egyptian leaders was the Egyptian-Jordanian Mutual Defence Treaty, Article 1 of which emphasised that, *'The two contracting powers consider any armed attack on either state or its forces*

King Hussein and President Nasser signing the Egyptian–Jordanian Mutual Defence Treaty in Cairo on 30 May 1967. (UIP)

an attack on both. Consequently … they commit themselves to the assistance of the attacked state and immediately take all measures … including the use of the armed forces to repulse the attack.'

Furthermore, Article 7 of this Treaty stipulated that the Jordanian armed forces were to be placed under the command of the Chief of Staff of the United Arab Republic (FM Muhammad Fawzi). As a representative of Fawzi, the Egyptians appointed Lt Gen Abdul al-Moneim Riyadh as the commander of the Eastern Front UAC (EFUAC). Headquartered in Amman, the EFUAC was to cover the Israeli–Jordanian–Syrian frontiers and operate in coordination with the C-in-C of the Egyptian Armed Forces, FM Amer.

King Hussein further demanded that the defences of Jordan be considerably bolstered – in exchange for a number of concessions regarding Egypt and Syria (including a withdrawal of Jordanian troops from the border with the latter country, as well as cooperation with the Palestinian organisation Fatah). Correspondingly, he agreed to the entry into Jordan of Egyptian Army commandos as well as significant contingents of troops from Iraq, Syria and Saudi Arabia.[1]

In addition to receiving military aid from Egypt and other Arab countries, King Hussein reportedly warned Nasser that war with Israel was inevitable, that the Arab forces were not ready for such a confrontation and that Israel was likely to initiate the war by launching a surprise attack with the objective of destroying the Arab air forces and the Egyptian air arm in particular. Nasser apparently replied, *'That's obvious. We expect it …'* According to the Jordanians, AM Sidki Mahmoud even added that for the last few days, *'squadrons of Egyptian aircraft had been flying into Israeli airspace unchallenged'* and expressed his belief that this indicated that the Israeli fear of the UARAF was sufficient to prevent them from challenging it. Egyptian confidence and the strength of their air force clearly impressed the Jordanian Prime Minister Saad Juma, who left the meeting convinced that winning the battle would not be difficult.[2]

According to Jordanian sources, King Hussein and other Jordanian politicians did not share such views, even though Jordan's military leaders were allegedly confident that they could at least fend off an Israeli attack until a ceasefire was declared, which was expected to happen within 48 hours of opening hostilities.

However, many Jordanians insist that it was 'well known' that their military faced severe problems in organising the defence of their own country. The Jordanian Army was relatively small and possessed inadequate resources to cover the long front line with Israel, and it also faced immense political and topographical difficulties. The loss of parts of central Palestine and the West Bank to Israel in the 1948 War, the raid on Samu, and fierce Egyptian and Syrian propaganda against King Hussein had resulted in a situation where the Jordanian military could not afford to leave a single square metre of the West Bank unprotected. The Jordanian Army therefore deployed five of seven infantry brigades available for defence in a very visible fashion along the 630km (391-mile) armistice line in the West Bank. This meant that each brigade had to cover front lines of between 50 and 100km (31 and 62 miles) across mountainous terrain. As a result, their positions lacked the necessary depth.

The terrain also badly hampered the movement of the two armoured and two infantry brigades held as a reserve in the rear, making movements both slow and highly visible, and exposing them to air attack. The only area in which Jordan expected to launch a very limited offensive operation was the Israeli side of Jerusalem, which was to be taken according to a plan entitled Operation Tariq.[3] Therefore, even after Lt Gen Riyadh's arrival in Amman and the reactivation of the UAC, Jordanian war plans remained purely defensive in nature. This would not change even once the Iraqi and Saudi contingents had arrived.

Following the signing of the Egyptian-Jordanian Mutual Defence Treaty, Lt Gen Abdul al-Moneim Riyadh was reappointed as commander of the Eastern Front UAC on 30 May 1967, and was provided with an HQ in Amman. At his disposal were primarily Jordanian military assets, but Iraqi, Saudi and Syrian units were expected to arrive in the following days. (via M. T.)

Rush Hour in Mafraq

The RJAF was only put on alert for a possible war with Israel on 31 May 1967, and the mobilisation could not have caught it in a more precarious position. Not only was it the smallest of the four major Arab air forces facing Israel, but practically all RJAF combat assets were concentrated at King Hussein air base, outside Mafraq, in the north of the country. Its flying units were therefore much closer to Israel than any other Arab air forces. Furthermore, and as described in *Volume 2*, as of spring 1967 the major combat asset, No. 1 Squadron, had been much weakened. In fact, the unit was actually in the process of reorganising and re-equipping when the crisis erupted. Although theoretically outfitted with 23 Hunters, only 19 of these were available and 18 were operational, since at least two were undergoing overhauls and modifications in the UK. Worse still, the majority of Jordan's fast-jet pilots were still undergoing conversion courses for the Lockheed F-104 Starfighter in the US. Five of these fighters had arrived only weeks before, together with a US Air Force team that was to supervise the training of Jordanian pilots and ground personnel.[4] One of the RJAF pilots in the process of conversion to the Starfighter, Jasser Zayyad, recalled:

'I was in the cockpit of an F-104, in Texas, when the signal came to cut engines: we were all recalled to Amman and were to leave within seven hours. With me were Jasser, Nasri, Jihad and Samir. We arrived in Amman on 3 June, but without flying gear and having not flown Hunters for six months. The Egyptian commander [Lt Gen Riyadh; authors' note] *gave us 24 hours of leave. I went to Jerusalem the following day and then on to my village, but was back to Mafraq on 4 June. I feared the*

outcome of the war that was looming, but was eager to see action. My grandfather, who was hard of hearing, caught me by the hand and showed me where the Israelis had been for the last 20 years. He said I should be shot in the front of the head, between the eyes, not in the back. That meant: 'Jasser, do your duty!'

According to King Hussein, once he realised that the war with Israel was approaching, and because his own pilots had not yet completed their training on the type, he requested the Americans to evacuate the remaining Starfighters. Hussein explained that the F-104s were insured with a Lebanese-Swiss company, but that the insurance did not cover war risks, and that they were therefore of little value in the case of conflict.[5] Therefore, on the morning of 4 June, US instructors flew the Starfighters to Turkey and all associated US personnel were evacuated with the help of Lockheed C-130 Hercules transports of the USAF. This was around the same time that the second group of RJAF pilots who were undergoing training on the type returned to Jordan from the US.[6] Zayyad explained:

'I got up early that day and arrived at the squadron at around 06.40. Everyone was in flying gear – except the four of us that returned from the US. Therefore, I decided to read the aircraft manual for the Hunter, to refresh my training. Then we received a briefing from Maj Firas Ajlouni, who had already flown along the Jordan Valley and said everything looked quiet … The Americans flew out four F-104s followed by C-130s, between 09.30 and 10.00.'

The RJAF was thus left not only without any supersonic fighters, but also with only 14 qualified pilots for its fighter jets. In order to bolster this diminutive force, the C-in-C RJAF, Brig Gen Ibrahim Othman, issued a request via official channels for the two Pakistani Air Force instructors who served with No. 1 Squadron, Flt Lt Saif-ul-Azam and Flt Lt Sarwar Shad, to be 'recruited' by his force. An appropriate permission was eventually granted, and the two Pakistanis were thus to fly with the RJAF during this war. However, by the morning of 5 June Shad was hospitalised: in fact, he did not fly a single sortie during the following week.[7]

Despite increasing tensions and all the movements described above, Nasri Jumean recalled that no other measures were undertaken to improve the situation at Mafraq air base:

'Although plenty of AAA was deployed, no arrangements or plans had been made for a war. Very few trenches, no sandbags, no protection for the aircraft, nothing.'

As of the morning of 5 June, the RJAF was organised as follows:

Table 1: RJAF order of battle, 5 June 1967

Unit	Base	Equipment	Remarks
HQ Amman			
Commander of the RJAF Maj Saleh Kurdi			
The Royal Flight	Amman IAP	Dove, Riley Dove, Herald, Heron, Viking, Alouette III	CO unknown; established 15 April 1950
No. 1 Squadron	King Hussein AB (Mafraq)	19 Hunter F.Mk 6	CO Maj Firas Ajlouni; unit slated to re-equip with F-104
No. 2 Squadron			Unit not active; slated to receive remaining Hunters once F-104s were operational; Vampires stored at Mafraq since 1962 but apparently no longer present

No. 3 Squadron	Amman IAP	Dove, Riley Dove, Herald, Heron, Viking, Ambassador, C-47, Whirlwind, Alouette	CO unknown; originally established as No. 2 Squadron in mid-1950s, re-designated as No. 3 Squadron in 1959; operating miscellaneous transports and helicopters
No. 4 Training Squadron	Mafraq	Chipmunk	CO unknown; unit established 1960 with Chipmunks but deactivated at an unknown date
No. 9 Squadron			Originally planned to operate Hunters after No. 1 Squadron became operational on F-104s; finally established only in 1969

Unaware of Jordanian military weakness, the population of Jordan was jubilant at the prospect of their country playing a significant role in the coming battle against Israel. As a result there was widespread support for the King's announcement of the call-up of Army reserves. This order was issued immediately after he returned to Amman, on 31 May.

Uncertainty in Baghdad

Lt Gen Riyadh arrived in Amman on 1 June, bringing with him a staff including Brig Mustafa Shalabi el-Hinnawy, a well-known Egyptian pilot and officer who acted as the Head of Air Operations of the UAC, and a signals officer whose duty it was to keep in constant contact with FM Fawzi in Cairo.[8] Senior Iraqi officers were soon expected to follow, particularly since Riyadh had visited Baghdad and Damascus on his way to Amman, a day earlier. During the meeting between Nasser and King Hussein on 30 May, a telephone call had already been made to President ar-Rahman Arif in Baghdad with a request for the Iraqi armed forces to start deploying to Jordan in coordination with Lt Gen Riyadh. President Arif agreed to deploy one armoured division and three squadrons of fighter-bombers immediately.[9]

President Abdel ar-Rahman Arif was swift to order deployments of significant contingents of the Iraqi Army and Air Force to Jordan in late May and early June 1967. Unknown to him (and the Jordanians and Iraqis at large) was the fact that the call for support came far too late.

(Nour Bardai Collection)

By the time the call from Nasser came, the Iraqis had already been waiting for months for the Eastern Front of the UAC to be 'opened'. Indeed, specific units of the Iraqi military had been put on alert for a possible deployment to Jordan and/or Syria as early as 24 March. On that day the GHQ in Baghdad received a request from the Syrian government to deploy one of its brigades to Syria. The Iraqis reacted immediately by mobilising their 2nd Mechanised Brigade – reinforced by a tank battalion – and redeploying it to Habbaniyah, pending transfer to Syria. On 17 May, the same day Egypt declared general mobilisation, the Iraqi Army alerted two additional Army brigades as well as Nos 6 and 17 Squadrons IrAF for deployment to Jordan. However, King Hussein turned down a corresponding offer from President Arif.[10]

When the situation changed following the treaty between Egypt and Jordan, and after Riyadh's visit to Baghdad a fortnight later, some of the Iraqi units were therefore ready. However, the contingent that Riyadh demanded from Iraq was significantly larger than the Iraqis expected, while the urgency for its deployment only increased. Unavoidably, this caused immense logistical problems. Moving a (reinforced) armoured division of the Army plus three air force fighter squadrons across 1,000km (621 miles) of desert

An Egyptian delegation visited Rashid on 1 June 1967. These photographs show the then CO of No. 11 Squadron, Lt Col Hashem Manhal al-Azawi, shaking hands with Egyptian officers. In the background is a row of MiG-21F-13s, including serial number 530. Notable is the presence of famous Egyptian pilot Mustafa Shalabi el-Hinnawy (brigadier and the Head of Air Operations of the UAC at the time), in the centre of the first photograph, wearing sunglasses.
(David Nicolle Collection)

from Baghdad to Amman was no mean feat and could only be accomplished within the following three days. Nor did confusion and ad-hoc planning within the ECUAC help increase the speed of this deployment.

Isolated Queen's Pawn

As of 17 May 1967, most of the IrAF was either involved in a renewed war against the Kurds in northern Iraq, which had broken out earlier that year, or was busy training on new MiG-21s that were in the process of delivery from the USSR. Others, meanwhile, were working up on the last batch of Hunters that was arriving from the UK. These

Prior to the June 1967 War with Israel, Iraqi Hunter pilots trained and fought almost exclusively for air-to-ground warfare. They therefore lacked experience in air-to-air combat. In the course of a rare air combat exercise, two Hunters from No. 6 Squadron collided over Habbaniyah air base in late May 1967. Fortunately, both aircraft – including the example flown by 1st Lt Hassan al-Khither, shown here – landed safely. Notable are two No. 10 Squadron Tu-16 bombers in the background.
(Ahmad Sadik Collection)

three efforts were hampered by Moscow's stance, however. Despite extending friendship to the government in Baghdad, the USSR strongly disagreed with the renewal of hostilities against the Kurds. Curiously, in order to significantly expand the IrAF, but being left with few alternatives outside Moscow, the Iraqis turned to Czechoslovakia. Contact had already been established in 1964, and the Czechoslovaks had supplied spares for Iraq's MiG-15s and MiG-17s the following year. Indeed, in 1965, Iraq attempted to order 20 MiG-21F-13s (and 50 T-54 MBTs) from Prague, but corresponding negotiations were fruitless in the face of Soviet pressure.

The Soviets then changed their minds and offered new MiG-21FLs at better conditions in terms of payment (see *Volume 2* for details). Nevertheless, contacts between Baghdad and Prague remained intact and in late 1966 a delegation led by the then C-in-C IrAF, Brig Gen Jassam Muhammad ash-Shaher visited Czechoslovakia in order to request delivery of Aero L-29 Delfin jet trainers. Corresponding negotiations were nevertheless protracted, despite serious Czechoslovak efforts and interest. The government in Prague knew that its existing business practices were all condemned to failure as long as the USSR and other communist countries in Eastern Europe offered their arms at better terms of payment. Furthermore, the Czechoslovaks concluded that they had to pay bribes to some important officials within the Ministry of Defence in Baghdad in order to win their favour.[11]

In other words, the top commanders of the IrAF were distracted by completely different priorities when the crisis with Israel – taking place far away from their bases – erupted. The situation was little different at the squadron and wing levels, where commanders were either busy with training or with the war against the Kurds. Nevertheless, as of 31 May 1967, Maj Gen ash-Shaher, C-in-C IrAF, had the following flying units of the Iraqi Air Force available:

Maj Gen Jassam Muhammad
ash-Shaher, C-in-C IrAF from 22
September 1966 until 17 July
1968.
(Ahmad Sadik Collection)

Table 2: IrAF order of battle, 5 June 1967[12]

Unit	Base	Equipment	Remarks	
HQ Baghdad				
C-in-C Maj Gen Jassam Muhammad ash-Shaher				
No. 1 Squadron	Al-Hurriyah (Kirkuk)	20 Fury FB.Mk 1	CO unknown	
No. 2 Squadron	Firnas (Mosul)	4 Mi-1, 9 Mi-4	CO unknown	
No. 3 Squadron	Rashid (Baghdad)	2 Dove, 2 Heron	CO unknown	
No. 4 Squadron	Rashid	11 Wessex HC.Mk 2	CO Lt Col Hassan Sharif; unit deactivated 1962 but re-established 1965 as a helicopter squadron	
No. 5 Squadron			Unit deactivated December 1963	
No. 6 Squadron	Habbaniyah	10 Hunter F.Mk 59A/B	CO Lt Col Adil Suleimany; two additional Hunters damaged in collision over Habbaniyah in late May 1967 and not repaired by 5 June 1967	
No. 7 Squadron	Al-Hurriyah	20 MiG-17F and MiG-17PF	CO Lt Col Masroor Bahaedin, Maj Jassam al-Jabouri took over during the war	
No. 8 Squadron	Al-Hurriyah	11 Il-28, 2 Il-28U	CO Lt Col Mehdi Mahsun as-Sabbah; unit redeployed to Firnas, 25 August 1967	
No. 9 Squadron		MiG-21PFM	In the process of being re-established	
No. 10 Squadron	Habbaniyah	9 Tu-16	CO Capt Farouk al-Tail	
No. 11 Squadron	Rashid	11 MiG-21F-13	CO Lt Col Hashem Manhal al-Azawi	
No. 14 Squadron		8-9 MiG-21PFM	In the process of being established	
No. 17 Squadron	Rashid	8-9 MiG-21FL	Acting as OCU for crews of Nos 9 and 14 Squadrons	
No. 23 Squadron	Rashid	8 An-2, 6 An-12BP	CO unknown	
No. 29 Squadron		12 Hunter F.Mk 59A/B	CO Lt Col Ismail Wakti	
Hunter OCU	Habbaniyah	9 Hunter F.Mk 59 and T.Mk 66	CO 'Capt Crow' (British pilot; real name unknown)	
Air Force Academy	Wahda (Shoibiyah)	Chipmunk, Jet Provost, MiG-15UTI	CO unknown	

Most of the IrAF pilots serving in May 1967 had seen active service in recent years during the war against the Kurdish rebels, and were familiar with frequent redeployments from their air bases to the airfields in the north of the country. However, many experienced fliers were away on conversion courses, and even the number of 'novices' was relatively low for similar reasons. Nevertheless, the IrAF was very swift to follow the orders from the Ministry of Defence in Baghdad and prepare its aircraft, personnel and bases for a war with Israel.

Four pilots with one of the IrAF's Jet Provosts as seen at Wahda air base in 1967 or 1968. This type was relatively recently delivered and served as an advanced trainer with the IrAF Academy.
(Mohammed Ahmed Collection)

Airfield 'H-3'

All the No. 6 Squadron Hunters as well as two Hunters from No. 29 Squadron IrAF transferred from Habbaniyah to the airfield known as 'H-3', in western Iraq, during the afternoon of 31 May. They found the local conditions and installations to be rather poor, as one of them recalled:

'Although originally constructed during the 1930s, to serve a major pumping station on the H-pipeline, connecting central Iraq with the port of Haifa, and although considered for major expansion by the British and Americans in the late 1950s, and despite various plans developed at the time the UAC originally came into being in 1964, as of 1967, H-3 was still a relatively small airfield, with only one metalled runway, a small fuel depot, and a bare minimum of other installations. As such, it was better suited to the purpose of transit airfield than an outright 'air base' that could support sustained combat operations. All personnel had to sleep in tents distributed around their aircraft. We did not think this a critical problem, however: we expected to soon redeploy to Mafraq AB in Jordan, where an advanced party of IrAF ground personnel was to arrive on 5 June 1967.'[13]

In expectation of the Hunters moving to Jordan, on 5 June the IrAF ordered the MiG-21FL interceptors of its newly established No. 17 Squadron to H-3, while Capt Farouk al-Tail, the newly-appointed CO No. 10 Squadron, received an order to keep four of his Tu-16 bombers on alert and ready for action, 24 hours a day. Furthermore, Maj Jassam al-Jabouri, CO No. 7 Squadron that flew MiG-17s, received an order to prepare his unit to move to H-3 as well, which meant that the IrAF actually decided to send not three but five of its units to Jordan. Obviously, subsequent developments precluded this deployment. Still, the Iraqis did manage to bolster the defences of H-3, even though only one AAA regiment equipped with 100mm guns of Soviet origin arrived in time to take part in the June 1967 War. As a result the airfield continued to lack effective low-altitude protection.

Meanwhile, on 3 June, an IrAF lieutenant colonel arrived in Amman, where he was to serve as liaison officer to Lt Gen Riyadh's HQ and facilitate joint operations with the RJAF and SyAAF as well as the UARAF. To his considerable surprise, once there, the

President Arif visits the IrAF 'Hunter Wing' at Habbaniyah, shortly before the pilots and their aircraft were deployed to H-3 on 31 May 1967. Sadly, only this blurred scan of a photograph published in a contemporary Iraqi newspaper serves as a reminder of the occasion, when the President apparently shook hands with Lt Col Adil Suleimany, CO No. 6 Squadron.
(Ahmad Sadik Collection)

officer in question was informed that Egypt had decided not to be the side to initiate hostilities, and that the Arabs would wait for the first Israeli strike.[14]

Unaware of the fact that they had to wait for a signal from Riyadh to go into action, on 4 June the IrAF pilots at H-3 received a briefing on their targets for the first day of the war: Israeli airfields at Lod and Kfar Sirkin, as one of them recalled:

'Our Intelligence informed us that we were to take part in Operation Rashid, and that we would attack Israeli air bases in cooperation with Jordanians and Syrians, while Egyptian troops would march into the Negev Desert ... Only later did we learn that this plan actually envisaged that the Israelis would open the war but get mauled while attacking Egyptian air bases, and that we were actually to take part in a counteroffensive.

'The target information we received was unusually poor. All the maps and intelligence on Israeli airfields were based on information from the times before 1948! They told us to expect Mirages in the air and US-made SAMs on the ground and therefore we needed to approach at low level to avoid being detected by Israeli radars.'

Ultimately, as of 5 June the two Hunter squadrons were still at H-3, and therefore – except for ground-based AAA – the 16 pilots and 19 Hunters of No. 1 Squadron RJAF at Mafraq represented the sole force that could effectively protect Jordanian airspace.

Last-minute Preparations

In the course of 3 June, as the first Iraqi Army units approached the border with Jordan on their march in the direction of Amman, Lt Gen Riyadh toured the West Bank to inspect the local Jordanian Army defences and draw up a defence plan. Within the short period of time left before the hostilities began, he was only able to develop very basic ideas for action in the case of an Israeli attack (and even less so for an offensive into Israel). Various Jordanian sources later claimed that their armed forces not only had the best knowledge and understanding of the IDF prior to the June 1967 War, but also that the Jordanian Intelligence was among the best informed as regards Israeli intentions and plans. Regardless of this, Lt Gen Riyadh was left facing a major problem: the information he received concerning the Israeli military was generally of very poor quality. For example, on the same day Riyadh toured the West Bank, Jordanian military intelligence reportedly monitored the Israeli build-up and forward concentrations west of Latrun and in the Afullah region, opposite Jenin. In turn, they are alleged to have informed the GHQ of an imminent Israeli offensive. However, it remains unknown exactly how much the Jordanians really saw in terms of details, or how they assessed the Israeli movements.

Later the same day, King Hussein received the Turkish Ambassador, who informed him that Israel would start its offensive on 5 or 6 June with an air strike on Egyptian air bases.[15] If this was the case, the question remains as to why the information the Jordanians possessed was not impressed upon President Nasser, FM Amer and AM Sidki Mahmoud with necessary urgency. Similarly, the reasons why the Egyptian leaders effectively ignored Jordanian and Turkish warnings, as well as similar information from India, remain unclear. For their part, the Jordanians claim that they conveyed three warnings to Cairo, and that each time the Egyptians replied that they were expecting exactly such an attack and were prepared for it.[16]

▶ A map of the air bases in Jordan and Iraq that saw action during the June 1967 War. Also shown is the H-pipeline, which proved not only a catalyst for the emergence of many airfields in this part of the Middle East, but was also used by pilots from both sides (including Israelis) to ease navigation.
(James Lawrence)

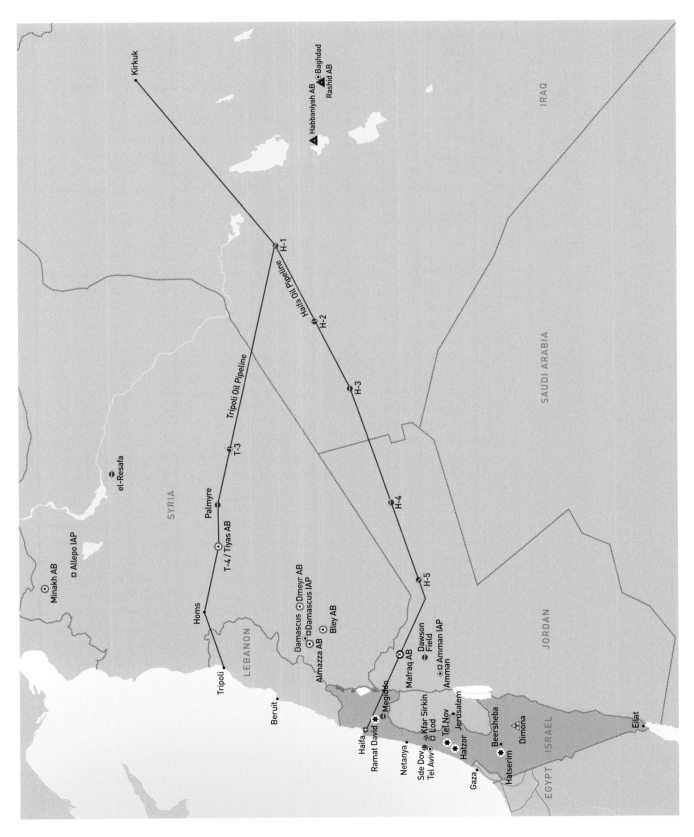

1   Mutawi, *Jordan in the 1967 War*, p109.

2   Ibid., p109.

3   Ibid., p115.

4   According to the personal notes of Patricia Salti, the first batch of Starfighters delivered to Jordan consisted of six aircraft, of which five arrived in Jordan in early June. However, one of the RJAF pilots was killed in an F-104 during training in the US, and a second crashed in his Starfighter only days after delivery of the aircraft to Jordan. Therefore, only four examples were evacuated to Turkey. Note that in his memoirs, *My War with Israel*, King Hussein recalled that six F-104s were delivered to Amman in early June – which is contradicted by practically all US sources that provide more information about this topic.

5   The RJAF is one of very few air forces in the world – Sudan is another – that insures its military aircraft.

6   Sources differ in regards to the timing of this evacuation of Starfighters to Turkey. According to King Hussein, this occurred on 4 June. According to most other sources – primarily 'Timely Withdrawal of US Mission', *Flight International*, 29 June 1967, p1082; O'Ballance, *The Third Arab-Israeli War*, p61 and Bowen, *Six Days*, p96 – it occurred on 3 June. Note that because they cited King Hussein, O'Ballance and Bowen both mentioned six F-104s as delivered to Jordan and then evacuated to Turkey, while *Flight International* mentioned only four. It is possible that the difference was caused by the loss of one example during training in the US, and the other in Jordan, both losses occurring shortly before the war. Certain is only that the RJAF pilots returned to Mafraq from their training in the US on 4 June, around 23.00.

7   Saif-ul-Azam, e-mail interview, April 2008.

8   For details about Shennawy's earlier career with the EAF/UARAF, see *Volumes 1 and 2*.

9   Mutawi, *Jordan in the 1967 War*, pp108–109, and Sadik, various interviews, 2004–07.

10 Sadik, various interviews, 2004–07; Al-Abbosi, interview with Group 73, January 2011; *History of the Iraqi Armed Forces, Part 17* (various chapters).

11 Based on documents VÚA-VHA, MNO, 1969 and VÚA-VHA, MNO, 1970 from the Military Historical Archive, Prague, Czech Republic; as well as Zídek, P. and Sieber, K, *Československo a Blízký východ v letech 1948–1989*, Ústav mezinárodních vztahů, Prague, 2009 (ISBN 978-80-86506-76-0) and Púčik, M., 'Vývoz zbraní a špeciálnej techniky do záujmových krajín bývalej ČSSR v sedemdesiatych rokoch', *Apológia* magazine (exact volume unknown).

12 Based on *History of the Iraqi Armed Forces, Part 17* (various chapters).

13 M. S. – a former IrAF Hunter and MiG-21 pilot, interview provided on condition of anonymity, March 2007; this and all subsequent quotations – as far as related and unless explained otherwise – are based on transcriptions of the same interview, also used as the basis for the article 'Nahostkrieg 1967 – Die Basis H-3', published in *Fliegerrevue Extra* magazine, June 2007. Note that the authors decided that, with a few specific exceptions, the names of all former IrAF pilots interviewed in the course of research for this book should be withheld. The reason for this decision is a series of assassinations of former IrAF pilots and officers in progress since 2003 (in the course of which more than 160 pilots and officers have been assassinated), as well as their prosecution by the new Iraqi, as well as Iranian, Israeli, Jordanian and Syrian authorities.

14 Ibid. and Sadik, series of interviews, 2004–07.

15 Mutawi, *Jordan in the 1967 War*, pp111–122.

16 Ibid, p122.

Chapter 4

TWO HOURS OVER JORDAN

As mentioned previously, the RJAF radar station at Ajloun began tracking intense aerial activity over Israel starting from 07.15 on the morning of 5 June. This information was forwarded to Lt Gen Riyadh, who immediately passed it on to the Egyptian High Command. However, the latter did not receive the message in time to alert its own air arm, and the destruction of much of this force practically sealed the fate of all the involved Arab armies.

According to Jordanian sources, nobody in Amman was aware of this fact until several hours later, and thus the RJAF missed a significant opportunity to – at least in theory – cause considerable problems to the Israelis. Worse still, left without support from the Iraqis and Syrians, both of which were supposedly unduly slow to move into action, the small Jordanian air arm subsequently lost too much time to launch any kind of effective action and was then wiped out during the course of slightly more than one hour of intensive Israeli air raids on its two airfields. Heavily dependent upon Egyptian and Iraqi air cover, the Jordanian Army was thus left exposed to merciless Israeli air attacks and in turn suffered heavy losses, as the result of which it was forced to withdraw across the Jordan River.

That is the picture created in a number of Jordanian accounts published since 1967 (and therefore in most other Western accounts), and often accepted uncritically by various Israeli and Western reports. However, as we are going to see, not everything happened exactly the way the Jordanian accounts suggest.

Contradictions in Amman

No. 1 Squadron RJAF was among the first Jordanian military units to be alerted for action, at 05.00 local time on the morning of 5 June 1967, and its pilots expected to take off as soon as the news came that the war had started. Between 06.00 and 06.30 that morning, Maj Firas Ajlouni, CO No. 1 Squadron, gathered his pilots for a briefing, instructing seven of them to prepare for air defence sorties, while he was to lead the others into an attack on Israeli airfields. Nasri Jumean recalled what was happening that morning:

'Firas was not happy because of previous incidents [not only involving Israel but also in the US; authors' note] *that had taken place, which had affected him. But he was happy to see me: we had not flown Hunters for six months and Firas arranged some training sessions and a few flights. Between 09.00 and 09.30, Khaled Mohammed Ali* [CO Mafraq air base; authors' note] *called for a meeting with Firas and me.*

Pilots of No. 1 Squadron RJAF prior to the June 1967 War with Israel, together with King Hussein and his two sons. Flt Lt Saif-ul-Azam (PAF) and Ihsan Shurdom can be seen standing first and second in the front row, to the left of the King's shoulder.
(Saif-ul-Azam Collection)

We decided to divide the pilots into two groups. Firas was assigned to north Operational Readiness Plan (ORP, on Runway 13) and me to the south ORP. Firas was to lead the strike section and me the fighter escort. He was to fly in formation with Mohammed Shiab, Ghazi Smadi and Jihad Irsheid, but the latter went sick. I was to fly with Farouq el-Abdeen, Wasfi Amari, Saif-ul-Azam, Ihsan Shurdom, and Hanna Najjar. George Matta was to act as a link between the base commanders and fighter pilots …'

Jasser Zayyad was still in need of a flying overall, helmet and a g-suit. He recalled:

'Firas told us that our task would be to provide cover for the Iraqi Army that would deploy inside Jordan. Then I saw Awni and made him strip so I could use his overall and helmet. That left Awni crying with frustration …'

Until just a few days before the war, the RJAF had planned to raid Israeli airfields at the onset of any kind of hostilities with Israel. However, since King Hussein had signed the treaty with Nasser, the Egyptians reserved the right to order and fly such attacks for themselves. The Jordanians thus concluded that they were expected to fly air defence and only minor attacks on targets inside Israel. Otherwise, they were to wait to link up with the Iraqis and then the Syrians. Once again confirming the poor state of Arab intelligence concerning the dispositions of the IDF/AF, Ihsan Shurdom summed up the state of mind of the RJAF Hunter pilots:

'Our air force was small but good. We knew that we would have to take on the Israelis and we had great respect for them. In the event of war we planned to bomb six or seven key Israeli airfields, but when the war approached, the Egyptians told us we would not be required. They would knock out the airfields and we would have a minor air defence role … But I knew that in those days MiGs could only fly as far as you could spit.'[1]

Jumean continued, revealing the pilots' strikingly poor targeting information:

'The briefing went on and Ali was asked about the armament. He said guns only, while Firas said guns and rockets. Asked if the rockets were ready – as they needed to be fitted to the aircraft – Ali said, 'No problem, it will be fixed'. Some 20 minutes later, Ali said to Nasri that their formation should be ready to attack Netanya. Nasri asked what they should look for, but was told just to look for 'anything' and fire at it.'

A row of No. 1 Squadron Hunters of the RJAF, as seen before the June 1967 War. Most of these aircraft were originally Hunter F.Mk 6s, re-conditioned to FGA.Mk 9 configuration, and primarily intended for use as fighter-bombers.
(RJAF, via Patricia Salti)

According to the Jordanians, at 08.50 Jordanian time (09.50 Egyptian time), FM Amer passed the following (coded) message to Amman:

'Israeli planes have started to bomb air bases of the UAR and approximately 75 per cent of the enemy's aircraft have been destroyed or put out of action. The counter-attack by the Egyptian Air Force is under way against Israel. In Sinai, UAR troops have engaged the enemy and taken the offensive on the ground. As a result, FM Amer has ordered the commander-in-chief of the Jordanian Front to open a new front and to launch offensive operations according to the plan outlined the day before.'[2]

However, as already explained in Chapter 1, at the time the Jordanians say they received this message, FM Amer was still on board an Il-14 that was searching for a safe place to land. He was nowhere near his HQ and could not have sent any such orders to Amman for at least another hour. Even assuming that Amer might have sent such a message immediately after landing at Cairo IAP, around 10.30 Egyptian time (09.30 in Amman), he would have been forced to use an open telephone line instead of other means, which – according to available Jordanian accounts – was not the case. Given that no Egyptian officers dared issue any kind of orders even to UARAF units without Amer's word, it is quite obvious that this was even less likely to be the case when it came to orders from Cairo to Amman. Therefore, the available Jordanian accounts raise a number of questions, ranging from whether the Jordanians indeed received any kind of orders from Cairo at 09.00 Jordanian time that morning, or whether this was an attempt by King Hussein to provide an excuse for the inaction of his military. Alternatively, if there was such a message, then who in Cairo would have been in a position to issue any kind of orders in the name of FM Amer? Is it conceivable that this message actually came from an Israeli source, as a means of prompting the Jordanians into action and thus giving the Israelis an excuse to occupy Jerusalem and the West Bank?

This was not the only inconsistency related to Jordanian reports concerning their actions on that day.

The next problem from the Jordanian standpoint stemmed from the fact that the supposed message arrived from Cairo around 09.00 Jordanian time, but the first report from Ajloun that morning – the one citing a large number of Israeli aircraft flying in the direction of Egypt – was *ignored*. In fact, Maj Firas al-Jouny immediately demanded permission to take off and attack Israeli air bases, arguing that the Israeli fighters would be returning from attacks on Egypt short on fuel and would thus present easy targets. However, his request became mired in lengthy discussions between superior officers in Amman and was eventually denied. The reason for this refusal was that the radar at Ajloun subsequently reported a large number of aircraft coming out of Egypt and flying towards Israel. Due to the Egyptian announcement that the war had begun with an Israeli attack, the Jordanians claimed to have wrongly concluded that the UARAF was in the process of launching a counterattack on Israel.[3] King Hussein explained this decision as follows:

'[When] *our radar screen showed planes flying from Egypt towards Israel, we didn't give it a thought. We simply assumed they were from the UARAF on their way to a mission over Israel. They weren't. They were Israeli bombers* [sic] *on the way home, their first mission against Egypt accomplished.*'

According to Jordanian sources, around 11.00 their time (12.00 Cairo time), a second message from Cairo arrived in Amman, this time apparently genuinely from Amer, who stated that Israel's air offensive was continuing but that 75 per cent of its air force had meanwhile been put out of action. He claimed that the UARAF had put many Israeli air bases out of action and that ground forces had penetrated the Negev. It is at least interesting to note that the essence of this message is actually the same as the one that supposedly arrived two hours previously.

Furthermore, at around 12.00 Amman time, President Nasser supposedly telephoned King Hussein and repeated the same statement to him, requesting Jordan to quickly take action pending a UN intervention that would impose a ceasefire.[4] Finally, sometime before 13.00, yet another message arrived from Amer, this time instructing Lt Gen Riyadh and the Jordanians to move the 60th Armoured Brigade to Hebron to provide support to an Egyptian division advancing towards Beersheba in the Negev. The 40th Brigade, near the Damia Bridge, was to replace it in positions in the hills west of Jericho. According to this message, a Syrian brigade would protect the northern sector of Jericho vacated by the 40th as previously instructed by Cairo.

Although supposedly 'horrified' by the latter order, and despite their agreement with the Egyptians not to enter the 'active phase of operations' until after the arrival of all the reinforcements from other Arab nations, King Hussein maintained that his generals now call their counterparts in Damascus to coordinate their actions. However, the Syrians – none of who are mentioned by name – supposedly responded with the following:

'*The outbreak of the war has taken us by surprise. Our pilots are on a training flight … They asked us to give them first a half-hour, then an hour, and so on until 10.45* [Amman time; authors' note], *when they asked us for yet another delay which we also granted. At 11.00, we couldn't wait any longer*'[5]

However, this explanation poses yet more questions, the most significant being: if the Jordanian military was expected to wait and Jordanian politicians were not eager to instigate offensive operations or 'seize Israeli territory', why were they then complaining that they had to wait for action from other Arab nations?

In the absence of precise answers to all these questions, the only logical conclusion is that the Jordanians did not receive any orders to attack Israel at 09.00 their time, and indeed not before around 10.00 (11.00 in Cairo) – at the earliest. That was around the time that FM Amer reached the GHQ in Cairo. King Hussein and Lt Gen Riyadh

Hunter F.Mk 6 K/709 (formerly XF379) of No. 1 Squadron RJAF, as seen before the June 1967 War. Notable are the large portions of the nose and wingtips (possibly also the entire fin) painted red. As Patricia Salti discovered in the course of her research, this measure was based upon agreements reached within the UAC back in 1964, and was intended to provide easier identification for the several Arab air forces expected to operate over Israel in the case of a major war.
(Albert Grandolini Collection)

did not issue any kind of orders for an attack on Israel until at least a few minutes later, and most likely after 11.45, once they had learned that the first wave of the IrAF was on its way towards Israel. Therefore, it is not as if the Jordanians were 'reacting to orders from Amer' or 'waiting for the Iraqis and Syrians', as usually claimed. Much more likely, King Hussein, Lt Gen Riyadh, and the Jordanian generals at the GHQ in Amman (C-in-C Jordanian Army FM Habes Majali, his deputy C-in-C Maj Gen Sharif Nasser Ben Jamil, the GOC Western Operational Command Jordanian Army Maj Gen Muhammad Ahmed Salim, the GOC Eastern Operational Command Jordanian Army, Brig Mashour Haditha al-Jazzi, and Atef Majali, Riyadh's Director of Military Operations) were informed about the outbreak of war. They then spent two valuable hours waiting for an order from Cairo to act, at the same time exchanging threats with Israel (via the CO of the UN contingent in Jerusalem, the Norwegian Gen Odd Bull) and quarrelling about whether the Jordanian Army should follow Amer's orders and Riyadh's idea of attacking al-Mukkaber Hill south of Jerusalem, or implement the Jordanian plan for Operation Tariq. The latter envisaged the 'encirclement of the Jewish-held part of Jerusalem to gain an excellent bargain for the return of any land Israel might have seized'. A heated debate clearly developed, in the course of which Riyadh and Salim exchanged insults, further increasing confusion.[6] Eventually, the generals at HQ EFUAC failed to reach an agreement and ordered the Jordanian military into action only once they were prompted to do so – probably by FM Amer's next message, and certainly in accordance with his orders, which were soon to prove disastrous.

Lost Keys

This is not to say that no No. 1 Squadron Hunters were airborne during the morning of 5 June. On the contrary, two fighters had been held on the CAP station between Mafraq air base and the armistice lines with Israel since 06.00 local time. George Matta and Ghazi Smadi flew the first pair. They were then replaced by Nasri Jumean and Farouq el-Abdeen. When Jihad Irsheid became sick, he was sent to the control tower, and replaced by Matta, who flew his second CAP together with another pilot. However, as no orders for an attack against Israel came, most of the No. 1 Squadron pilots had to wait in frustration. The only news they received later during the morning was to expect an Iraqi MiG-21 squadron to arrive in Mafraq during the early afternoon.

An indirect confirmation that no orders for an attack on Israel were issued by King Hussein or Lt Gen Riyadh before 11.00 Amman time is provided by recollections of Jasser Zayyad. He explained the reason:

'Just after 09.00 I was told to go to the aircraft. Then things began to change. First they wanted to load our aircraft with rockets, but there were no keys to the ammunition depot where these were stored. While Bader Zaza took off in an Alouette to meet the vehicle and get the keys, we heard news on the radio of Egyptians shooting [down] so many aircraft. We knew this was impossible and that this war was already turning into a mess ...'[7]

Another pilot confirmed Zayyad's recollection as follows:

'I went to Firas to tell him about our poor target intelligence for the attack on Netanya, only to hear that we could not go as there were no rockets. These were still in the stores and the doors were locked, the keys being with Saleh Kurdi – in Amman! Saleh sent the keys via a messenger, but to shorten our waiting, Bader Zaza took off in an Alouette to look for the latter, finding him just before the village of Mafraq. He landed and got the keys. Our Armament Officer, Shaher Shahin, took the keys, opened the doors and found the rockets still packed in their boxes ... Because of this postponement, that morning our ground crews managed to outfit only four Hunters with Hispano-Suiza rockets of 3in calibre. These should have had high-explosive warheads, but later on it turned out they were all practice rockets, with solid warheads ...'[8]

During the wait for the keys, a decision was taken to slightly adapt the composition of the two attack formations, and Ihsan Shurdom as well as the Pakistani Flt Lt Saif-ul-Azam – himself a veteran of the 1965 Kashmir War between India and Pakistan, in which he scored one confirmed kill – were assigned to the formation that was to fly the attack against Israel. However, only moments after this meeting was over, they were re-tasked back to air defence. Azam recalled the reason for this change:

'Official Pakistani clearance for me to fly air defence missions only was received on the morning of 5 June, and thus I had to hurriedly switch roles on the tarmac. After waiting in the cockpit for half an hour I learnt that the Israeli Air Force had struck Egyptian airfields. Sitting helplessly on the ground waiting for orders was nerve-racking and all pilots squirmed in their cockpits to seek revenge ...'[9]

The Jordanian pilots thus had to keep on waiting next to or inside their aircraft, ready to launch at the shortest possible notice, but valuable time lapsed without an order for take-off. Although the RJAF was on alert and supposedly ready for combat operations, and despite receiving a (supposed) order from FM Amer to attack Israel as early as 09.00 that morning, the Jordanians simply failed to act.

Targeting Controversy

The next controversy surrounding Jordan's involvement in the June 1967 War concerns the issue of the targets assigned to RJAF and Jordanian Army units. Various Jordanian reports (and Western sources) mention attacks on a number of different targets rang-

This photograph of Flt Lt Saif-ul-Azam was taken in spring 1967 during his tour of duty in Jordan. Of Bengali origin, Azam served with distinction with the Pakistani Air Force during the 1965 War, in Jordan and then again in Pakistan, until joining the newly established Bangladesh Air Force in the 1970s. (Saif-ul-Azam Collection)

ing from northern to central Israel. Curiously, according to Iraqi sources, some of the targets usually said to have been attacked by the Jordanians were actually hit by IrAF fighters. Ironically, the Israelis have not made the situation any clearer, with reports that usually completely ignore the Iraqi side and instead support the Jordanian reports, while at the same time only stressing attacks on civilian objectives.

From what can be ascertained, Lt Gen Riyadh's orders dictated the following:

- The air forces of Iraq, Jordan and Syria were put on combat alert and ordered to commence air strikes 'immediately'. Ironically, no source cites any specific timing, nor targets actually hit by the RJAF. This might indicate that the target selection was left at the discretion of the responsible commanders of the forces in question, which were to act according to the plan for Operation Riyadh.
- Two batteries of US-made M59 'Long Tom' 155mm long-range howitzers were instructed to take forward positions near Qalqilya and Latrun – and to bombard selected targets in Israel, primarily the air bases of Tel Nov and Ramat David, starting at 11.30 Amman time. As far as is known from Israeli sources, neither of the two air bases was shelled around this time.
- The Egyptian commando battalions (known as Saiqa) attached to the Jordanian brigades around Jenin and Ramallah were ordered to infiltrate Israeli territory at dusk and attempt to destroy Israeli 'air bases' named as Hertzlia, Ein Shamer, Kfar Sirkin, Lyda, Ramle, and Aqir, and their associated radar stations.[10]

Two fine studies of Hunter F.Mk 6 E/712 (formerly WW507), delivered to Jordan in 1958. Re-coded as N/712, and having large parts of its fin and wingtips painted red, the fighter is known to have been flown by Ihsan Shurdom during the air battle with Israeli Mirages in November 1966. Sadly, its eventual fate remains unknown. (Albert Grandolini Collection)

This list provides clear evidence that the military decision-making in Amman was based on even poorer intelligence than that in Cairo: were the Jordanians indeed in possession of superior intelligence, they would have been forced to order their air force into all-out attacks on Tel Nov and Ramat David – which was not the case. It also provides evidence that King Hussein's argument that, '… *without the help of the Syrian MiGs the bombing of Israeli bases would have had a negligible effect'*, was similarly shaky, to put it mildly. After all, even if the RJAF launched its Hunters to attack Israel at an earlier time that morning, these were unlikely to cause any serious damage because – as we will come to see – they would have hit the wrong targets. Namely, except for Tel Nov and Ramat David air bases, both of which had been assigned to Egyptian commandos and Jordanian artillery, respectively, none of the Israeli airfields attacked by the RJAF were important for the IDF/AF's ability to continue its operations. Meanwhile, the third major Israeli airfield used during this war – that in Hatzor – was not mentioned on any lists of Jordanian targets, despite its proximity to the West Bank. In other words, Lt Gen Riyadh and the Jordanian military had very little knowledge concerning the genuinely important Israeli military installations. Despite Jordanian insistence that they possessed superior intelligence about Israel compared with that available to the Egyptian military, in reality the work of Jordanian military intelligence was as poor as that of their colleagues in Cairo.

Raid on Kfar Sirkin

The morning of 5 June found the Egyptians and Jordanians quarrelling about how best to attack the wrong targets, and irrespective of King Hussein's complaints, it was the Iraqis who were first within the UAC to decide to act in reaction to the Israeli attack on Egypt.[11]

Iraqi pilots deployed at H-3 were waiting for orders to move to Jordan and flying familiarisation flights around their new base. Around 10.30 Baghdad time (10.30 in Cairo, 09.30 in Israel), all the pilots were called to a briefing, as recalled by Faysal Abdul Mohsen:

'*1st Lt Najdat an-Naqeeb and me were on a familiarisation flight near H-3 when the order came for us to land. Immediately after we were told that war had broken*

This ex-Belgian Hunter F.Mk 6 (formerly IF07) – upgraded to F.Mk 59 standard and given the serial number 580 prior to delivery to Iraq – was photographed in 1963. At the time, these were some of the most advanced ground-attack fighters in the Middle East, armed with four 30mm ADEN cannon and various combinations of unguided rockets.
(Albert Grandolini Collection)

Hunter F.Mk 59A serial number 668 (note the serial number applied on the door of the nosewheel bay) as seen at Habbaniyah, before the June 1967 War. Notable is the fact that this aircraft is parked inside a shallow blast pen covered by camouflage netting – very unusual practice for most Arab air forces at the time. This measure had been introduced by the IrAF in 1963, and was bolstered by Indian experiences from the 1965 war with Pakistan.
(Ahmad Sadik Collection)

out between Egypt, Syria and Israel, that we should help push our aircraft into blast pens, and then to expect orders to attack Kfar Sirkin airfield, near Tel Aviv, as ordered by Lt Gen Riyadh in Amman. The time-on-target was set for 12.55 Baghdad time.'[12]

Eight No. 6 Squadron pilots were selected to fly this mission, organised in two formations, one of five and the other of three aircraft. Led by Lt Col Adil Suleimany, the first group included 1st Lts Faysal Abdul Mohsen, Hazem Hassan Kassem, Hassan al-Khither and Fadhil Mustafa, and received the task of attacking Kfar Sirkin 'air base'. The second formation was to launch one hour after the first and hit Lod International Airport. Its pilots included Maj Mumtazz Abdel Ali al-Saydoon, 1st Lt Najdat an-Naqeeb and 1st Lt Emad Ahmed Ezzat.[13]

By the time the pilots returned to their aircraft, the Hunters were already parked outside their blast pens and were fully armed, each carrying 24 British-made rockets of 3in calibre and two drop tanks in addition to a full load of ammunition for their four 30mm ADEN cannon. The Hunters' air-conditioning systems were also working at full power to ensure their cockpits remained comfortable despite the simmering heat outside. The targeting information they received followed the original plan for Operation Riyadh, yet portrayed a rather confused picture, as one of the involved pilots recalled:

'The intelligence was that the objective of our formation – Petah Tikva airfield east of Tel Aviv – was constructed as Royal Air Force 'Kfar Sirkin' by the British in 1941, and used by the RAF until 1948. We were told that ever since 1948 it had been an air base of the IDF/AF and that we should expect to find numerous transport aircraft there, as well as to expect strong air defences. In fact, as we learned only years later, this was a small airfield, in use by the Flying School of the IDF/AF from 1949 until 1955, and by the Paratrooper School thereafter, but only used for the dispersal of units equipped with transport aircraft.'[14]

Despite poor intelligence, the pilots were enthusiastic:

'*We took off at 12.30* [Baghdad time; authors' note] *and completed the first leg of our flight without any problems. We climbed to 23,000ft* [7,010m] *and continued to Mafraq AB in Jordan. Once there, we saw the Hunters of the Royal Jordanian Air Force – still on the ground. We did a circle while descending to low level, and then turned in the direction of the Jordan River. It was a textbook mission like the many we had completed in the war against Kurds: no technical problems, everything was fine. Some of us were singing while under way.*'

Barely one minute after passing the Jordan River, Lt Col Suleimany and his wingman popped up to start their attack. One of the participating Iraqis recalled what happened next:

'*In front of us we saw two runways, a control tower and several scattered buildings – together with a number of transport aircraft parked on the tarmac: [Douglas] Dakota and Noratlas transports painted in silver. The first pair dove to attack, each aircraft unleashing all of their 24 unguided rockets at once, as per instructions we received during the briefing. Suleimany and his wingman reported hits on two Noratlas transports and one Dakota ... The second pair followed in the same fashion, one releasing its rockets towards the control tower and the other at the runway intersection. But while number 4 was diving towards his target he saw a trace of thick white smoke streaking into the sky and shouted, 'Missiles!'. As soon as the last of his rockets was away, he made a hard turn to the right. We later concluded that the number 4 came under attack from the Israeli MIM-23 HAWK SAM site protecting Tel Nov ...*'

An Iraqi Hunter pilot gives the thumbs-up to his ground crew, prior to flying a training sortie before the June 1967 War. Iraqi pilots had gathered considerable experience during the fighting against Kurdish separatists and considered themselves ready for a war with Israel.
(Nour Bardai Collection)

MIM-23 HAWK SAMs seen during a military parade in Israel before the June 1967 War. At that time, this was the most advanced weapon of its type anywhere in the Middle East. (IDF)

Faysal Abdul Mohsen specified:

'Suleimany pounced upon two Noratlas, his wingman a Dakota; all three destroyed. Me and Mustafa destroyed a Noratlas each, parked next to the control tower.'

Disengaging, the Iraqis returned over the Jordan River at low level, sighting columns of Israeli armour moving in the direction of Jenin, and Jordanian artillery rounds exploding around them. Without further disturbance, the formation then climbed back to 23,000ft (7,010m) for its return to H-3. Unaware of the disaster in Egypt, the pilots were in such high spirits that they tuned their receivers to radio stations, to listen to popular and martial music, and national anthems.

In summary, these five pilots claimed to have destroyed or damaged seven Dakota and Noratlas transports on the ground. Mohsen specified the source for this conclusion:

This very rare photograph shows an IrAF Hunter flying at very low level over the Judean Hills while withdrawing towards Jordan, following the raid on Kfar Sirkin, in the early afternoon of 5 June 1967. The Iraqi attack caught the Israelis by surprise and no Mirages managed to intercept the intruders. However, HAWK SAMs fired from the site protecting Tel Nov air base might have disrupted the attack runs by the last two Hunters. (IDF)

This pre-war photograph shows paratroopers about to embark in IDF/AF Noratlas transports. It is possible that this scene was photographed at Kfar Sirkin, sometime in the late 1950s. (IDF)

Apparently released by mistake – in the belief that it showed the wreckage of an Arab transport destroyed by the IDF/AF – this photograph from an Israeli publication printed shortly after the June 1967 War clearly shows the wreckage of a Noratlas. Remnants of the cockpit are in the centre, below the mid-section of the wings and between the two engines. If Israeli reports that only one Noratlas was destroyed at Kfar Sirkin are correct, this aircraft was registered as 4X-FAX. (IDF via Albert Grandolini)

'Two days later we captured two Israeli pilots. One of them said that the attack on Kfar Sirkin delivered a painful blow, because we destroyed transport aircraft full of paratroopers.'

On the basis of this and other information subsequently obtained, the IrAF became convinced that this raid prevented a paratrooper assault on el-Arish, which the Israelis are known to have planned for the early hours of 6 June. However, the results of the Iraqi attack not only remain disputed, but have also been ignored to this day. Initially, the Israeli media reported only an 'aerial attack' on Kfar Yavetz, in the Tel Mond area (some 20km/12.4 miles north of Tel Aviv), by 'Jordanian Hunters', supposedly taking place around 13.15.[15] Ever since, the Israelis and Jordanians have claimed – in near-unison – that the raid on Kfar Sirkin was flown by Jordanian Hunters. This despite the fact that it is well known that all the RJAF Hunters were still on the ground when the first Iraqi formation passed over Mafraq.[16] The Israelis also claim that only one Noratlas (registered as 4X-FAX) and a civilian Piper Super Cub were destroyed, several people being injured on the ground – and that their assault on el-Arish was cancelled because it became unnecessary.[17]

Attack on 'Netanya Air Base'

While the differences between the Iraqi and Israeli accounts about the attack on Kfar Sirkin are almost unavoidable, the situation is very different in regards to targets attacked by the RJAF Hunters. While practically all the Jordanian – and thus also the Israeli – accounts state that these hit Kfar Sirkin and Megiddo, the pilots involved recall something entirely different.

The first formation of three RJAF Hunters – flown by Firas Ajlouni, Jasser Zayyad and Mohammad Shiab – launched between 11.50 and 11.55 Amman time and thus entered Israeli airspace close behind the first Iraqi formation.[18] However, its target was not Kfar Sirkin, but 'Netanya Air Base', as recalled by Jasser Zayyad:

'We received no intelligence briefing … While taking off, we heard a radio call from King Hussein: 'Hashemite Red Section: good luck to you all!'… Firas, Shiab and me went low level, and then pulled up. Firas said he was going for the runway and I felt sick: what can rockets do to a runway? Then Firas said he was going for the hangar and Shiab should go for the control tower. There was lots of AAA, and I told Firas he was being fired on, but Firas replied, 'No, YOU are being fired on!' We did only one pass and headed home, the mission lasting just under 30 minutes. The second section followed shortly later and we were covered by three Hunters, flown by Ihsan, Hanna and Saif, but these did not cross the armistice line … We landed on the western end of the runway and started refuelling and rearming. That's when I clashed with Firas because I had stayed behind the formation and used my guns to strafe a troop movement on the highway east of Netanya. Firas did not like this and said I would be court-martialled if I ever went off the assigned target. Perhaps he wanted me to keep the ammo for protection.'

Exactly what had been the target of this formation is actually unclear: there was no, nor had there ever been, a 'Netanya Air Base' in Israel. The likelihood of Ein Shemer – a small airfield east of Haifa used by civilians only – being the target is virtually non-existent, not only for the reasons discussed below, but because there are no authentic Israeli reports about attacks on that location – only the Netanya and Tel Aviv areas. Reports from Netanya indicate that, *'… two or three RJAF Hunters penetrated the Israeli airspace undisturbed as deep as to reach Netanya. They unleashed their rockets at the ABIC Pharmaceutics factory in that town, killing one person and injuring seven.'*[19]

Unbeknownst to the RJAF pilots, on the way back towards Mafraq their formation was nearly intercepted by a pair of Israeli Mirage IIICJs from No. 117 Squadron, scram-

A formation of Hunters from No. 1 Squadron RJAF, based at Mafraq, seen before the June 1967 War. While it is usually claimed that these aircraft attacked Netanya, Kfar Sirkin and a number of other targets in Israel, currently only the first of these operations can be positively confirmed. Even so, the exact target in Netanya remains unclear, since there was never an IDF/AF air base there. (RAF Museum)

bled from Ramat David. In fact, the Mirages were late in trying to catch the Iraqis, and then their GCI provided an incorrect vector for the Jordanian formation. As a result they not only missed their intended target, but also received only a fleeting opportunity to fire at the Jordanians, while these were passing over Ramleh. However, the only Shafrir 1 air-to-air missile the Israelis managed to fire missed its low-flying target, and the pilots were then vectored to intercept another target. Thus, the Hashemite Red Section returned to Mafraq undisturbed.

Chaos over the West Bank

Currently available information does not allow a clear conclusion to be drawn as regards the target hit by the second formation of RJAF Hunters launched to attack Israel. Also unknown is if these fighters indeed reached any of their targets there – despite King Hussein's claim that:

'Three times, our Hawker Hunters attacked the bases at Netanya in Israel without a loss. And our pilots reported that they destroyed four enemy planes on the ground, the only ones they had seen.'

None of the RJAF pilots available for interview could recall any other attack sorties other than the one mentioned above. Nevertheless, it is at least likely that four Hunters – apparently flown by Wasfi Ammari, George Matta, Ghazi Smadi and, probably, Hanna Najjar – did reach Megiddo, another small airfield in northern Israel, though at least one with a 'secondary' military purpose.[20] There the Jordanians might indeed have destroyed one or two Piper Cubs – or wooden decoys – on the ground, as often reported by various Israeli and Western reports. However, while the aircraft that attacked Megiddo are said to have used rockets for that purpose, as explained by Jumean (see above) the ground crews of No. 1 Squadron RJAF managed to arm only four Hunters with such weapons by the time the RJAF went into action: the three aircraft of the Hashemite Red Section, plus the example manned by Ihsan Shurdom (see below for details). However, this latter did not participate in this mission because Shurdom, as Saif-ul-Azam's wingman, was rescheduled to fly top cover instead. Furthermore, it is now widely known that Syrian MiG-17Fs attacked Megiddo.

All that can be said with certainty is that by the time the next two Jordanian formations approached Israeli airspace, at least two (but more likely four) Mirage IIICJs of the Ramat David-based No. 117 Squadron IDF/AF were already airborne. According to Zayyad, one of these two RJAF formations – including Ihsan Shurdom, Hanna Najjar and Saif-ul-Azam – was not even to enter Israeli airspace, but provided top cover only as far as the armistice lines:

'The strike formation had air cover, consisting of three Hunters flown by Ihsan, Hanna and Saif but they received the order not to go over Israel.'

Furthermore, neither Shurdom nor Azam ever mentioned Wasfi flying in formation with them on that day, even though they did confirm that Hanna Najjar and Ghazi Smadi were airborne around the same time. On the contrary: while some Jordanian sources indicate that Azam was paired with Wasfi, while Shurdom flew with Najjar, Shurdom and Azam recalled flying their mission only as a pair. Whatever happened, under as yet unclear circumstances, the Hunter flown by Capt Wasfi Ammari eventually ended up over Israel and was engaged by a Mirage IIICJ flown by Israeli Capt Oded

RJAF Hunter J/708 following its conversion to FGA.Mk 9 standard, at the SBAC show in Farnborough, England, in July 1965. Lacking the capability to maintain supersonic speed (except in a shallow dive), the Hunter was obsolete as an interceptor by 1967, but remained a powerful ground-attack asset and an aircraft beloved by its pilots. (Albert Grandolini Collection)

Sagee while under way at low level over the Beit Shean Valley. The only presently available account about the action that followed was provided by an Israeli source:

'Flying east, they [two Mirages from No. 117 Squadron; authors' note] *approached the enemy aircraft at high speed. The Hunters broke away, apparently having received warning from their radar. Oded's partner attached himself to one of them and they both dived and disappeared for a moment. The controller directed Oded towards the other, and he entered the duel with the advantage. He fired a Shafrir missile ... but it dropped downwards, below the enemy's engine ... Oded had no choice but to rely on his cannon.*

'They crossed the Jordan River, and the chase quickly headed toward Amman. Oded shifted around and again came up behind the Hunter. He closed in his range, almost too fast, to 200m [656ft]. Aiming carefully, he fired one long burst. The Hunter's wing broke off, and the aircraft began spinning ...'[21]

Wasfi Ammari bailed out over Jerash but landed hard, suffering injuries to his back that ended his career with the RJAF.[22]

Like a Bolt from the Blue

Meanwhile, a pair of Hunters flown by Saif-ul-Azam and Ihsan Shurdom reached a position high over Barmah, a village next to Ajloun. Shurdom recalled a very important detail about the start of his mission:

'I took off with an aircraft armed with 24 rockets and had to shoot them off to get rid of them, as my aircraft was too heavy for air combat.'

Saif-ul-Azam continued:

'After take-off, I contacted the radar for further instruction. The controller announced a vector and we headed in the required direction. Soon, another vector was announced and we changed our heading again. It was not long before the controller declared that there were too many aircraft and it was difficult to make out who was who. We were asked to be on our own. Noting the controller's dilemma I called my wingman to stay close. The visibility in the hot, dusty desert was barely a mile and there were no signs of enemy aircraft. Re-checking with the controller if there were any aircraft approaching Mafraq, my concerns were confirmed when he received an affirmative reply.'

RJAF Hunter F.Mk 6 E/704 in
the landing pattern to Mafraq
in the mid-1960s. The aircraft
was photographed carrying
four 100-Imp gal (455-litre)
drop tanks (made of phenol-
asbestos). Much larger 230-Imp
gal (1,046-litre) drop tanks
(made of steel) were available
to the RJAF as of June 1967, but
were seldom used.
(Albert Grandolini Collection)

Turning around, Azam and Shurdom headed for their base. Minutes later, contact
with the radar in Ajloun was lost. This was the moment that the first Israeli formation ordered to attack Jordan – four Super Mystère B2s from No. 105 Squadron IDF/
AF, originally scrambled to attack el-Mansourah airfield in northern Egypt, but then
diverted – reached its target and knocked it out. The RJAF was thus left without its
'eyes' right at the opening of the Israeli onslaught.

By 13.40 Amman time, all but four of the Hunters – those flown by Azam, Shurdom,
Najjar and Smadi – were on the ground in Mafraq, and in the process of refuelling and
re-arming. Like most of the other air forces of the time, and not precisely informed
about what was going on in Egypt that morning, the RJAF operated according to
widely accepted norms of preparing its aircraft for the next mission with turnaround
rates of one to two hours. This was clearly far too slow: by that time two formations of
four Mystère IVAs each were already approaching the RJAF's main base at low level.
They were to reach their target almost simultaneously.

Around this time Jasser Zayyad was still preparing for the next sortie to Israel:

'Another target was assigned to us – Ein Shamer – and we went to the same three
aircraft. Then Firas got a telephone call. Target changed: instead of Ein Shamer we
should go for Lydda. Firas said there was no plan, but I knew the area (I used to see
it from my home). But, Firas wanted a detailed plan. After another briefing, we got
back to the aircraft and started. Because Samir [Samir Mutawi; authors' note] joined
us, our formation consisted of four aircraft.'

The pilots were in the process of readying themselves for their next sortie when the
first eight Mystères appeared over Mafraq to hit the runway and claim destruction of
three Hunters on the ground. Much too late, air raid sirens began to wail, announcing
the tragedy that was to follow. Zayyad continued:

'That's when the sirens went on and someone motioned us to shut down the
engines. I got down and then saw three, then four, then five aircraft ... Some on

the ground said these would be the Iraqis. I said they were Mystères, so we ran to the trenches, while Firas called Shiab to man his aircraft. George was there too and he asked Firas if he wanted him and me instead, but he said no. Thus, only Firas and Shiab started their engines. Firas moved for the runway as the first Israeli aircraft was diving in that direction. The second Israeli attacked Firas' aircraft and it caught fire. The third Israeli attacked Hunters near our trenches. I looked up from there and saw Shiab walking back. I told him to get in the trench but he said, 'Firas!' I brought him to the trench ...'

Jumean explained what happened next:

'The Israeli leader dropped two bombs in the middle of the runway, while his wingman fired at the Hunters manned by Firas and Shiab: the tower held them on the ground much too long, to wait for instructions. Firas decided not to wait: he reached the runway when his aircraft was hit, and then jumped out, but was burned to death by the exploding fuel. Samir attempted to help and opened a CO_2 bottle on him, but he was just a cinder ...'

The next formation of Israeli Mystère IVAs hit Mafraq only seconds later. One of them was damaged – by ground fire, according to Israeli reports – right at the start of this attack, and had to disengage. Another first aborted his mission but then returned to strafe, claiming four Hunters destroyed on the ground. The other two Israelis reported engaging Hunters in air combat. Jumean recalled their attack:

'Farouq el-Abdeen and me had barely landed when the Israeli attack came. I told Farouq to get into the aircraft and ordered the fuel bowser away. We rolled towards the northern ORP [Operational Readiness Platform] for take-off in the direction of the Baghdad Road. However, while under way there, we saw four Israeli fighters and I called Farouq to warn him. We jumped out of our aircraft and shouted at the AAA people to fire ... There were many AAA guns around but their crews were waiting as they thought these would be the Iraqis. Then the guns opened up, left, right and centre, even when there were no enemy aircraft around.'

Left without the radar station in Ajloun, it was around this time that Azam and Shurdom approached Mafraq. Once there, they spotted four aircraft flying in battle formation at low level. Through the haze, the camouflage of these aircraft appeared similar to that of the Hunters of the Iraqi formation that had passed by minutes before, while returning in the direction of H-3.

Azam was thus led to believe that the aircraft in front of him must also have been returning from a raid on Israel. Following them for a while, he watched with amazement as they changed into echelon formation – getting ready for an attack! Realising his mistake, the Pakistani promptly manoeuvred behind the trailing attacker, the number 4 in the Israeli formation:

'As the aircraft was turning for the attack, I closed in and let off a fusillade from my four cannon. The Mystère caught fire and pieces started to fly off: I had to pull up to avoid hitting the debris.'

Ihsan Shurdom, who lost sight of Azam's Hunter while returning towards Mafraq, recalled:

'I had a bet with Saif that if he shot down an Israeli, I would get him a girl ... As we approached the area mentioned by the GCI, I saw a Hunter following two Mystères and I said, 'I am going to give you cover'. Saif said, 'Allah-u-Akhbar', and shot the Israeli down.'

Maj Firas Ajlouni, CO No. 1 Squadron RJAF, was mortally injured when the Hunter which he attempted to scramble from Mafraq caught fire due to an Israeli air raid.
(via ejection-history.org.uk)

This ex-RJAF Hunter was put on a pole in front of the RJAF Museum in Amman several years ago. It was delivered to Jordan only after the 1967 War, but is decorated with two kill markings commemorating claims by Ihsan Shurdom from air battles over Mafraq on 5 June 1967.
(Oscar Ruf Wilson)

While pulling up, Azam looked around for other attackers:

'I noticed the smoke trail of two Mystères charging off towards the west at full power. As I turned hard for them Ihsan called a bogey to the right. I directed him to go for a singleton while I went for the pair on the left. I managed to get behind the trailing Mystère, which had started to manoeuvre, about to spoil my aim. During the frantic turn reversals, I fired four times but my bullets stayed off the mark. Then the enemy loosened the turn and straightened out in the direction of Israel. Closing in to about 600ft [183m], I squeezed the trigger for a fifth time. The Mystère started to trail smoke from its right wing and then ducked down before I could confirm if it had been terminally dispatched. Then the leader of the enemy pair attacked me. By this time, I was low on fuel and ammunition and decided to disengage and turn for Mafraq …'

In summary, Azam claimed one Israeli as shot down and the other as damaged, while Shurdom claimed two kills:

'The Hunter was a very agile jet and our aim was to drag the Israelis into a low-level, low-speed dogfight in which their air-to-air missiles would be less effective. Saif and me shot down four and drove the rest away.'

It seems that this air battle was quite confusing for all the pilots involved, since it resulted in quite a lot of over-claiming on both sides. Indeed, Azam's and Shurdom's claims for at least three Israelis shot down were only slightly closer to reality than the claims of their counterparts to have shot down two Hunters. However, contrary to the RJAF, the IDF/AF never officially recognised the claims of its pilots as 'confirmed'.

The Israeli pilots certainly did better in their strafing runs: although claiming up to 24 Hunters, they actually destroyed or badly damaged 13 Jordanian fighters. In turn, their first formation is known to have lost one Mystère, serial number 94, flown by Lt Hananya Boleh, who was killed. According to Israeli reports, Boleh reported he was hit shortly after the leader of his formation bombed the runway at Mafraq, and then disappeared, never to be seen again. Foreign observers generally concluded that Boleh became the victim of the more experienced Azam and was shot down before the other Israeli pilots saw what happened to him. While another Mystère was – according to

The crew of a Jordanian 40mm Bofors L/70 anti-aircraft gun. Although initially taken by surprise by the Israeli attacks, and confused by orders not to open fire, these gunners soon recovered and began causing considerable damage to those attacking Mafraq air base and Amman IAP.
(Patricia Salti Collection)

the Israelis – hit by ground fire, all three surviving fighter-bombers from this formation successfully returned to their base.[23]

Zayyad continued his description of the Israeli attack on Mafraq as follows:

'Khalid Mohammad Ali came in a Land Rover to check for us, and drove us away. Then the next Israeli wave came in and finished everything. Our AAA was not effective and the Israelis even hit the main hangar.'

In fact, Jordanian AAA proved quite effective. The third Israeli formation to hit Mafraq consisted of four slow and vulnerable Ouragans. They encountered no opposition other than AAA fire and flew three attack patterns to claim the destruction of two Hunters on the ground. Then the number 3 was hit by ground fire and forced to disengage. While this formation was withdrawing in the direction of Israel, it became obvious that the number 4 was also damaged: the pilot failed to respond to calls from other formation members and eventually ventured straight into the 'no-fly zone' over the Dimona complex, where his aircraft was shot down by Israeli MIM-23 HAWK SAMs.[24] Shortly afterwards, two other Ouragan formations, one consisting of three and the other of four aircraft, completed the destruction of Mafraq air base. Finally, the sixth Israeli formation to attack Mafraq again suffered a loss to AAA, having its number 1 damaged badly enough for the pilot to eject safely over the Mediterranean Sea. With this, Mafraq air base and most of No. 1 Squadron RJAF were finished in a matter of only 45 minutes.

Nasri Jumean summarised the effects of this series of blows as follows – noting that to the Jordanians it appeared as if there were 'only' five attack waves, since the first two Israeli formations attacked almost simultaneously:

Gun-camera film recording an Israeli attack on one of the RJAF Hunters parked at Mafraq in the early afternoon of 5 June 1967. (IDF)

'Five attacks in waves of three to four aircraft. First Mystères then Ouragans. They dropped delayed timed bombs so there were explosions for the next 30 minutes. We crawled to the squadron ready room where there were a couple of trenches and Khalid Mohammad Ali told us that Firas was killed ... Everything around us was burning, aircraft and stores ... When we got to the tower this was hit by four Ouragans too. Eventually, we decided to evacuate our base and our families to Mafraq village.'

Light Work in Amman

The reason why successive formations of Ouragans met no Jordanian fighters was that the pilots of the last four RJAF Hunters still in the air decided not to land in Mafraq, as recalled by Azam:

'Reckoning that the Mafraq runway had been rendered unfit for use, I called all aircraft to hold north while checking the feasibility of landing there. The runway was hit by several bombs and we decided to divert to Amman IAP ...'

Shurdom further recalled – and Azam confirmed – how his presence of mind saved the pair from the trap set up by Israeli intelligence:

'By the time our air battle was over, I had been hit by our ground fire. My aircraft was not handling right and I asked Saif to cover me. While trimming my aircraft, I called Mafraq to see if I could land. The answer was positive but I became suspi-

Gun-camera film showing an attack on two RJAF Hunters parked at Amman IAP in the early afternoon of 5 June 1967. All four fighters that landed there were swiftly destroyed, leaving the RJAF without a single operational fighter. (IDF)

cious and thus asked the controller for the name of my dog. There was no reply, so we headed for Amman. Once there, I called Abdel Haleem Majali in the tower to tell him I was having problems with my aircraft and to keep the guns tight. I landed with my Hunter jumping all over the runway and overshot by a few metres. Saif landed after me … Next I saw Hanna taxiing in as if in peacetime. He got out of his aircraft only once the attack came.'

However, the international airport outside the Jordanian capital did not offer any safety. The first Israeli formation to reach Amman IAP consisted of four Mirages from No. 119 Squadron IDF/AF that had originally scrambled to attack Hurghada air base in Egypt. The fighters approached their target at high level in order to conserve fuel and were already descending when an order from the GCI turned them in the direction of Jordan. As the Mirages approached Amman IAP, they encountered no opposition in the air or from the ground. Not only had the last four RJAF Hunters meanwhile been forced to land because they were out of fuel, but the local AAA gunners had a strict order not to open fire. Jiries Shoubat, then a communications officer serving with the RJAF, recalled what light work the four Israeli Mirages had:

'In the Operations Room, Saleh Kurdi ordered all the anti-aircraft artillery not to fire as they were expecting the arrival of our own aircraft and then the Iraqis. After some Hunters landed, Fouad Jamal took my bicycle to go off and try to refuel them. Then we saw some aircraft, apparently coloured in silver, and we all thought these would be Iraqis. Everyone cheered – but then they attacked us for nearly 40 minutes …'[25]

A rare colour photograph of RJAF Hunter F.Mk 6 serial number L/710 (formerly XF380). The aircraft is known to have been destroyed in the course of Israeli attacks on Jordanian airfields on 5 June 1967, but whether this happened at Mafraq or Amman remains unknown. Application of red paint on the nose and fin was intended to provide easier identification, but the meaning of the white-painted wingtips remains unknown.
(Albert Grandolini Collection)

Baris al-Hadid, then the head of the Technical School in Amman and in charge of 700 students, walked down the runway watching the Hunters land. He had already heard that the Israelis had attacked Egypt but thought that the USSR had mediated and there would be no war:

'I was walking by the runway towards the place where Ihsan had landed, as if in a dream. Then Ihsan and Farhan Sa'adi came and pulled me into a trench. I was half in and half out when the first Israeli attacked and [I was] covered in earth within moments ... Ihsan was worried because his aircraft was loaded: it could blow up. He wanted to return to his aircraft and I thought he wanted to scramble again – but it was actually for his gun-camera film, containing images of an attack on Israel. Farhan attempted to stop him but I cannot recall what happened ... Meanwhile I saw Hanna get out of the aircraft and fall from the ladder: I thought he was dead ...'[26]

The Mirages first bombed the runway then returned to strafe, hitting one parked Hunter and two that appeared to still be taxiing. They then continued to knock out various transport and passenger aircraft parked around the airfield, as Shoubat recalled:

'They burned the UN Dakota, one of the RJAF [Westland WS-51] Widgeons, the Dove of the British Attaché and one [Beech] Bonanza. They hit another RJAF Dove but it did not burn ...'

Ahmad Juweiber, serving as a transport pilot with the RJAF, was also present at Amman IAP when the Mirages came, followed by four Ouragans that struck some 10 minutes later:

'We were all on standby but did not think that war would happen. Our only plan for the case of a war was to hide our aircraft ... When the attack came, most of us were in trenches. Two Israeli waves hit us. Despite the damage, we already had four Dakotas flown to Azrak airfield in the desert, by Awni Alaeddin, Farhan Sa'adi, Radi Monomey and Zeid Toukan. Marwan Nooreddin flew one of the Alouettes to Ruseifa, while Awni Maher – the King's personal pilot – took off in another in the middle of the Israeli attack and thus disregarding his own safety. Ducking the strafing Israeli jets, he took off and manhandled the small aircraft to safety behind the nearby hills. Three other Alouettes escaped any damage, together with one of the Hunters that landed at the IAP.'

Meanwhile, Ihsan Shurdom was under way from Amman back to Mafraq, in an attempt to rejoin his unit:

'As next we drove to the hospital to find out what happened to Firas. The hospital knew nothing. Together with Samir, I drove back to Mafraq to get Firas. We arrived there to find him still lying on the ground, very burned except for a small area between his shoulders that was slightly burnt. Samir used the fire extinguisher –

After the small RJAF fighter component was destroyed in the course of attacks on Mafraq and Amman IAP, the Jordanian Army was left exposed and without effective air cover. As a result, it suffered extensive losses to IDF/AF air attacks. This photograph shows a column of Israeli tanks (left) passing by a knocked-out and abandoned M48 Patton of the Jordanian Army, somewhere on the West Bank.
(IDF)

actually a CO_2 bottle from the dinghy – on his smouldering body. Then he was taken to the hospital.'

The Jordanians had put up a spirited battle, but could not keep up with the pace of successive Israeli attacks, which took them by surprise and destroyed the combat power of the RJAF. Theoretically, the Royal Jordanian Air Force was thus out of the war. In practice this was not the case, since despite the shock and confusion there was still much fighting to do. Illustrating this, the second formation of IrAF Hunters, including Maj as-Saydoon and Lts an-Naqeeb and Ezzat, was to attack Lod IAP exactly one hour after the first formation of five fighters had hit Kfar Sirkin. Although entering Israeli airspace entirely unopposed, the three pilots in question found themselves over unknown terrain. Having only completely obsolete maps for navigational aid, they failed to find Lod.[27]

Nevertheless, the two raids flown by the IrAF Hunters impressed the IDF/AF sufficiently for its High Command to issue the order for an attack on H-3 airfield.

1 Shurdom, interviews with Patricia Salti, May 2007, January and February 2012; this and all subsequent quotations from Shurdom are based on transcriptions of the same interviews.

2 Mutawi, *Jordan in the 1967 War*, p123, citing King Hussein from Vance and Lauer's book *My War with Israel* (New York: Morrow Publishing, 1969). Interestingly, the latter book remains the only available source for the existence of such a message from Cairo to Amman.

3 Bowen, *Six Days*, p113; note that some of the former RJAF pilots interviewed privately pointed at the commander of the RJAF, Maj Saleh Kurdi, as a source for this decision.

4 Mutawi, *Jordan in the 1967 War*, p123.

5 Hussein, *My War with Israel*, p66, and Mutawi, *Jordan in the 1967 War*, pp123–124.

6 Mutawi, *Jordan in the 1967 War*, p124.

7 Zayyad's statement in this regard is also supported by the recollections of Saif-ul-Azam and Ihsan Shurdom.

8 When interviewed by Patricia Salti and asked about this incident in 2008, Saleh Kurdi denied all knowledge and stressed that this was the first time he had heard this story. He further said that there was no reason for him to hold the keys to ammunition depots in Mafraq. Nevertheless, the same story has been provided to the authors by several independent sources.

9 Azam, interview, April 2007, and Yasin Khan, *A Sword for Hussain*, published on the Internet, 30 September 2004.

10   Mutawi, *Jordan in the 1967 War*, p126.

11   Indeed, according to many eyewitnesses, Radio Baghdad was the first Arab media outlet to report an Israeli attack on Egypt, doing so already around 08.50 Cairo time on the morning of 5 June.

12   Mohsen, interview with Group 73, October 2010. Additional details in this sub-chapter are from Sadik, interview, March 2007.

13   Note that Mohsen and Sadik recalled the composition of these two formations differently, Mohsen not recalling that al-Khither flew with him, but Sadik providing notes based on al-Khither's logbook in support of his version.

14   M. S. – former IrAF Hunter and MiG-21 pilot, interview provided on condition of anonymity, March 2007.

15   'As the News Broke', *Jerusalem Post* (English edition), 6 June 1967.

16   See Hussein, *My War with Israel*, where the author clearly stated that the IrAF Hunters passed over Mafraq while the RJAF Hunters were still in the process of rolling for take-off. Furthermore, Saif-ul-Azam recalled seeing Iraqi Hunters on their way to Israel before he took off, and Wasfi Ammari also saw them, as did Maj Gen Saqer (ret.), who served at the Ajloun radar station on that day.

17   Ilan Warshai and Noam Hartoch, 'Nord 2501 Noratlas in IAF Service', *Kne-Mida* ('In Scale', IPMS Israel Magazine), No. 47 (12/2007), and Cohen, *Israel's Best Defence*, pp218–219.

18   Note that in an interview with Patricia Salti in 1994, Maj Gen Saqer, former air controller of the RJAF, recalled this formation to have consisted of four Hunters flown by Firas Ajlouni, Jasser Zayyad, George Matta and Ghazi Smadi.

19   For an example, see '7 Hurt in Air Attack on Netanya', *Jerusalem Post* (English edition), 6 June 1967; the article in question cited Hunters that attacked the ABIC insecticide and animal pharmaceutical plant with unguided rockets. 'One rocket sailed clear through the production room three metres off the floor and out the other side. Another exploded inside, leaving four lightly injured and Miss Daisy Nathan hospitalised in Hadera. A fire set off by the shells [sic] caused heavy fire … one house was demolished by a rocket shell. Another shell blew a sun heater off a roof and the pieces fell and injured two persons slightly …' The area hit by RJAF Hunters on 5 June 1967 is now occupied by a large IKEA warehouse.

20   Nasri Jumean and Farouq el-Abdeen are known to have flown a sortie around this time as well. Sadly, while helping the authors with a number of answers to their other questions, Mr el-Abdeen never answered the question about this mission. Hanna Najjar is known to have been the last Hunter pilot of No. 1 Squadron RJAF to take off from Mafraq on that day, and the last to land at Amman IAP; see below for details.

21   Cohen, *Israel's Best Defence*, p221.

22   Mr Ammari's logbook – put on display in the museum at Mafraq air base – registered two missions on that day. A CAP in the early morning, lasting 55 minutes, and another mission around noon, lasting 35 minutes. The latter ended following an encounter with four Mirages, after which he had to bail out. Ammari subsequently flew airliners for Alia Airlines.

23   Aloni, *The June 1967 Six-Day War*, pp140–141; Jasser Zayyad recalled seeing the wreckage of Boleh's Mystère IVA with the body of the dead pilot still inside the cockpit. He recalled that inside one of the pockets in Boleh's flying overall were intelligence maps of Amman IAP and Mafraq; these were so up-to-date that they showed buildings constructed only after Jasser left for F-104 training in the US in early 1967.

24   Aloni, *The June 1967 Six-Day War*, pp145–146.

25   Shoubat, interview with Patricia Salti, Amman, 2007; Shoubat retired from the RJAF in 1981.

26   Barjis al-Hadid, interview with Patricia Salti, Amman, 2007.

27   According to Faysal Abdul Mohsen, the leader of this formation failed to find Lod and thus attacked an alternative target in the Tel Aviv area. According to Ahmad Sadik, the formation only strafed an Israeli military column on the road to Jerusalem, but in essence returned with most of its rockets and gun ammunition still intact.

Chapter 5

THE H–3 SAGA

Dozens of accounts of the Israeli attack on air bases in Egypt, Jordan and Syria have been published in Israel and the West since the end of the June 1967 War. In addition, there are at least a dozen accounts concerning the series of attacks by the IDF/AF against H-3 airfield in western Iraq. With one exception, all of these concentrate on reports concerning three Israeli raids and the flight of a single Iraqi Tu-16 bomber over Israel, on the morning of 6 June 1967. It is only in the last five years that at least a part of the true story behind this affair has become known. Clearly, the Israeli attack was provoked by the two raids flown by IrAF Hunters against Israel, as described in Chapter 4. The following is in fact the first reconstruction that can be considered as anywhere near complete.

Spoiled Revenge

While unable to hit any other air bases inside Iraq, the Israelis were determined not to let the Iraqis use H-3 for additional attacks on Israel. The order for an attack on this airfield was issued while Mystères and Ouragans were still busy destroying No. 1 Squadron RJAF. With no other aircraft available for this task, a formation from the Ramat David-based No. 110 Squadron IDF/AF was selected. The four aircraft in question were led by Capt Gideon Magen, flying two-seat Vautour IIN serial number 66 (with Capt Alexander Inbar-Meltzer as navigator). Meanwhile, Lts Ran Goren, Ya'acov Tal and Dan Ilan flew single-seat Vautour IIAs.

Israeli sources usually insist that this was an ad-hoc operation. An attack against H-3 was not a part of the plan for Operation Focus, and Capt Magen's formation was initially scheduled to hit Tsaykal air base in Syria, before being re-tasked to attack Dmeyr, and finally Ras Banas in Egypt. It was only in the final moments before take-off that the force were ordered to attack Iraq. Correspondingly, the pilots involved were poorly prepared, having received no reconnaissance photographs of their target. Instead, they were instructed to follow the old H-pipeline from Haifa via Mafraq to H-3 as a navigational aid. They were told to expect Hunters, MiG-21s and bombers as opposition. Ilan had to abort due to technical problems shortly after take-off, but the other three Vautours continued.[1]

Following an ingress at only 15m (49ft), the Israelis approached H-3 around 15.00 their time (16.00 in Iraq). Faysal Abdul Mohsen recalled the situation at the Iraqi airfield:

A pre-war photograph shows an unknown Iraqi pilot behind a row of Hunters at Habbaniyah. Despite frequently mixing in politics and their involvement in several coup attempts (a number of IrAF pilots that saw action during the June 1967 War were sent to their units almost 'straight out of prison'), the Iraqis were reasonably well-trained and possessed experience from the war with the Kurds. They were confident fighters and on 5 June their spirits were very high.
(Nour Bardai Collection)

'Around 13.30, while we were still under way attacking Israel, MiG-21FLs from No. 17 Squadron arrived at H-3. After our return and post-mission debrief, I was standing on the tarmac next to Adil Suleimany, watching the Hunters from the Lod attack returning to land and two MiGs taking off. Suleimany then ordered two Hunters to take-off and establish a CAP some 5 miles [8km] west of the airfield. As the Hunters rolled for take-off, we saw several aircraft in the west and thought these must be Jordanian Hunters, trying to land on our runway. Less than half a minute later, we recognised two Vautours ...'

Having problems with target identification, Capt Magen climbed to have a look around and find H-3, but as soon as he did so, his formation came under attack by the two MiG-21s that were already airborne. Without knowing that their opponents were not armed with any cannon, the Vautour pilots began to manoeuvre hard, in turn spoiling firing solutions for the R-3S missiles carried by the Iraqi MiGs. After several such manoeuvres, they managed to free themselves sufficiently to strafe some of the aircraft on the ground and then bomb the single runway. Mohsen continued:

'They first opened fire on an Antonov transport and then hit a row of MiG-21s and a Dove. Then another Vautour hit one of two Hunters that returned from the attack on Lod IAP and were still parked near the runway. The resulting detonation caused injuries to several of our pilots, and 1st Lt Najdat an-Naqeeb barely escaped the explosion of his aircraft ...'

Taken at Habbaniyah during the June 1967 War, this photograph shows a Hunter F.Mk 59B (serial number 628 or 633) in front of a sandbag revetment covered by camouflage netting. Due to the 'temporary' nature of the IrAF deployment to H-3, no such protective measures were introduced there.
(Ahmad Sadik Collection)

The wreckage of this
de Havilland Dove (serial
number 267) was discovered
at the former Habbaniyah
air base in March 2006. The
aircraft likely ended its service
still wearing the same colours
as the example destroyed by
the Israelis in the course of
their first attack on H-3, on the
afternoon of 5 June 1967. The
IrAF acquired a total of seven
Doves, which were flown by
No. 3 Squadron.
(Tom Cooper Collection)

As the Vautours pressed home, they came under repeated attack by the two MiG-21s, the pilots of which finally found targets that were flying steady enough to be targeted with R-3S missiles. However, none of the four missiles they fired hit: all missed since the Vautours were flying much too low and the missile seeker heads were distracted by the heat emitted by the hot desert below. The first air battle over H-3 therefore remained inconclusive.

The situation in regard to the results of the Israeli attack on the parked IrAF aircraft was quite different. The IDF/AF pilots involved exaggerated by a considerable margin, Capt Magen claiming the destruction of between nine and 12 aircraft, and Lt Ran no fewer than six MiG-21s, five Hunters, two MiG-17s and a 'large transport'.[2] Citing an official IrAF report about this attack, Ahmad Sadik summarised:

'The attack caught our pilots by surprise but the Israelis exaggerated a lot. Our records were very specific and cited three MiG-21s, one Hunter, one Dove and a single An-12 (that was carrying R-3S air-to-air missiles and spare parts for MiG-21s), as destroyed. There were no MiG-17s at H-3: they did not deploy there during the June 1967 War. The runway was damaged but ground crews rapidly prepared an alternative and thus the airfield was operational by the next morning.'[3]

Apparently, the Israeli commanders were neither impressed nor convinced by the reports filed by their pilots and drew similar conclusions to the IrAF. Thus, CO 1st Wing IDF/AF, Col Yezekiel Somech, subsequently received the order to fly another

An IrAF Antonov An-12B (serial
number 505) as seen in the UK,
while still wearing its original,
'overall grey' livery and picking
up spares and armament for
Hunters, in the second half of
the 1960s. This example entered
service with No. 23 Squadron
in 1963 and survived the June
1967 War.
(Albert Grandolini Collection)

strike against H-3, on the following morning.[4] What the Israelis did not know – or did not expect – was that the IrAF planned to return the favour earlier that morning.

Iraqi Counterattack

By sunrise on 6 June, six Hunters from No. 6 Squadron IrAF – each armed with eight rockets with 60lb warheads and a full load of 30mm ammunition for their cannon – were prepared for their next combat sortie from H-3. Acting according to orders from the UACEC HQ in Amman, CO Suleimany distributed them into two formations, one of four and the other of two aircraft, of which the former was to attack Israeli ground units, while the other received the order to hit Ramat David air base, as Sadik recalled:

'The orders Suleimany received were very unclear and provided no useful details about the target, which was to be some Israeli artillery position near Jenin. Contrary to the usual practice within the IrAF, there was no direct communication between No. 6 Squadron and Jordanian ground troops, and we had no forward observers deployed on the West Bank. We also still knew next to nothing about the importance of Ramat David air base.'

The reason the IrAF did not send more fighters over Israel that morning was quite obvious. At that time, H-3 was not only a small airfield with very primitive support facilities, but was also already overburdened by the presence of a squadron each of Hunters and MiG-21s. Positioned in the middle of the barren, rocky desert between Baghdad and Damascus, and nearly 500km (311 miles) away from the Iraqi capital, it was also very isolated. Apart from lighter and more sensitive items, such as weapons, the IrAF had to truck-in most supplies – including fuel and water – along the highway from its depots in the Baghdad area. H-3 was also not expected to serve as a front-

Fine studies of Hunter F.Mk 59As serial numbers 571 and 575, photographed prior to and during their delivery to Iraq in March 1964, respectively. Both aircraft saw combat while in service with No. 6 Squadron during the June 1967 War. (David Nicolle Collection)

line base for attacks on Israel, but only as a staging post for units ordered to deploy in Jordan. Therefore, the supply situation for Nos 6 and 17 Squadrons did not permit anything more substantial than offensive sorties by six Hunters and a CAP consisting of two MiG-21FLs.

The first formation of four Hunters lost one of its number early, when the fighter, flown by an unknown pilot, had to return to H-3 due to mechanical problems. Flying at low level, entirely undisturbed, the other three pilots reached the designated target area near Jenin by around 05.00 Israeli time. Failing to find their target in the area expected, the three Iraqi pilots were quick to find an alternative. Faysal Abdul Mohsen flew as number 2 in this formation and recalled what happened next:

'Our formation consisted of Capt Mohammed Abdel Wahed Yuzbaki, myself, and 1st Lt Abdul Latif Abdul Karim. We hit a group of tanks parked in an open field next to the road from Nazareth to Haifa. Their U-shaped formation was surrounded by many cars and trucks and apparently in the process of loading ammunition and refuelling. It was nearly impossible to miss and all our rockets hit the target area, causing an impressive volume of radio chatter on the Zionist networks ...'

According to a post-war investigation by the IrAF Intelligence Department, this attack – not reported in any known Israeli account of the June 1967 War – apparently left five Israelis killed and eight injured, although the exact extent of the damage caused to various tanks and other vehicles remains unknown.[5]

Around the same time, another Iraqi jet appeared over the West Bank, having met as little resistance as the three Hunters that preceded it. Namely, the IrAF was in possession of assets capable of attacking Israel when operating directly from their bases: these were the Tu-16s of No. 10 Squadron based at Habbaniyah. Put on alert as early as around noon on 5 June, early morning the following day the CO of the squadron ordered four of his aircraft to attack Ramat David air base, each armed with six

A rare photograph of an Iraqi Tu-16 bomber, apparently taken in the late 1960s, while the aircraft was undergoing overhaul in the USSR, and before all the aircraft received a coat of disruptive camouflage colours.
(via Albert Grandolini)

Top and bottom left: The crash site of the Iraqi Tu-16 shot down on the morning of 6 June over Israel. Israeli sources vary, but as well as the IrAF crew of five, between 11 and 14 IDF soldiers were apparently also killed when the bomber hit their base.
(IDF)

Bottom right: The wreckage of the ill-fated Iraqi Tu-16 bomber.
(IDF)

FAB-500 bombs.[6] Once again, the targeting intelligence provided to the crews involved was very poor. Furthermore, each bomber was to operate as a single-ship, without providing mutual protection with the help of their three defensive barbettes, each of which was equipped with two 23mm cannon, and without any fighter escort. Instead, one bomber was to follow the other at an interval of an hour.

The first Tu-16 to take off was piloted by Capt Farouk al-Tail with 1st Lt Majid Turki as co-pilot. It reached Mafraq air base flying at low altitude, then climbed to 25,000ft (7,620m) while crossing the Jordan River and searching for its target.[7] The crew reported to have found Ramat David and released its bombs without any disturbance, around 05.05 local time. However, it seems that Capt al-Tail's report was overoptimistic and his crew released its bombs upon a military installation near Taamach, 10km (6.2 miles) southeast of Afula, where – according to Iraqi intelligence reports – several buildings were demolished, two Israeli soldiers killed and five injured.[8]

Left: Pilot of the IrAF Tu-16 shot down over Israel on the morning of 5 June 1967 was Sqn Ldr H. M. 'Kaka' Hussein. (Ahmad Sadik Collection).

Right: Flt Lt Alwan was Hussein's co-pilot. (Ahmad Sadik Collection)

Left: First Navigator of the Iraqi Tu-16 shot down over Israel was 1st Lt Rashid. (Ahmad Sadik Collection)

Right: Second Navigator and responsible for manning one of the 23mm cannon barbettes in the downed Tu-16 was 1st Lt Kargoli. (Ahmad Sadik Collection)

The next two Tu-16 crews were less lucky: both were forced to abort due to technical difficulties and return to Habbaniyah. Therefore, only the fourth Tu-16 was left to attack Israel. Flown by Sqn Ldr Hussein Mohammad 'Kaka' Hussein with co-pilot Flt Lt Alwan, navigators 1st Lt Rashid and 1st Lt Kargoli, as well as rear-gunner 1st Lt Sabih, the aircraft missed Ramat David and continued climbing until over the Mediterranean Sea, whereupon Sqn Ldr Hussein decided to turn around and try to find another suitable target. Around 08.35 local time, for unexplained reasons and despite a clear order not to attack civilian targets, the crew released its warload over the centre of Netanya, hitting the main street and causing a number of civilian casualties.[9]

Seconds later, Hussein's bomber was intercepted by two Mirage IIICJs from No. 117 Squadron. As the Mirages approached, 1st Lt Sabih opened fire with his two 23mm cannon, forcing them to break and reposition. Sqn Ldr Hussein then entered a right turn and began a descent that finally brought him directly over Ramat David – just at the moment that the crews of the four No. 110 Squadron Vautours and two No.117 Squadron Mirage IIICJs were preparing for their second attack on H-3.

Still pursued by two Mirages, the Tupolev thundered low over the Israeli air base, making a right turn that enabled Sabih and Kargoli to open fire from their barbettes on the aircraft at the installations below. The bomber was then hit by one of two missiles fired by the Mirages: Hussein reported to H-3 over radio that the aircraft was still controllable and that he was attempting to escape in an easterly direction. However, while trying to do so, he flew his bomber directly over the IDF barracks near Megiddo airfield, where the Tu-16 was apparently hit again, this time by the Mirage flown by Capt Amnon Arad and ground-based Bofors 40mm L/70 cannon. Finally, the bomber crashed into a military storage complex hidden within a pine forest west of Afula, destroying three barracks and two teams of 120mm mortars, and killing its entire crew as well as 11 or 14 Israeli reservist soldiers (sources differ) and injuring eight.[10]

Almost simultaneous with Hussein's Tu-16, the two remaining Hunters from H-3 also arrived over the Ramat David area. Flown by 1st Lt Samir Yousif Zainal and 1st Lt Waleed A. Lattif, they reached their target by flying at low altitude and without encountering any kind of opposition. However, the results of their attack remain unknown: available Israeli sources mention only an air raid that apparently hit the villages of Nahalal and Migdal Haemek, though without causing any damage or casualties. Curiously enough, these locations are due north and east of the sprawling Ramat David complex, respectively, barely a few kilometres away.[11]

Second Attempt Frustrated

Shortly after Hussein's Tu-16 was shot down, and after Zainal and Lattif had left Israeli airspace, the second Israeli attack on H-3 was launched. This time the formation was led by Maj Moshe Sa'ar with Capt Inbar as navigator in Vautour IIN serial number 67, with Lt Goren as wingman. Capt Ben-Zion Zohar flew as number 3 in Vautour IIA serial number 17, with Lt Herzle Budinger as number 4. Behind them followed two Mirages, led by Capt Yehuda Koren. The aircraft followed the same route as the first formation that attacked H-3, and the same as that used by all the Iraqi Hunters. The Israelis arrived over H-3 just as Zainal and Lattif were about to land. In order to make sure that the returning fighters would be well protected, four IrAF fighters were ordered to scramble. These included two MiG-21FLs, flown by Majs Khalid Sarah and Mumtazz Abdel Ali al-Saydoon, and two Hunters, flown by Capt Yuzbaki and 1st Lt Namik Saadallah.

Already airborne and in the process of developing their attack, the Israelis proved quicker off the mark. Koren positioned behind Lattif's Hunter that was still in the landing pattern and followed him down towards the runway, while Sa'ar turned to attack the two MiGs as these were accelerating for take-off. Barely within firing range of his target, Koren was surprised to see Lattif tucking in his landing gear, braking and then accelerating away – having received warning from the ground, the Iraqi did his best to avoid the Israeli attack.

Turning around, the leading Mirage then attempted to attack the two Hunters that were still on the runway. Under pressure to get airborne as soon as possible, Capt Yuzbaki made the fatal mistake of pulling too hard and too early on his stick, while kicking the right rudder: lacking the speed to lift off, his Hunter stalled, yawed and then struck the main water tank of H-3. The pilot was killed instantly.

Mumtazz Abdel Ali al-Saydoon, seen earlier during his career, while disembarking a two-seat Hunter T.Mk 66. By the June 1967 War with Israel, as-Saydoon was already a very experienced pilot, and had converted to the MiG-21FL. (Nour Bardai Collection)

The other Israelis all missed the three remaining IrAF fighters and these then managed to became airborne and engage the enemy in a somewhat confused air battle. Pulling his Hunter above the debris left by the detonation of Yuzbaki's jet, Saadallah first attacked the Vautour flown by Capt Zohar but was then counterattacked by Koren – before the engine of the latter's Mirage stalled. Undisturbed, Sadallah proceeded with his attack on Zohar and claimed his jet as 'damaged'. In turn, the Israeli claimed to have outmanoeuvred his opponent and then hit him with 30mm cannon fire: according to Zohar, the Hunter crashed seconds later. Sadallah's Hunter was indeed hit this time, and the pilot injured, but nobody had been shot down so far: Namik Saadallah managed to land safely back at H-3.[12]

Meanwhile, the two MiG-21s made a wide turn around and then accelerated to attack the Israelis that now began to withdraw from H-3. This attack came just around the time Koren managed to recover his Mirage from a stall by dropping the nose of his fighter and relighting the engine. Sarah now attacked Zohar's Vautour as the latter was pulling up from a strafing pass. While doing so he had to make several manoeuvres, as his MiG was armed only with R-3S missiles, which possessed a very narrow engagement envelope. Zohar spoiled Sarah's attack by turning west to escape in the direction of Israel, but the Iraqi major followed – in turn presenting his tail to Koren. The Israeli Mirage pilot subsequently claimed that a short burst from his cannon was sufficient to cut off the right wing and cause the Iraqi fighter to crash. In fact, several rounds hit Sarah's MiG-21FL, one of which caused his braking parachute to pop open, in turn confusing his Israeli opponent. However, the next turn and subsequent acceleration of the MiG caused the parachute to break away and Sarah subsequently managed to land safely. The Israeli formation then hurriedly disengaged and disappeared in a westerly direction. The second Iraqi MiG-21 attempted to pursue one of the Vautours but both

Capt Abdel Wahed Yuzbaki, veteran of the Kfar Sirkin raid, was killed while scrambling from H-3 airfield when this came under a second Israeli attack on the morning of 6 June 1967. (Ahmad Sadik Collection)

of his R-3S missed, Maj as-Saydoon later bitterly complaining about the poor quality of the Soviet-made missiles.

Back at Ramat David, Zohar, Koren and the other Israeli pilots rather optimistically claimed the destruction of two MiG-21s and six Hunters on the ground, as well as a MiG-21 and a Hunter in air combats. Once again, the IDF leadership was unconvinced: this raid was nothing short of chaotic, with the sole result of one Iraqi Hunter crashing on take-off, and two other IrAF fighters damaged in the air. A third attack was thus ordered for the morning of 7 June. This time Col Somech was to fly the mission too.

Jordanian Contingent

For the Israelis, the action did not end there: following their rather hasty departure from Iraq they flew along the Baghdad-Amman highway when they sighted a large column of military vehicles. These they identified as belonging to the Iraqi 8th Brigade, sent as an expeditionary force to the Jordanian front. Unchallenged in the air, the Vautour pilots vented their frustration by exhausting their remaining ammunition with random strafing.

In fact, the convoy they hit consisted of Jordanian vehicles, under way in the opposite direction – towards Iraq. It also included the buses carrying the surviving RJAF Hunter pilots. Nasri Jumean explained how this came about:

'On the evening of 5 June, we gathered at the HQ in Amman. There we met King Hussein twice and then the PAF Assistant Chief of Staff (Operations), Air Cdre Ahmad Rahim Khan, who was visiting Jordan at the time. The second visit of His Majesty, around 22.00, boosted our morale considerably. He told us that he had contacted our brothers in Iraq and that we were to go to H-3 and continue the fight. I would be in command of that detachment, consisting of Jihad, George, Jasser, Samir, Farouq, Smadi, Shiab, Ihsan, Saif and another Pakistani. Several engineering officers joined us in the bus that was to bring us to H-3 …'

Around midnight a convoy of buses with Jordanian personnel was on its way from Amman to Iraq. After driving the entire night, early in the morning, while approaching H-4 in eastern Jordan, this column met a convoy of the Iraqi 8th Brigade. Jumean continued:

'Under way towards the east we met an Iraqi brigade and its commander asked us what was happening. I replied that we didn't know much. He told us that H-3 had been hit the previous day, but was still operational. At 08.30 two Vautours and two Mirages buzzed our column. I told the Iraqis to disperse their people and vehicles, as the aircraft would certainly come back. Fifteen minutes later they did come back and strafed …'

Meanwhile, Col Hamid Sha'ban at-Tikriti, CO Hunter Wing at Habbaniyah, arrived at H-3 in a two-seat Hunter to find his pilots excited and exhausted from battles with the Israelis. He was also confronted by a number of damaged and destroyed aircraft parked around, and the main runway still undergoing repairs. With insufficient equipment and installations at hand, Sha'ban ordered all the remaining Hunters and MiGs to be evacuated back to Habbaniyah.

Under way towards H-3, one of the vehicles from the Jordanian column broke down. Therefore, one group of RJAF pilots – including Nasri Jumean – arrived first,

A beautiful study of Hunter F.Mk 59A serial number 570, photographed prior to its March 1964 delivery. The aircraft was to enjoy a very long and distinguished career with the IrAF, surviving combat sorties in no fewer than five wars, as well as service with the IrAF's jet display team.
(David Nicolle Collection)

and put themselves at the disposal of Col Sha'ban. The Iraqi could not do much for them, as Jumean recalled:

'*When we reached H-3, it was smoke and chaos. Col Hameed told us he had got no aircraft and no station and we should continue to Habbaniyah.*'

Jasser Zayyad arrived with the second Jordanian group, several hours later, by which time Sha'ban had managed to bring the situation under control:

'*The Iraqis lost one pilot and a few aircraft at H-3 but they repaired the damage quickly. We had a lunch and were then told to go to Habbaniyah. Our bus broke down again and we got on a lorry. We had only flying overalls on and it was a very cold drive to the old quarters.*'

Moving out again, one group of Jordanians – including Saif-ul-Azam – reached Habbaniyah around 21.00 on 6 June, tired, hungry and thirsty. At first, nobody knew what to do with them. But then King Hussein of Jordan phoned Iraqi President Arif, finally informing him that he had sent his pilots to Iraq, and hoping they could join the IrAF in the fight against Israel.[13] Agreeing to arrange for their attachment to No. 6 Squadron IrAF, President Arif issued corresponding orders directly to Col Sha'ban. Finally, arrangements were made for their housing and a dinner was served. The second group of Jordanian pilots, including Jumean, arrived at Habbaniyah only around 03.00 on 7 June, as he recalled:

'*Everybody went straight to bed, but half an hour later, we were woken and told to go to the Operations Centre. The Iraqis told us they wanted to stop the Israelis from taking Jordan and that we had 50 Hunters at our disposal, because there were only two Iraqi pilots there. The others were to arrive during the day, after evacuating other aircraft out of Israeli reach ... Eventually, we decided to organise ourselves into two formations of four aircraft, the first consisting of Jihad, Farouq and two Iraqis, and the second of Nasri, Ihsan, Saif, and George.*'

Zayyad and his group followed the same pattern, several hours later:

'*We went to the old quarters. I took off my boots, swept the bugs off the bed and fell asleep ... At 03.00 in the morning I heard a commotion outside and got up. I saw the Iraqis going to the squadron ready room and followed them, but could not eat break-fast. I was the only Jordanian around. The Iraqi squadron commander told me not to fly. However, around 06.30 the Iraqi that was going to fly the CAP over H-3 said he had a bad stomach so I was assigned to fly with an Iraqi as number 2. I asked the Iraqis for a map, but there was none so I took one off the wall ...*'

The morning of 7 June thus began with more than a little chaos at Habbaniyah.

Col Hamid Sha'ban at-Tikriti was the CO Habbaniyah air base and in overall charge of operations from H-3 during the June 1967 War with Israel. He subsequently enjoyed a very successful career with the IrAF, becoming the C-in-C on two occasions.
(Ahmad Sadik Collection)

Disastrous Third Raid

Around 07.00 on 7 June, Jasser Zayyad launched from Habbaniyah as leader of a quartet of IrAF Hunters:

'Under way towards H-3 I wanted to check my Iraqi number 2 and I told him to attack me. He was so poor in air combat manoeuvring, I was quickly behind him and he could not shake me off. It was obvious that this guy was not trained and this made me very nervous. By the time we came back to Habbaniyah, other Jordanians were around as well and it was decided that we would lead the sections.'

Around 10.15 it was the turn of the next division of four Hunters to take off for their patrol over H-3. This formation was led by Flt Lt Saif-ul-Azam (in Hunter serial number 570), with 1st Lt Ihsan Shurdom as number 2. The combat-experienced Iraqi 1st Lt Samir Yousif Zainal was to fly as number 3 (Hunter serial number 585), with youngster 1st Lt Galeb al-Hameed al-Qaysee as number 4. Jumean recounted the original plan for their mission:

'They were to patrol H-3, then land and refuel there, fly another CAP and then return to Habbaniyah.'

As the Hunters approached H-3, Iraqi Army units moving along the highway between Baghdad and Damascus called the HQ at Habbaniyah to report a formation of eight Israeli fighters under way at low level, heading east. Immediately, Col Sha'ban made a call to his deputy, who was still at H-3, to warn him about the enemy. Jumean continued:

Vautour IIA serial number 17 of
No. 110 Squadron IDF/AF was
flown in two attacks on H-3
airfield.
(via Zvi Kreissler)

'The base commander climbed on to the roof of an old fortress near the airfield. Using his eyes, telephone and radio he then directed the incoming Hunters. He was fantastic: he had just been let out of jail and went straight to command the base.'

Azam's division was thus alerted to the incoming Israeli raid in a timely fashion and ordered to engage.

Calculating that all previous Iraqi air raids were launched from H-3, Col Somech elected to shut down this airfield once and for all. Despite previous negative experiences, and the high probability of aerial opposition, it is surprising that this mission was so poorly planned. The attack formation was to use the same ingress route as before; the Vautours were to go in at low level, but instead of providing top cover, the following four Mirages were to be armed with bombs as well, and would hit the runway. The Israelis expected to surprise the Iraqis again.

Taking off at 10.22, Capts Shlomo Keren and Alexander Inbar led the formation in Vautour IIN serial number 65, with Col Somech as number 2 in Vautour IIA serial number 17, Capt Yitzhak Glantz-Golan as number 3 in Vautour IIA serial number 14, and Lt Avshalom Friedman in Vautour IIA serial number 03 as number 4. Capt Ezra Dotan, Capt Gideon Dror, Lt David Porat and Lt Reuven Har'el flew the escorting No. 117 Squadron Mirages.

The Israeli formation appeared over H-3 at low altitude. At around the same time, the four Iraqi Hunters were only some 10km (6.2 miles) from the airfield, on directly the opposite side and at high altitude. A major air battle was now inevitable.

Advised of the Israelis' appearance by the Iraqi base commander on the ground, Saif-ul-Azam dove towards the enemy, ordering his formation members to arm their guns and jettison their drop tanks in the process. The Pakistani and his Jordanian wingman manoeuvred behind two Vautours, while the two Iraqis attacked two Mirages, jumping them only seconds after Capt Dror has dropped his two bombs on the H-3 runway. Pulling up, Dror noticed two Hunters behind the rear pair of Mirages, and turned to attack. Still in a dive, Azam decided to cross over his formation: he and Shurdom were now to attack the Mirages, while Zainal and al-Qaysee were to attack the Vautours.

The Mirages were faster: Dror closed upon the rear Iraqi pair and opened fire first, hitting the Hunter flown by 1st Lt al-Qaysee. Spinning out of control, the aircraft crashed into a fuel tank, instantly killing the pilot. Undaunted, Azam attacked the same Mirage, his 30mm shells causing a big ball of flame to appear at the rear end of the Israeli fighter. When the controls went dead, Dror ejected. He was taken prisoner by Iraqi troops only minutes later. In return, Ezra Dothan attacked one of the Hunters

1st Lt Galeb al-Hameed
al-Qaysee was another veteran
of Iraqi Air Force raids on Israel,
in the June 1967 War. He was
killed when his Hunter was hit
by Dror and it crashed into a
fuel tank at H-3, during the
third Israeli attack.
(Ahmad Sadik Collection)

According to Iraqi records, Ihsan Shurdom flew Hunter F.Mk 59A serial number 578 during his sortie over H-3 airfield on 7 June 1967. (David Nicolle Collection)

behind Dror, claiming it as shot down seconds later. However, his effort was in vain: not only did his target escape undamaged, the Israelis were now about to receive a series of return blows.

Breaking off to the right without looking back at his first target, Azam spotted a Vautour approaching head on, but below his flight level:

'I had just shot down a Mirage III in flames and came across a Vautour closing head on, 2,000ft [610m] below me … I inverted the Hunter and pulled through a split-S. I pulled back on the stick to the point of blacking out and on levelling found myself within 150ft [46m] of the Vautour, and again closing fast in spite of the fully extended airbrakes and throttle at idle. Only on this occasion I did not hesitate and fired a burst with the immensely powerful 30mm cannon. Simultaneously, I broke hard to the left. There was a violent shudder right across the aircraft. I was hit by flying debris from the exploding Vautour …'

Meanwhile, 1st Lt Zainal positioned himself behind a Vautour as well, recalling in his post-mission report:

'The big Israeli fighter did several shallow manoeuvres, avoiding three bursts from my cannon, but then steadied on a western course. I carefully positioned the target in my crosshairs and then fired for the fourth time, hitting the wing and fuselage. Pouring smoke, the Israeli plane pulled up and two ejection seats separated from it: at that moment the empty plane exploded.'[14]

Whether shot down by Azam or Zainal, Capt Glantz-Golan ejected from one of the two disintegrating Vautours to become the second Israeli PoW in Iraq. Indeed, this series of clashes occurred within such a short period of time that Dror and Golan ejected almost simultaneously, Dror ironically still 'escorting' Golan as they descended towards the ground under their parachutes!

Rescue Attempts

With his formation leader and one of the escorting Mirages shot down, and at least one other aircraft on fire, Somech finally ordered the survivors to disengage immediately. However, they were given no respite. Zainal attacked both remaining Vautours and then a Mirage, claiming hits on all of them. According to his post-mission report, at least two Israeli aircraft were last seen trailing smoke when the Iraqi disengaged upon realising he was already well inside Jordanian airspace and very short on fuel.

Back over H-3, Saif-ul-Azam decided to return to Habbaniyah, which he reached safely, even though he was now on his last drops of fuel:

'On landing I saw a large piece of debris from the Vautour embedded in the fuse-lage. An amusing story went around Habbaniyah, 'The Pakistani, when running out of ammunition, rammed the enemy aircraft and brought it down ...''

On the way to Habbaniyah, Ihsan Shurdom fell back behind Azam:

'I could not find Habbaniyah and landed at a small airstrip on a plateau nearby with only 50lb [23kg] left in my fuel tanks.'

His Hunter was only slightly damaged on landing. Swiftly repaired and refuelled by a party of IrAF ground technicians, Shurdom was able fly the fighter back to Habbaniyah.

Following his pursuit of the Israelis deep over Jordan, 1st Lt Zainal was so short of fuel that he was forced to land at H-3, despite new damage on the runway. He rejoined his unit in Habbaniyah slightly over an hour later.

Although it was obvious that H-3 was not yet knocked out, and could still be used by the IrAF for staging attacks on Israel, the IDF/AF never again attacked it. Neverthe-less, lacking knowledge about the fate of its downed crews, and in the hope that one or two of them might have avoided becoming PoWs, in the late afternoon of 7 June, three Mirages were sent to orbit the area along the Iraqi–Jordanian border. After listening on their radios for some time for possible transmissions from downed crews, the pilots returned without having found anybody.

The IrAF remained active over western Iraq, sending additional CAPs out of Habbaniyah throughout the afternoon, and also launching pairs of Hunters over Jordan, as recalled by Mohsen:

'I flew two missions that brought me over Jordan that day. One with Jassam Mohammed Juburi and the other with the Jordanian pilot George Matta. The second mission was in support of the Iraqi Army brigade that was still under way towards Amman. We saw smoke columns caused by Israeli air raids against our ground troops but encountered no opposition and returned to Habbaniyah safely.'

On 8 June, four Jordanians were sent from Habbaniyah to Rashid air base, where they met Col Sha'ban again.[15] Nasri Jumean recalled one of the worst injustices suf-fered by any Arab pilot in the course of the June 1967 War or immediately after:

'Sha'ban informed us that the Israelis had taken the Golan and were going for Damascus. He wanted four aircraft to launch and hit the advancing Israeli ground units. I told him, 'You want four aircraft – what can they do?' But, he insisted and thus we prepared ourselves. On the order from Col Sha'ban, all rocket launchers were taken off our Hunters, to make us lighter. Meanwhile, we calculated a flight plan and found out we could reach the Golan but not get back. I told this to Col Sha'ban, but he continued insisting. Thus, we decided to try and land at Dawson's Field or bail out. Then Sha'ban told us to stand down: the war was over.

'Eventually, the story came out that we had refused orders, but we did not know what kind of repercussions this might have ... We remained in Iraq until 17 June and then returned to Amman, requesting an inquiry. The next day, we – including George, Jihad, Issa Qandah, Raja Abu Zeineh, Nasser Sa'adi, Radi Monomy and me – met Sharif Nasser bin Jamil at the GHQ. We expected to get decorated for our efforts. Instead, Raouf Abdeen, Chief of Legal Affairs, appeared to say that four of us were up for trial and four for interview. He said, 'Major Jumean, effective from this

moment you are released from the Air Force and on pension. George, Nasser and Raja, you are released from the Air Force. Your services are not needed …' Others received minor punishment. We were marched out without being allowed to say a word and do not know the reason for our release until this very day.'

The Israeli pilots involved were far luckier. On the evening of 8 June, after their Intelligence had intercepted an Iraqi radio message erroneously reporting that three IDF/AF pilots had been captured, they were sent over Iraq again. A Noratlas transport configured as a communications relay platform, and supported by three Super Frelon helicopters, was launched in a search and rescue attempt the same evening. Failing to find any of the downed crews, the aircraft eventually attracted the attention of Syrian air defences and came under attack from a MiG-21, as described in the next chapter. The Israelis then beat a hasty retreat.[16]

Finally, a decision was taken to launch a rescue operation under the command of Zuri Saguy, a paratrooper officer who previously worked with Iraqi Kurds. Saguy first carried out a reconnaissance deep inside Iraq, in order to prepare a complex raid involving an incursion into an Iraqi prison, and an escape with the help of Super Frelons. Eventually, he concluded that an adventure of this type would almost certainly end in failure, with many casualties, and explained this to his superiors; a plane ticket to Iran, he said, would be cheaper and more efficient. Once in Iran, Saguy met the Israeli military attaché, Yaakov Nimrodi, and several leading Kurds that had fought against the Iraqi government. However, before he could organise any kind of operation, the Iraqis released their captives.[17]

Second Ezra

What exactly happened over H-3 shortly before noon on 7 June 1967 remains partially unknown. Except for the fate of 1st Lt Galeb al-Hameed al-Qaysee, who was killed, and the fact that Dror and Glantz-Golan were captured almost immediately after landing under their parachutes, the remainder of the action remains unclear.

In the course of only two missions flown on 5 and 7 June 1967, Saif-ul-Azam (left) and Ihsan Shurdom claimed a total of eight Israeli fighters shot down or damaged. (Saif-ul-Azam Collection)

Saif-ul-Azam was highly decorated for his achievements during the June 1967 War with Israel. Here he is seen together with several Iraqi dignitaries, while receiving one of the highest decorations for valour. (Saif-ul-Azam Collection)

Flt Lt Saif-ul-Azam claimed one Mirage and a Vautour shot down, and his recollections are described above. He was subsequently officially credited with two kills and was highly decorated by the Iraqi government.[18] 1st Lt Samir Yousif Zainal claimed a Vautour and a Mirage (in that order), and was similarly credited with two kills and highly decorated. Finally, 1st Lt Ihsan Shurdom claimed a Mirage and a Vautour, which exploded, while the sole 100mm AAA battery deployed at H-3 claimed another Israeli fighter as shot down. Shurdom's conclusion is as follows:

'We arrived at 20,000ft [6,096m] over H-3, jettisoned drop tanks and then engaged. Farouq Abdeen was down on the ground and watched all of this. I shot down a Mirage and the pilot bailed out. Then I shot down a Vautour, which exploded. Then my guns jammed. Saif meanwhile shot down a Mirage that hit an Iraqi pilot and who then went straight into the fuel tank. Then Saif shot down a Vautour too.'[19]

Other Iraqis and Jordanians who were at Habbaniyah to hear the post-mission reports recalled the events somewhat differently – and foremost lower Israeli losses. Faysal Abdul Mohsen explained:

'Ihsan Shurdom felled a Mirage flown by a pilot named Ezra, who was killed, and damaged another Israeli plane. Saif-ul-Azam shot down a Mirage, the pilot of which was captured: he was of Romanian descent. Our pilot Samir Zainal shot down a Vautour of the Israeli formation leader and killed him and his navigator.'

Recollections of Jordanian pilots that were in Iraq at the time tend to confirm Mohsen's version: Nasri Jumean:

'The Iraqi pair bounced the Vautours but the Iraqi number 2 was caught by a Mirage and crashed. This Mirage was then shot down by Saif. The second Iraqi then shot down a Vautour and a Mirage, and another Israeli was shot down by the AAA.'

Jasser Zayyad recalled the events differently:

'… Saif got one, Ihsan got one and Samir Zainal got one …'

The reason the IrAF eventually concluded that all three pilots' claims were 'correct' is likely to come as a surprise to almost anyone familiar with Israeli accounts published so far. However, it is based on evidence collected by the Iraqi military after the air battle. During the afternoon an Iraqi Army patrol found the wreckage of a third

Dror (left) and Glantz-Golan as PoWs in Iraq.
(Ahmad Sadik Collection)

Israeli fighter – they described it as a 'Mirage' – not far from H-3. The aircraft was completely destroyed and the pilot dead: according to IrAF reports, his body was still strapped to his ejection seat, which had not separated in time, and was nearly completely burned. What was left of his papers showed that he held the rank of a major and that his first name was Ezra – the same name as recalled by Mohsen.[20]

Later on 7 June, Saudi border guards called Habbaniyah to report finding wreckage of an Israeli Vautour, together with the bodies of pilots identified as 'Capt Keren' and

Glantz-Golan (right) and Dror as seen during their return to Israel, in the course of a POW exchange on the River Jordan, on 26 June 1967.
(Ahmad Sadik Collection)

'Capt Meltzer'. Keren's body was still inside the cockpit, while Meltzer's was found several hundred metres away: he had obviously been fatally injured in an unsuccessful ejection attempt from less than the 600m (1,969ft) minimum safe altitude.

For the IrAF at least, the situation thus very soon became quite 'clear': its Hunters had shot down five Israeli fighters in combat on 7 June, with three Israelis being killed in the process, while two were captured alive.

Exactly who this 'second Ezra' was remains unknown, since the Iraqis were left with insufficient time to find out. Immediately after the ceasefire with Jordan, Israel began exerting fierce pressure upon King Hussein for the return or release of its pilots – dead or alive – from Iraq. Furthermore, the IDF demanded the return of its five pilots via the International Red Cross. Dror and Glantz-Golan, as well as the bodies of three Israeli pilots, were exchanged for Jordanian PoWs as early as 26 June 1967.[21] Clearly, the 'unknown Ezra' could not have been Ezra Dothan: he is known to have made it back to Israel and to have continued his career with the IDF/AF after the war.

The official IDF/AF documentation available so far, as well as nearly all the accounts of the air battle published in Israel or based on Israeli sources, only mention the loss of three aircraft – one Mirage and two Vautours – during the third attack on H-3. According to these accounts, Dror flew the downed Mirage serial number 60 and Glantz-Golan the downed Vautour IIA serial number 14. The Vautour IIN serial number 65, found inside Saudi Arabia, had been flown by the formation leader, Capt Shlomo Keren, with navigator Capt Alexander Inbar. The name 'Meltzer' reported by the Saudis was the Hebrew family name of Capt Inbar (a fact all the interviewed Iraqis deny until this day, questioning why there should be any difference, since both names are Hebrew). Therefore, according to Israeli sources, no fourth or fifth IDF/AF fighter was ever shot down over H-3 on 7 June 1967.

The exception to this rule was an article published in the Israeli newspaper *Haaretz*, on 24 December 2005, citing for the first time in 38 years that, '… *Israel suffered a loss of three pilots killed and two captured …*' during the third raid on H-3. Whether a mistake or an unintended revelation, this statement was never retracted.

Whatever the truth of the details, the third battle over H-3 was all but over by 11.35 on 7 June 1967, and it ended with a clear Israeli defeat.

1   The Iraqi officers interviewed for this project were quite surprised by the lack of Israeli intelligence concerning H-3. For example, it is fairly well known that none other than Moshe Dayan 'visited' H-3 in 1941, while serving with the British Army. Furthermore, Brig Gen Ahmad Sadik – who formerly served with the IrAF Intelligence Directorate – recalled that several times during the 1950s and 1960s Israeli Boeing B-17s overflew H-3, and that the IrAF concluded that they had taken reconnaissance photographs of the base. Finally, in May 1967, a man subsequently uncovered as an agent of Mossad is known to have travelled from Baghdad to Amman by car, and to have taken photographs of H-3 while passing by (at that time the highway was only few metres away from the boundary of the H-3 compound).

2   Aloni, *The June 1967 Six-Day War* and Bowen, *Six Days*, pp157–158.

3   Sadik, interview, March 2007. The An-12B destroyed by the Israelis during their first attack on H-3 was serial number 508.

4   There is still much uncertainty – perhaps even controversy – concerning the background of the orders for subsequent IDF/AF attacks on H-3. Sadly, after granting an interview to Lon Nordeen in November 1987, Mr Somech turned down all subsequent requests for interviews regarding this and other missions against H-3.

5   Sadik, interview, March 2007.

6   Ibid. This relatively light warload might surprise some readers, but a load of 3,000kg (6,614lb; i.e. six FAB-500 bombs) was considered 'normal' for a Tu-16 sent on a very dangerous mission over 800km (497 miles) distance, without any kind of escort. There remains some contradiction over the precise type of FAB-500s used: the few photos of – supposedly Iraqi – unexploded bombs that appeared from Israel so far show FAB-500M46s – obsolescent weapons with low-pressure casings, unsuitable for use from high-speed aircraft like Tu-16s. On the other hand, Iraqi sources report that the more modern FAB-500M54s were used for this attack, the reason being that their target was to be the runways of Ramat David.

7   Majid al-Turki continued a successful career with the IrAF for two years longer. Sadly, he was executed on the order of Saddam Hussein al-Tikriti in 1969, under the pretext of conspiracy against the state.

8   The IrAF report in question apparently leant upon at least some Israeli media reports, as well as various printed publications. The best available example of media reports is 'Killed in Explosion of Bomb they were Guarding', *Jerusalem Post* (English edition), 8 June 1967. This cites, 'Afula – Two men were killed on Tuesday night by the explosion of a Syrian bomb (sic) they had been told to guard and keep away from. The bomb was one of several which belonged to the Syrian Ilyushin bomber (sic) that crashed here in the early morning. Experts had begun to dismantle them, but had not completed their job by nightfall. The two, Arieh Glaser, 43, and Salomon Buchriss, 28, of here, were ordered to warn everyone off. The investigation revealed that one of them had tampered with the bomb, setting it off. The two were killed instantly ...' Printed publications used by the Iraqis included Zeif Sheif, *The Israeli Military Encyclopedia*, 1988, translated into Arabic and English and republished by Dar el-Jaleel for Publishing & Palestinian Research & Studies, in Amman, a year later.

9   'Woman killed, 21 wounded in Netanya bombing', *Jerusalem Post* (English edition), 7 June 1967. The report cited: 'One woman was killed and 21 persons wounded when an Iraqi Tupolev 16 plane dropped several bombs on the city shortly after six o'clock yesterday morning. The plane was downed on its way back to base. The casualty was Mrs Violette Dayan, 36, mother of four. Eyewitnesses said she was killed when going to the balcony of her home. Fourteen of the injured were hospitalised of whom five are reported to be in serious condition. The bombs fell on the main street, Rahov Herzl, damaging a number buildings (sic). Hardest hit were the offices of Solel Boneh, Bank Hapoalim and Ulamel Netanya. Also damaged was a Paz petrol station and cars parked nearby. Shop windows on both sides of the street were smashed. Other windows were thrown through the air together with their frames. Haga workers had the injured at first aid stations within minutes. Shops opened later in the morning ...'

10 According to the IrAF post-mission report, as cited by Sadik during an interview in March 2007, Hussein's Tu-16 was first hit by a Matra R.530 missile (not by a Shafrir 1, as reported by the Israelis), which proximity-fused and caused some damage to one of the engines. Eventually, according to the Iraqi conclusion, it was

shot down by a HAWK SAM site protecting Ramat David. The same report concluded that the Israelis credited this Tu-16 to the crews of their Bofors guns because so many of these were killed in the crash of the bomber on their base. Interestingly, Israeli reports about the operations of these two Iraqi Tu-16s are quite confused and it is therefore hardly surprising that until the Arab-Israeli negotiations in the 1990s, the IDF was convinced that only one Tupolev attacked. The confusion began already on the following day, when Israeli media initially misidentified the Iraqi Tu-16 as a Syrian Il-28. A good example of this is the report 'Syrian Plane Crashes on Petrol Station Kills 9', from the *Jerusalem Post* of 7 June 1967, which describes the following events from the Afula area, on the morning of 6 June: 'Nine (unreadable) were killed and a number were wounded when a Syrian Ilyushin bomber was shot down by an Israeli fighter at 05.35 yesterday morning before it could drop any bombs. The bomber was flying very low in a southerly direction over the rooftops of the buildings at Rehov Habanim and the Government housing quarter. Hit by the Israeli plane, the bomber fell in flames near a petrol station, on the outskirts of the town (Afula; authors' note) and exploded together with its load of bombs. Nine Israelis were killed instantly. The pilot and the co-pilot were also killed'. Notably, the bodies of the Iraqi Tu-16 crew were returned to Iraq during a PoW exchange on the River Jordan on 26 June. In the course of our research on the Iraqi-Israeli air battles in 1967, the authors were contacted by the brother of 1st Lt Rashid. He told us that he once saw a BBC documentary showing his brother alive and as a PoW in Israel after his aircraft was shot down. Nevertheless, on 26 June, Israel handed over his body to the ICRC. Finally, according to an anonymous source in Israel, an internal study by the IDF/AF concluded that the Iraqi Tu-16 pilot attempted to make an emergency, wheels-up landing at Megiddo, but was prevented by the AAA protecting this site and the busy military complex nearby.

11 'As the News Broke', *Jerusalem Post* (English edition), 8 June 1967.

12 As we are to see in subsequent volumes of this series, Namiq Saad Allah continued a successful career with the IrAF until the October 1973 War with Israel – something that would have been quite unlikely if Koren's claim is correct: chances of a successful ejection from a Hunter at an altitude of less than 100m (328ft) were next to non-existent.

13 As recalled by Azam, interview, April 2008. From his and Jumean's descriptions of events at Habbaniyah, it appears that King Hussein did not make any calls to President Arif on the evening of 5 June, as promised when meeting the survivors of No. 1 Squadron RJAF, but did so only after his pilots arrived in Iraq.

14 According to the IrAF post-mission report, as cited by Sadik during an interview in March 2007.

15 Col Hamid Sha'ban continued a particularly successful career with the IrAF, being appointed its CO for two terms. Two of his Hunter pilots from the June 1967 War, 1st Lt Hassan al-Khither and 1st Lt Najdat an-Naqeeb, rose almost as high. Al-Kither reached the position of Director of Operations IrAF (effectively a Deputy CO of the Air Force), and was replaced by an-Naqeeb. 1st Lt Sadallah served with the IrAF until the October 1973 War with Israel, when he claimed a kill against an Israeli fighter during an air battle over the Golan Heights. Sadly, he was killed in action only a few days later. 1st Lt Zainal served during the October 1973 War with Israel as well, when he claimed a kill against an F-4E Phantom II of the IDF/AF. Most of these and many other of their subsequent adventures will be described in future volumes of this series.

16 Some Israeli sources reported that the Noratlas was fired upon by SA-2s – even though neither Iraq nor Syria operated these weapons at that time.

17 Sadik, interview, March 2007.

18 Following the June 1967 War, Flt Lt Saif-ul-Azam was decorated with the Wisam-al-Istigal (Order of Independence Medal) in Jordan, as well as the Nowt al-Shuja'a (Medal of Bravery) in Iraq, and the Sitara-i-Basalat (Star of Courage) in Pakistan. Having already scored a kill against a Folland Gnat lightweight fighter of the Indian Air Force during the 1965 Kashmir War, he became one of the few pilots to score kills while flying fighters of three different air forces. After the Indo-Pakistani War of 1971, as a born Bengali, Azam eventually donned the uniform of yet another air force when transferring to his new homeland, Bangladesh, where he still lives today.

19 Shurdom, interview with Patricia Salti, May 2007. Ihsan Shurdom continued a successful career with the RJAF, eventually reaching the rank of major general and the position of Chief of Staff RJAF. He is still living in Jordan.

20 According to the IrAF post-mission report, as cited by Sadik during an interview in March 2007, and Mohsen, interview with Group 73, October 2010.

21 According to Sadik, Capts Dror and Glantz-Golan were transferred to the Iraqi Military Intelligence HQ, in Baghdad, immediately after their capture. Separated from each other, they were interrogated by an Iraqi Hebrew linguist. Dror refused to cooperate, while Glantz-Golan explained 'quite a lot' about his training, 'for a year and a half on models that were exact replicas of the objectives they would have to attack', about the results of Iraqi attacks on Kfar-Sirkin and Ramat David, and about the first two Israeli attacks on H-3. Furthermore, both Israelis had with them small books with detailed intelligence on all the major air bases in Egypt, Jordan and Syria, and showing all the routes used by their units to attack these. Notably, in the course of the same PoW exchange when Dror and Glantz-Golan were returned to Israel, Israel returned the bodies of the IrAF Tu-16 crew killed when their aircraft was shot down near Megiddo on the morning of 6 June.

SYRIA ALONE

The Syrian response to Nasser's calls for activation of the UAC, and to Lt Gen Riyadh's visit (see Chapter 3) was somewhat reserved. Damascus openly expressed its unhappiness at the Egyptian-Jordanian Mutual Defence Treaty and not only maintained its propaganda attacks on the Jordanian government, but also refused to send even a liaison officer to Amman. For all practical purposes, the Syrian military and political leadership isolated the country from the UAC, resulting in the Syrian Arab Republic Air Force (SyAAF) fighting this war entirely on its own. The reason for this situation was that Syria's top military – and by extension political – leadership was heavily factionalised.

Egyptian reports about the Israeli attack reached Damascus around the same time they reached Amman and Baghdad. Around 09.30 local time, the government and leading military commanders held a conference that resulted in a major dispute between leading figures – the result of a simmering power struggle between two cliques within the upper ranks of the Syrian military. The major protagonists of this struggle were the de facto Syrian strongman, Gen Salah Jadid, and Minister of Defence and Commander of the SyAAF, Maj Gen Hafez al-Assad. As the head of the government and Chief of Staff, Jadid was the most powerful figure in Syria, but his hard-line policies caused unrest and economical difficulties and coalesced many around al-Assad. Together with civilian members of the government, foremost President Nureddin al-Attasi, Jadid propagated calls for the destruction of Israel. It was mainly because of their bombastic public speeches that Syria lost any sympathy in the Western world. The forces on the Golan were under the command of Jadid's favourites, including Col Ahmad el-Myr, supervised by newly appointed Assistant Chief of Staff Army, Lt Gen Ahmad Suweidany.

Al-Assad took no part in this battle talk favoured by Jadid and al-Attasi, but also took no actions to prevent or at least mitigate their words. Instead, he waited for them to embarrass themselves. Simultaneously, al-Assad was concerned about a possible coup attempt supported from abroad, since his Intelligence reported the activity of a Druze officer in Jordan, Salim Hatum, who was reported as preparing a new coup attempt.[1]

While preparing for his actions, al-Assad could foremost count on support from lower-ranking officers, a few of whom – such as his Assistant Commander of the SyAAF, Brig Gen Mohammad Assad Moukiiad – were well-trained professionals, but most of whom lacked the necessary military education and field experience.[2]

Extensive factionalism made all decision-making processes particularly problematic, and the meeting in Damascus on the morning of 5 June brought the worst of this

The 'true strongman' in the Syria of the mid-1960s was Gen Salah Jadid. Together with President Nureddin al-Attasi, his calls for Israel's destruction resulted in Syria losing any sympathy in the Western world. (Nour Bardai Collection)

to the fore. Al-Assad suggested Syria attack before Israel could launch an invasion on its own. However, Suweidany – supported by President al-Atassi and el-Myr – suggested striking Israel via Lebanon in order to lessen the danger of a counterattack on Syrian territory. Corresponding telephone calls were made to Beirut but the Lebanese proved resistant to the idea. After nearly two hours of fruitless discussions, Jadid one-sidedly issued the order to launch Operation Nasr at 05.45 on the morning of 6 June.

The original plan for Operation Nasr envisaged brigade-sized attacks to the north and south of the Sea of Galilee, followed by a major advance on Haifa. However, al-Assad opposed this idea and effectively sabotaged this plan, firstly by banning the SyAAF and elite Army units from participating and then issuing countermanding orders to his favourites on the Golan.[3]

The situation changed only very slowly towards noon, apparently in response to requests from Cairo and Amman. What exactly prompted al-Assad to change his opinion remains unknown, but he eventually permitted the SyAAF to launch limited attacks on Israel, deploying only the aircraft and pilots that were ready. This decision could not have had more adverse effects. Such an operation was sufficient to allow Israel to claim that Syria 'attacked first', and then prepare its long-sought 'revenge' while dealing with Egypt and Jordan at its own convenience. Syria, the loudest enemy of Israel and the centrepiece of the original crisis that led to the June 1967 War, thus failed to become involved in this conflict while there was still time to make an impact. However, even if the SyAAF had launched attacks in the morning, poor intelligence would have rendered the result of such missions highly questionable.

Expecting Victory

As of 5 June 1967, only the Syrian Army was mobilised and ready for action. It included a total of four infantry brigades – each reinforced by one armoured battalion – and these were well entrenched along the armistice lines with Israel. One armoured and six infantry brigades held the second line of defence. Encamped near Qunaitra, together with the bulk of artillery, engineers, observers and a single SyAAF AAA regiment, were two additional infantry brigades. Even further to the rear, one armoured and seven infantry brigades were held in readiness to launch a counterattack in response to any Israeli penetration.[4]

The SyAAF was neither mobilised nor put on alert. Its commanders felt that their four Il-28Rs and a small fleet of MiG-17s were insufficient and ill-equipped to fly close air support for the Army, and the Air Force had no clear idea of how to deploy its assets for attacks on Israel. Furthermore, al-Assad's power pretensions dictated that the Air Force be conserved and held back for home defence.

Contrary to the usual Western reports, the SyAAF suffered no shortage of pilots. It had 115 fully qualified pilots provided with fewer than 100 operational aircraft – roughly the same aircraft-to-crew ratio as the IDF/AF. The three squadrons of Air Brigade 3 that operated MiG-21s possessed 42 aircraft (34 operational) and 47 pilots, Air Brigade 7 had two squadrons with 33 MiG-17Fs (all operational) and 32 pilots, and an independent unit operated four Il-28R reconnaissance-bombers. Except for its combat aircraft, the SyAAF also operated seven AAA regiments, six for the protection of major air bases and one deployed in the Qunaitra area, where it was to play a very prominent role.

These were powerful formations, each of which included three batteries of four 61-K (M1939) AA guns of 37mm calibre and three batteries of four S-60 AA guns of 57mm calibre.[5] As of 5 June, the SyAAF was organised and deployed as follows:

Table 3: SyAAF order of battle, 5 June 1967

Unit	Base	Equipment	Remarks
HQ Damascus C-in-C Maj Gen Hafez al-Assad Assistant C-in-C Brig Gen Mohammad Assad Moukiiad			
Air Brigade 3	Dmeyr		CO Brig Gen Muwafak al-Assasa; operated total of 42 MiG-21s (34 operational) flown by 47 pilots
No. 5 Squadron	Dmeyr	MiG-21F-13	CO Lt Col Abdul Razzak
AAA Regiment ??	Dmeyr	37mm and 57mm AAA	CO unknown
No. 9 Squadron	T.4/Tiyas	MiG-21F-13	CO Lt Col Naseh Khalid al-Olwany
AAA Regiment ??	T.4/Tiyas	37mm and 57mm AAA	CO unknown
No. 67 Squadron	Tsaykal	MiG-21FL	CO Lt Col Khalid Marwan Zain ed-Dien
AAA Regiment 42	Tsaykal	37mm and 57mm AAA	CO unknown
Air Brigade 7	Almazza		CO Lt Col Fayez Mansour; operated total of 33 MiG-17Fs (all operational) flown by 32 pilots
No. 3 Squadron	Almazza	MiG-17F	CO unknown
AAA Regiment 725	Almazza	37mm and 57mm AAA	CO Col Duqaq al-Emad
No. 8 Squadron?	Bley	MiG-17F	CO unknown
AAA Regiment ??	Bley	37mm and 57mm AAA	CO unknown
Air Force Academy			
Elementary Flying School	Minakh	Chipmunk, 10 Yak-11	Unknown number of Chipmunks operational until late 1960s
Basic Flying School	Minakh	10 Yak-18	Some Spitfires possibly still in use as advanced trainers
Advanced Flying School	Minakh	L-29, MiG-15UTI	First of eventual 78 L-29s delivered 1965
AAA Regiment ??	Minakh	37mm and 57mm AAA	
Balance of SyAAF			
No. 19 Squadron	T.4/Tiyas	4 Il-28	CO unknown; only two aircraft operational
No. 22 Squadron	Almazza	6 C-47, 6 Il-14	CO unknown
No. 18 Squadron	Almazza	4 Mi-1, 10 Mi-4	
AAA Regiment ??	Nayrab/ Aleppo	37mm and 57mm AAA	

| AAA Regiment ?? | Hama | 37mm and 57mm AAA |
| AAA Regiment ?? | Qunaitra | 37mm and 57mm AAA |

The morale of this force was very high, and not shaken by the loss of four MiG-21s to the Israelis in April 1967: the Syrians claimed five kills during that incident and thus considered themselves victorious. Many of their pilots possessed combat experience from earlier skirmishes with the IDF/AF and, together with their superiors, they were convinced they had consistently made considerable progress towards efficiency. In fact, although most had no clear idea why, Syria at large was convinced of a certain victory against Israel.

Despite improved readiness and eagerness for combat, due to both Syrian command shortcomings and poor Soviet advice, the relatively strong and compact SyAAF was left to remain vulnerable to an Israeli attack. No measures are known to have been introduced to reduce the exposure of aircraft parked on its air bases, even though a significant number of decoys – usually in the form of aircraft withdrawn from service – were positioned and air defences deployed. However, crucial for preventing the SyAAF from experiencing the same fate as the RJAF was the development of plans for the dispersion of all fighter assets to airfields in the north of the country, apparently devised during early June 1967.[6]

Photographs of early Syrian MiG-21s remain incredibly scarce. This still from a video shows a MiG-21F-13 passing low over the photographer – apparently for display purposes. Flying low was still an activity that neither Syrian squadron commanders nor their Soviet advisers approved of. (David Nicolle Collection)

MiG-21s at T.4

During the night to 6 June, the SyAAF Central Headquarters decided to regroup and concentrate its remaining MiG-21s in Aleppo, before returning them to air bases in central Syria for further action. Yasser Ajami recalled:

'The attack on the control tower at Tsaykal interrupted our communications with the Central HQ SyAAF in Damascus. It took several hours until some contact was possible again. Our squadron mates in Dmeyr had learned about the attack on Tsaykal by then and thought I was dead. In the evening, full communications had been re-established and our commander in Dmeyr ordered all pilots to return from Tsaykal. Seven or eight of us crammed into one car for that journey. When we arrived at Dmeyr, around 01.00 on the morning of 6 June, we reported to the command centre. I was welcomed with delight because I had been feared dead. Our commander then told us we should take a short break. Additional aircraft would be prepared by the morning and I was to fly one of these to Aleppo.

'I was the first to take off, so I did all the pre-flight checks and found the plane OK. I took off at dawn, around 04.00, using one of the taxiways because the works on repairing the main runway were still going on. While on the taxiway, all the time I kept a wary eye for possible Israeli aircraft above: the enemy was still active over Syria.

'I flew to Aleppo at 'zero' feet. This made me feel uncomfortable because we usually preferred to have plenty of space around us, including below. I reached Aleppo International – the airfield used by the military but also by civilians, not Minakh AB, the base of the SyAAF Academy – without problems.'

This stylised photograph shows Lt Col Naseh Khalid al-Olwany, KIA when his MiG-21F-13 rolled off the runway at Tiyas and exploded on the afternoon of 6 June 1967.
(Courtesy al-Olwany Family)

The SyAAF thus spent the rest of the morning far away from the combat zone, and evacuating additional aircraft to northern airfields. Later in the day, it began returning pairs of MiG-21s to Tiyas. It was in the course of one of such flight that it suffered what was perhaps the most damaging loss of the entire June 1967 War. The MiG-21F-13 piloted by Lt Col Naseh Khalid al-Olwany rolled off the runway at Tiyas, turned upside down and exploded, killing the pilot. Al-Olwany, one of very few highly qualified and popular COs within the SyAAF at that time, was posthumously awarded the Medal of Hero of the Syrian Arab Republic for courage and dedication shown during the battles of 5 June 1967.[26]

Elsewhere, the Syrian Army did launch its 'offensive' over the Jordan River and 'into' Israel, early on the morning of 6 June, but deployed only two battalions for this purpose. Both attacks proved entirely useless and only exposed the involved units to fierce Israeli artillery and air attacks, which caused heavy losses. In fact, the II Battalion of the 4th Infantry Brigade, which was the first to attack, later report to have been under attack by the IDF/AF for 14 hours without interruption.

With the SyAAF away from the battlefield, it was left to the elements of its sole AAA regiment deployed near Qunaitra, as well as Army anti-aircraft units, to provide air defence over the front lines. In the course of the day, these claimed seven Israeli aircraft as shot down. The Israelis confirmed only one loss plus three of their fighters damaged by Syrian AAA, nearly all while attacking targets in the B'not Yacov Bridge area.

During the morning of 7 June, the SyAAF continued transferring additional MiG-21s to Tiyas, as recalled by Ajami:

'On my second day at Aleppo AB, I was ordered to take my aircraft to T.4 air base. Four other pilots had already flown their MiG-21s to T.4 the day before. We were to stay there for four days ...'

The intensity of Israeli air attacks on Syrian Army positions on the Golan Heights increased by a magnitude during that day, prompting officials in Damascus to claim again that *'British combat aircraft are flying with the Israelis and bombing many targets on the Golan'.*[27] Syrian ground defences reacted in force, claiming a number of kills, but the IDF/AF is only known to have suffered one loss during the day (the pilot being recovered safely). Eventually, calls for help from Army units resulted in the SyAAF launching a number of CAPs out of Tiyas. Around 16.00, a pair of MiG-21FLs under way near Damascus, piloted by Capt Mohammad Mansour and 1st Lt Mohammed Osama Mohammed Ameen Bayrouty, was informed by the GCI about the appearance of Israeli aircraft over as-Suwayda, a town in southern Syria. Mansour and Bayrouty requested an intercept vector and approached the Israeli formation from below before attacking with R-3S missiles. According to official Syrian releases, they should have shot down no fewer than three IDF/AF fighter-bombers, which crashed between al-Sheikh Maskin and Nawa, some 25km (15.5 miles) north of Dera'a. According to Israeli sources, there was only a pair of Mirages led by Ezra Dothan on the scene, and these were returning from a search for IDF/AF crews shot down during the frustrated third attack on H-3 airfield in Iraq. Only Dotan's Mirage IIICJ (serial number 29) was damaged, but the pilot managed to nurse it back for an emergency landing in Megiddo.[28]

According to official IDF accounts, this photograph shows the damage suffered by a Mirage IIICJ when hit by one of the R-3S missiles fired by Capt Mohammad Mansour during the afternoon of 7 June 1967. (IDF)

While other MiGs from Tiyas flew uneventful CAPs over Dmeyr, later the same evening two MiG-21FLs were scrambled to intercept a formation including one Noratlas transport and three helicopters that was searching for crews of other IDF/AF fighter bombers shot down over H-3 airfield, as described above. Inexperienced in night-time operations, the Syrians did manage to find the Noratlas and fire at least two R-3S at it, but the Israeli crew apparently evaded both missiles. According to Ajami, it was in response to these operations that on 8 June the IDF/AF returned to bomb the runway at Tiyas. In order to keep the enemy under the impression that this important air base was non-operational, this time the SyAAF decided not to repair the damage: for the rest of the war, the MiG-21s stationed there operated from the taxiway.

No SyAAF MiG-21s are known to have flown operations over the Golan on 8 June. Except for an attack on Tiyas, another likely reason for this was bad weather, which also prevented the IDF from launching its planned invasion of the Golan Heights the same day. In comparison, the IDF/AF continued bombing Syrian Army positions throughout the day, prompting the Syrian air defences to claim no fewer than 29 'Israeli and British aircraft' as shot down.[29]

Onslaught on Syria

Early in the morning of 9 June 1967, Damascus accepted the ceasefire with Israel. However, eager to 'punish' Syria, and bowing to severe pressure from the IDF leadership and Israeli settlers, Israel's military eventually launched its attack at the very time the war was supposed to be over. This attack was launched in the light of reports about continued shelling of settlements in northern Galilee, and in spite of possible repercussions for Israel's relations with the USSR – including a potential Soviet military intervention.

Beginning at 09.40, IDF/AF fighter-bombers returned to pound Syrian positions on the Golan Heights – some of them using Sakr rockets captured at Egyptian air bases in Sinai. Col Ahmad el-Myr later reported 163 Israeli sorties within the first three hours of this attack, killing 52 and injuring 163 of his soldiers. The major impact of the Israeli aerial onslaught was psychological: the SyAAF was nowhere to be seen, and under severe pressure from the IDF/AF at least two brigade commanders refused to move their units forward in order to reinforce front-line positions. Furthermore, in expectation of the ceasefire, Suweydani ordered his units to avoid shelling Israel.

A ground offensive followed soon afterwards. Taking the Syrians by surprise, the Israelis first assaulted Syrian positions near Kfar Szold, in the northern Golan. Struggling uphill along narrow paths that permitted no manoeuvre, and in the face of intense Syrian fire and mines, the Israelis advanced slowly, suffering extensive losses in the process. Despite the shock and confusion caused by fierce Syrian resistance, they crushed one fortification after the other before reaching the most accessible road to Qunaitra. Throughout, the IDF/AF continued to pound Syrian positions, and proved effective in knocking out several tank units that had been rushed in to support forward strongpoints held by reservists. Under such pressure, an increasing number of units led by Ba'athist officers refused to follow Suweidany's orders.[30]

Syrian air defence units once again attempted to provide protection against vicious IDF/AF attacks. Before long many of them were forced to level their guns and fight the

The scene of a typically vicious Israeli air attack on a forward Syrian position on the Golan Heights. (IDF)

Israeli ground units as well. Furthermore, after four days of incessant air attacks, many units had been left without food, water and fuel, and began running out of ammunition.

Recognising the seriousness of the situation, the SyAAF began launching ever more MiG-21s into the skies over the battlefield, and its pilots claimed a number of kills, including 'two Israeli bombers' in an air combat over northern Golan around 10.10, and another 'Israeli bomber over the eastern side of Jabel Sheikh' around 11.00 local time. In return, a pair of MiG-21s was intercepted while approaching the battle zone in the early afternoon and Yasser Ajami's friend Rifaat was shot down in an air combat with four Mirages. The pilot ejected safely over Syrian positions and returned to his unit the next day. The IDF/AF is known to have lost three fighters and three pilots over Syria on 9 June. These included one Magister, one Ouragan and the Super Mystère B2 flown by Col Shlomo Bet-On. The Israelis insist that ground defences shot down all three.[31]

Fall of the Golan

The Israeli attack into Syria continued through the morning of 10 June 1967, and now despite vague Soviet threats against Israel. While there are indications that the Soviet military did make at least a few preparations for a possible intervention on a limited scale, the Soviets actually neglected their concern that had initiated the whole crisis – the purported Israeli threat to 'overthrow the progressive Syrian government'. Not only did Moscow commit a number of severe diplomatic mistakes, but it also failed to follow up its threats with action. In fact, as of 10 June, Soviet policy turned from indirect involvement on the Arab side to political support from the sidelines. For all practical purposes, the USSR was now submissively betraying its Arab allies. That said, it is

Another film still shows a SyAAF MiG-21F-13 passing at low level. The aircraft appears to have been armed with UB-16-57 rocket pods for the occasion – a weapon mainly used for air-to-ground purposes, but also with a secondary air-to-air role. Whether the SyAAF MiG-21s flew any air-to-ground attacks during the June 1967 War with Israel remains unknown, but there is little doubt that they inflicted a number of painful losses on Israeli fighters.
(David Nicolle Collection)

doubtful whether Moscow could have done anything meaningful in support of Egypt or Syria – short of provoking a nuclear exchange with the US and thus triggering World War III. As of 1967, the Soviet Union possessed no large air-mobile or amphibious units with the required mobility, nor transportation facilities capable of putting these into action within the required time anywhere in the Middle East. Sure enough, the Soviet Navy deployed no fewer than 70 naval vessels in the eastern Mediterranean during the following days, but these had limited amphibious-landing and even less conventional war-fighting capabilities. Therefore, Moscow's threat of a military intervention was rather a gratuitous gesture aimed at regaining Arab political support.

On the contrary, precisely because of these Soviet military deficiencies, the administration of President Johnson felt free not only to continue providing nearly whole-hearted political support for Israel, but also to deploy warships of the US Sixth Fleet less than 150km (93 miles) off the Syrian coast, as a counterweight to Soviet Navy vessels gathering in the area. More significantly, Israel felt free to once again ignore its own word. Instead of respecting the ceasefire, the IDF ground units accelerated their advance, launching a full-scale attack into the Golan.

The IDF/AF ranged all over the Golan Heights, attacking the Syrian positions that were still holding out, but missing a large column carrying officers who were members of the Ba'ath Party, and who had begun abandoning their units. The final blow was delivered by an announcement from al-Assad, aired by Radio Damascus around 09.30, stating that the Israelis had captured Qunaitra. At the time, the Israelis were still kilometres away from this town and thus this report caused much confusion and uncertainty within the military, which was already weakened by Ba'athist defections. Subsequently, the majority of Army units fell back in the direction of Damascus, some completely disintegrating in the process.[32]

Only hours later, when the commanders that remained with their units reported that Qunaitra was still under their control, was the SyAAF scrambled in an attempt to provide assistance to the remaining Army formations. The MiG-21s from Tiyas were to fly more than 30 sorties that afternoon, mainly CAPs but also several attacks on advancing Israeli ground units. The first formation to approach the Golan Heights included MiG-21F-13s piloted by Lt Col Abdul Razzak and Lt Rafik Shorbaji. They later reported to have '*intercepted a group of Israeli Super Mystères*', engaged them in an air combat that '*lasted 10 minutes*' and shot one down. When the Army reported that Israeli helicopters were searching for their downed pilots, the SyAAF GCI vectored two pairs of MiG-21s in that direction. The first two MiG-21s attacked the helicopter carrying Gen David Elazar, CO of the IDF Northern Command, and forced it to dive sharply through a ravine towards Kibbutz Ein Gev, near Lake Tiberias. Minutes later, a MiG-21 from the second pair, flown by 1st Lt Sayd Younis, was shot down near Qunaitra. The pilot ejected safely and joined the SyAAF AAA regiment deployed nearby. Later in the afternoon, the unit claimed one IDF/AF fighter-bomber shot down, and attempted to capture its pilot, but the Israeli fired back and was killed in the ensuing firefight. Younis and most of the airmen from the unit he joined also fell while attempting to stop one of the final Israeli attacks that afternoon.

According to Syrian sources, the final SyAAF loss of the war was the MiG-21 flown by 1st Lt Bayrouty, shot down in the course of an air battle with 'several Mirages' over Khan Arnabeh (then a village 5km/3.1 miles east of Qunaitra), shortly before the final ceasefire came into effect, around 18.00.[33]

1   Salim Hatum already attempted one coup, in September 1966, but had to flee to Jordan, see *Volume 1*, p153. He returned to Damascus after hearing about the outbreak of the war on 5 June 1967, was immediately arrested and sentenced to death. The verdict was enforced on 26 June 1967, see Konzelmann, *Damaskus*, pp286–287.

2   A typical example of al-Assad's men was 1st Lt Habash, an elementary teacher and reservist officer. Badly under-qualified for the job, he was appointed Chief Intelligence Officer to el-Myr on 8 March 1967, and thus found himself in charge of a major post while lacking the skills necessary to complete his job. However, Habash was in a perfect position to follow el-Myr's work and report to al-Assad.

3   Mustafa, *The Fall of the Golan*, Chapter 3, and Konzelmann, *Damaskus*, pp277–278. Mustafa further mentioned that on 28 May 1967, Syrian Maj Gen Adel Sheikh Amin and the Iraqi Brig Gen Mahmoud Araim signed a memorandum concerning coordination of their military operations. While Mustafa did not mention any deployments of the Iraqi military inside Syria, or any possible plans for a joint Iraqi-Syrian offensive into Israel, it is quite obvious that subsequent developments quickly made all such decisions surplus.

4   Ibid., Chapters 1–3. Revealing entirely different unit designations than usually reported in Israeli and Western publications, Mustafa described the deployment of the Syrian Army on the Golan in June 1967 as follows: the 1st Line was held by (from north to south) the 6th, 2nd, 4th and 15th Infantry Brigades. The 2nd Line was held by the 11th and 19th Infantry as well as the 8th Armoured Brigade in the north, the 13th and 43rd Brigades in the centre and the 32nd in the south. The 80th and 123rd Reserve Infantry Brigades were concentrated in the Qunaitra area. The counterattack force, positioned further to the rear, consisted of the 18th, 19th (renamed as the 122nd Brigade during the war), 43rd, 70th, 72nd and the 90th Infantry Brigades (all Motorised), together with the 70th Reserve Brigade.

5   Moukiiad, *Autobiography*, pp141–154; Mustafa, *The Fall of the Golan*, Chapter 4 (these two sources provided most of the background for this sub-chapter); veteran SyAAF MiG-21 pilot from the time, the name of whom

has been withheld by the authors for reasons of his own safety and that of his family (for additional details provided by the same source, see *Volume 2*, pp167–170), and Yasser Ajami, interview, November 2006; for details about earlier career of Yasser Ajami see *Volumes 1 and 2*.

6   While Moukiiad provides circumstantial evidence for it, no other published source explicitly mentions such a plan: instead, this conclusion is based on interviews with several participants and eyewitnesses. These suggested that several days before the war, strict instructions were issued regarding how and where to evacuate what aircraft in the case of receiving a specific order. This leads to the conclusion that Brig Gen Moukiiad – the 'technocrat' within the SyAAF – developed a corresponding plan in advance. He could do so only on orders from al-Assad, who subsequently became renowned for doing his best to conserve the assets of his own service, the SyAAF, regardless of the circumstances and often despite dramatic repercussions for Syria. Indirectly, this is one of the reasons why ever since the outbreak of unrest and uprising in Syria in March 2011, the entire al-Assad family has been blamed by its opponents for having 'sold' the Golan Heights to Israel.

7   Even such Israeli sources as the *Israeli Military Encyclopaedia* (Arab translation), (Baghdad, 1988) and *Like a Bolt Out of the Blue*, pp478–491, differ over the results of the SyAAF attack on Megiddo. Similarly, although the MiG-17F claimed as shot down over Megiddo supposedly crashed well inside Israel, the IDF never released photographs of its wreckage or any details about its pilot.

8   Mustafa, *The Fall of the Golan*, pp96–100, and *The History of the Syrian Army*, Chapter 9; Hussein was born in Lattakia in 1941.

9   *Like a Bolt Out of the Blue*, pp478–491.

10   'As the News Broke', *Jerusalem Post* (English edition), 6 June 1967, and *The History of the Syrian Army*, Chapter 9.

11   According to *Like a Bolt Out of the Blue* (pp478-491), in response to Iraqi, Jordanian and Syrian air raids, by 15.00 local time, no fewer than nine pairs of Mirages – a total of 18 interceptors – were airborne over northern Israel, most of them from No. 117 Squadron, but a few also from No. 101 Squadron.

12   For details about this MiG-17F, see *Volume 2*, p41. Convinced that Hussein shot down his opponent, the Syrian Ministry of Defence posthumously decorated this pilot with the Hero of the Syrian Arab Republic Medal for courage (this decoration is equivalent to the Hero of the Soviet Union or British Victoria Cross). Also highly decorated for their success were Lt Col Fayez Mansour and Lt Col Naseh Khalid al-Olwany (he led the four MiG-21s that provided top cover for Mansour's formation), see *The History of the Syrian Army*, Chapter 9 and *Arab MiGs Volume 2*, p41.

13   *Volume 1*, pp179–180, and Mustafa, *The Fall of the Golan*, pp96–100.

14   This was the MiG-21 flown by Capt Adnan Ahmad Hussein, mentioned above.

15   Moukiiad, *Autobiography*, pp141–154, and Mustafa, *The Fall of the Golan*, pp96–100; according to Mustafa, Weiland was subsequently shown on Syrian National TV where he said that his target was Dmeyr and that he came from a base where '17 British bombers' were based to 'fight against the Arabs'. Notable is that from this period onwards and until spring 1970, practically every Israeli aircraft claimed shot down in Syrian media releases was described as a 'Mirage'. Nevertheless, when Adeeb al-Gar was decorated for his achievements following the October 1973 War with Israel, his official citation included credit for a 'Phantom' shot down on 5 June 1967 – at the time the IDF/AF was nearly three years away from operating any US-made F-4 Phantom IIs.

16   For details about these two related, and by that time highly experienced pilots see *Volume 1*, p96 and p100.

17   Nordeen, *Fighters over Israel*, pp68–70, and *The History of the Syrian Army*, Chapter 9; Khalid Marwan Zain ed-Dien and Ibrahim Saleem Zain ed-Dien were posthumously decorated with the Hero of the Syrian Arab Republic Medal.

18   AAA Regiment 725 claimed a total of no fewer than six 'enemy Mirages' on 5 June 1967, and its CO Col Duqaq al-Emad was subsequently highly decorated for his achievements.

19   See *Volume 1*, pp178–179.

20 Vatche Mitilian, *The Independent Guide To The Lebanese Air Force* website available at http://lebaneseair-force.info/index.htm, extracted in July 2010. This claim is based on an official FAL release from November 2008, which summarised the service history of the Hunter in Lebanon and included the observation that FAL Hunters shot down an Israeli Mystère. After being contacted by the authors, Mr Mitilian is attempting to gain access to the official FAL archives in order to retrieve additional details. Should any of these become available, they will be reported accordingly in future volumes.

21 According to available Lebanese accounts, and contrary to the usual Israeli explanations, no FAL Hunters attempted 'to have a look' at the fighting between Israel and Syria, nor did they enter airspace over northern Israel. Instead, the Israelis apparently directed their Mirages to attack FAL Hunters over Lebanon in order to extract revenge for the Lebanese shooting down one of their fighters while this was under way within Lebanese airspace. Vatche Mitilian, interview, July 2010.

22 *The History of the Syrian Army*, Chapter 9, and a veteran SyAAF MiG-21 pilot from the time, the name of whom has been withheld by the authors for reasons of his own safety and that of his family (for additional details provided by the same source, see *Volume 2*, pp167–170).

23 Aloni, *The June 1967 Six-Day War*, pp163–164.

24 Within the ranks of the SyAAF there is still a the legend circulating that Ghazy Abdulkader Wazwazy shot down Sigiri by 'ramming' his fighter into the Israeli aircraft. *The History of the Syrian Army* reveals the official position, as presented in *Volume 1*, p152.

25 Moukiiad, *Autobiography*.

26 *The History of the Syrian Army*, Chapter 9.

27 Mustafa, *The Fall of the Golan*, p167.

28 This negative experience seems to have led to renewed fierce discussions between SyAAF MiG pilots and their Soviet advisers. The latter first accused the pilots of deploying their missiles in the incorrect manner, firing too early and from too great a range. When Mansour and his wingman explained they fired at a range of 1200m (0.75 miles) from their non-manoeuvring targets, and while under way at a speed of Mach 1 – i.e. at targets that were nearly in the centre centre of the R-3S envelope – the Soviets changed their standpoint and began blaming Syrian ground crews for poor handling of the missiles. However, the Syrians possessed the knowledge required for proper handling, appropriate maintenance and safekeeping of these missiles in order for them to function properly. Like the Iraqis before them, by 1967 they had obtained copies of manuals such as *MiG-21F-13/MiG-21PF Aerial Tactics*, which emphasised that the effectiveness of an R-3S attack depended not only on 'accuracy of guiding the missile to the target, conditions of rocket-target encounter, zones of activation of the proximity fuse, type of the target and nature of its mobility', but also on the 'reliability of rocket apparatus and control system under tactical conditions' (see *Fishbed C/E Aerial Tactics*, p70). Still, it took the Syrians two more years to convince the Soviets of the need for a new, more reliable and capable variant of this weapon. Even so, the SyAAF was not to receive any more advanced model of Atoll AAM before summer 1973.

29 Among precise claims published by Syria on this day are the following examples: 'three Israeli aircraft over northern Golan, around 09.50, and one around 10.55'; 'one Israeli aircraft' shot down over Degania, around 11.45, 'three Israeli aircraft' shot down over al-Khalisa, Kfar Shirin and Nawot Nardachai, around 14.30, 'one Canberra and one Vautour' shot down over the northern Galilee around 15.00; 'one Israeli aircraft' over central Golan, around 16.50; 'two Israeli aircraft west of Ain Rif', around 17.20, and 'one Ouragan and one Mystère' supposedly shot down 'west of al-Qalla', around 17.45.

30 Mustafa, *The Fall of the Golan*, pp189–190; Mustafa cited the example of the CO 70th Brigade who disobeyed Suweidany's and then Jadid's direct orders, instead contacting al-Assad via telephone to inform him about his 'concerns'. Given the above-mentioned examples of Israeli cable-tapping operations, it is certain that this telephone call provided a true 'treasure trove' to the Israeli military intelligence.

31 Mustafa, *The Fall of the Golan*, p189-190; according to various Israeli publications, Bet-On attempted to nurse his badly damaged aircraft back to Ramat David, but crashed near Kibbutz Lahavot-Habashan.

32 Ibid. Mustafa further explained that the same column looted the gold reserves of the Syrian National Bank before continuing for Homs, but also bitterly complained that the units that received the most intensive training from Soviet advisors were the first to disintegrate in the face of Israeli attacks.

33 Oren, *Six Days of War*, p303; Mustafa, *The Fall of the Golan*, pp109–110; *The History of the Syrian Army*, Chapter 9; Bayrouty was posthumously decorated with the Hero of the Syrian Arab Republic Medal.

Chapter 7

REPERCUSSIONS

To say that the Arabs – or those that were aware of the extent of the catastrophe that befell their militaries – were stunned by defeat and gripped by shock, humiliation and anger following the June 1967 War is an understatement. The defeat of June 1967 was a shattering experience with far-reaching consequences for nearly all those in the Middle East. Despite efforts to explain it away, or refer to it as a mere 'setback', the reality of the defeat hit hard. Whereas the wars of 1948 and 1956 affected only some portions of the Arab nations, and then mainly the military, the defeat of 1967 affected all Arabs – and continues to do so today. The impact delivered was such that the search for reasons has continued until now. Irrespective of considerable oppression by a number of local governments, a reason has never been found to fully explain the circumstances leading to the catastrophe. With hindsight, it must be observed that the June 1967 War also marked the beginning of the most recent Muslim revival period, as many Arabs – unwilling or incapable of accepting Israeli military superiority – saw the defeat as 'God's retribution for their straying from the proper Islamic path.'[1]

Statistics

For all the political turbulence following the June 1967 War, certain aspects of everyday life in the countries of the Middle East remained constant. The Arabs as a whole continued to be denied representation and thus only a very few of their – largely military – rulers felt a need to account for their actions. By that time, the widespread use of personal privileges and patronage tended to establish networks that developed into a coercive apparatus that served the purpose of keeping new governments in power. The people in general were excluded not only from decision-making processes, but also from obtaining information about the reasons for the defeat of June 1967, or indeed the political instability of their countries.

Unsurprisingly, it was under such circumstances that an almost countless number of groundless rumours of 'conspiracies' that led to the defeat in the war against Israel came into being. Most of these legends circulate in Arab public life until today. Provided the 'everyday' Arabs would have had the chance to seriously study the reasons for their defeat in June 1967 War, many of them – as well as the majority of Western observers – would certainly have been surprised. Namely, while there is no doubt that the conflict was foremost lost because of major mistakes by military leaders, and almost inexplicable intelligence flaws, the Arab air forces actually fared much better than usually assessed.

On the basis of available information, the following can be said about the activity of the UARAF during the June 1967 War. The Egyptians flew a total of at least 168 combat sorties in five days of fighting with Israel. This total might have been much higher, since the Su-7s of Air Group 7 are said to have flown a total of 32 combat sorties (see Tahsin Zaki's statement cited in Chapter 2), although only 12 of these are known in detail. Similarly, ex-Algerian MiG-21s might have flown at least four combat sorties, but precise details of this mission remain unknown. In terms of aircraft type, MiG-17s are known to have flown 49 combat sorties, MiG-19s 39, and MiG-21s at least 65, and possibly 69; Su-7s flew at least 12, and possibly up to 32 combat sorties, and Il-28s flew a total of six combat sorties against Israel.[2] Additionally, no fewer than 21 or 23 repositioning sorties were flown by various aircraft on 7 June 1967 (four of these resulted in combat action), with similar numbers in the days that followed.

The total number of UARAF pilots and ground personnel killed or injured in the course of the war remains unknown, but the available details indicate that the figure is far lower than assessed by various observers immediately after the conflict. On the basis of information currently available it appears that 33 Egyptian pilots sacrificed their lives for the freedom of their country, while losses of ground personnel were much heavier.

In the course of 168 known combat sorties, UARAF aircraft became involved in at least 35 separate engagements with Israeli interceptors and fighter-bombers, during which their pilots are known to have claimed at least 18 kills while suffering 31 losses – at most. These figures also include aircraft that crashed after running out of fuel due to combat damage, and transport aircraft. At least five additional aircraft were shot down by friendly air defences, while at least five (and likely more) crashed due to fuel starvation. On the basis of available Israeli documentation it is believed that at least eight of the Egyptian claims from the June 1967 War can be considered as 'confirmed', five of which were scored on the first day of the conflict.

Of course, the total number of aircraft the UARAF was forced to write off during the June 1967 War was much higher after all the aircraft destroyed on the ground were added. As presented in Table 4, based on official Egyptian documentation, between 5 June and 1 August 1967 the UARAF wrote off a total of 15 MiG-15bis and MiG-15UTIs, 44 MiG-17Fs and MiG-17PFs, 16 MiG-19s, 78 MiG-21s, 25 Su-7s, 34 Il-28s, 23 Tu-16s, 19 Il-14s, two An-12s, and 10 Mi-6s – for a grand total of 178 aircraft and helicopters. However, it must be emphasised that these figures include losses the UARAF suffered during the first series of post-war 'incidents' with Israel, on 14 and 15 July 1967.[3]

Certain similar conclusions are also possible in the case of the Iraqi, Jordanian and Syrian air arms. On the basis of available information, the RJAF is known to have flown at least three, and possibly seven offensive sorties on the morning of 5 June 1967, as well as either three or seven top-cover sorties. Jordanian Hunters claimed three enemy fighters shot down in air combat over Jordan, of which the Israelis confirmed one loss. In return, Israeli fighters shot down one Hunter, its pilot ejecting safely. Additionally, Jordanian pilots (and the sole Pakistani instructor seconded to the RJAF) flew around 20 CAPs over Iraq between 7 and 10 June, and their pilots claimed four kills (of which the Israelis confirmed three) without any losses while there. One RJAF pilot was killed on the ground, during the first Israeli attack on Mafraq air base.

The Iraqi Air Force launched a total of 18 offensive sorties (14 by Hunters and four by Tu-16s) during the June 1967 War. Only five of these reached their intended tar-

gets, three aircraft returned to base without taking part in the attacks, while the other aircraft are known to have engaged various alternative objectives. Only one Tu-16 was shot down over Israel. Defensive operations were much more intense, many of the IrAF pilots (and, later on, RJAF pilots) flying at least two, often three CAPs over H-3 between 5 and 9 June 1967. In the course of these operations, the IrAF suffered the loss of one Hunter that crashed on take-off and a second that was shot down by Israeli fighters. Both pilots of these aircraft were killed, while one Hunter pilot and one MiG-21 pilot were injured. Two transports (a Dove and an An-12), two Hunters and eight MiG-21FLs were destroyed on the ground. Notable is that this total loss of 14 aircraft stands in stark contrast to Israeli claims for 24 or 26, particularly when it comes to losses in air combat, where the Iraqi fighters shot down at least three Israeli aircraft in exchange for one fighter lost and two damaged.

Information from all Syrian sources available to date indicates that the SyAAF flew at least 116 combat sorties in six days during the June 1967 War. This figure includes at least 36 combat air patrols flown deep within Syria, which saw no engagements with the enemy. In terms of types, MiG-17s are known to have flown at least 20 combat sorties and MiG-21s at least 76 sorties that resulted in contact with the enemy. In the course of these, the SyAAF admitted losing seven pilots KIA, and at least three injured. SyAAF pilots – primarily those flying MiG-21s – engaged Israeli fighters in at least 17 air combats and claimed no fewer than 13 kills, at least seven of which (plus one damaged Mirage) have been confirmed by the Israelis (even though Israeli sources do not always agree as to the reason for their losses). In return, the Syrians are known to have lost seven MiG-21s. The Israelis also claimed several SyAAF MiG-17s as shot down, and credited their pilots with at least two kills against these, but the Syrians have never confirmed any such losses.

Claims and Reality

Nearly every air war fought to date has resulted in major discrepancies between the claims issued by the pilots involved, and the losses actually suffered by the various parties. However, it is very likely that there is no better example for exaggerated claims than in the case of the June 1967 War between the Arabs and Israel.

While it is obvious that not all the information concerning the losses of the various Arab air forces is available, and that many of the above-mentioned figures are far from being definitive, it is already possible to draw at least a few important conclusions. Foremost, there is a huge gap between the number of Arab aircraft claimed by the Israelis as destroyed on the ground in the course of their onslaught on various air bases, and the number of aircraft the Arabs officially confirmed as written off. For example, IDF/AF pilots claimed no fewer than 337 Egyptian aircraft as knocked out or shot down between 5 and 10 June 1967 alone, while the UARAF actually wrote off some 176 aircraft and helicopters during the entire war. Similarly, in the case of Syria, the Israelis claimed nearly half of the SyAAF as destroyed or shot down on 5 June 1967 alone, while the Syrians admitted only 12 of its losses on that day (including four MiG-21s in air combats).

Sure enough, the bulk of the Egyptian air arm – especially its offensive capability – was destroyed, while the SyAAF did suffer a number of losses and was largely rendered ineffective for the rest of conflict. For example, the entire fleet of Egyptian Tu-16 bombers, three quarters of Egyptian Il-28 light bombers (as well as two Syrian Il-28s) and all ready-to-use Egyptian Su-7 fighter-bombers were written off. Furthermore, the Egyptians never made a secret of the fact that UARAF technicians were busy repairing dozens of various combat aircraft for months following the war. It is very likely that something similar was the case in Syria as well. It is meanwhile certain that practically the entire Jordanian Hunter fleet was wiped out. However, as the Israelis often insist that 'damaged is not destroyed' when denying specific Arab claims, it is necessary to apply the same, 'conservative' rule to Arab air forces in order to keep any review of this air war balanced. This leads to the conclusion that the most likely reason for Israeli exaggerations in regard to the numbers of Arab aircraft claimed as destroyed on the ground was that while pilots might have hit and damaged many MiGs, Sukhois and Ilyushins, these aircraft were subsequently repaired and returned to service.

However, there is no such explanation when it comes to the results of air combats. From the details provided above, it is certain that original post-war Israeli claims that the IDF/AF shot down some 48-50 Arab aircraft – including 29 Egyptian and eight Syrian MiG-21s – in air combats for no loss were completely unrealistic.

The information that has since become available from Arab sources indicates a much more realistic 'score' of 31:8 in the Israelis' favour over Egypt, 1:1 over Jordan, 1:1 over Lebanon, 1:3 in favour of the Arabs over Iraq, and around 8:7 in the Israelis' favour over Syria, for an overall total of 42:20.

Undeniably, measured on the number of sorties they flew between 6 and 10 June 1967, the Egyptians and Syrians suffered relatively heavy losses. It is also certain that, measured on their frequency of success in air combats, the Israeli pilots were more likely to shoot down their opponents, provided they found any. This in turn confirms the Israelis' better training and preparedness, as well as the availability of weapons better suited to this type of combat. However, it is at least as obvious that the Israelis did their best to deny the losses they suffered in air combats with the Egyptian and Syrian, as well as the Iraqi air arms. It was only much later that the Israelis showed a readiness to admit that 'some' of their fighters had been shot down by Arab interceptors. Even then, Israel hurried to explain that all these aircraft had been, '...*surprised while engaged in ground attacks and therefore did not constitute air-to-air combat losses*'.[4] Indeed, it took nearly 35 years for most of the IDF/AF losses (actually) suffered in air combats to become fully known. Even today a number of these losses remain fiercely disputed. The Israelis continue to 'prefer' crediting the majority of their losses to Arab ground fire, apparently in an attempt to emphasise the superiority of their pilots compared to the Arabs. The authors found it hard to avoid the conclusion that such a standpoint is badly misleading as well as unfair towards the Arab pilots. After all, the IDF/AF was more than willing to proudly credit its own pilots with kills scored against Arab fighter-bombers. Ultimately, the above-mentioned figures lead unavoidably to the conclusion that plenty of air-to-air missiles and many thousands of 30mm rounds were expended by all the air forces involved – for far more meagre results than claimed by their pilots.

Having said that, it is undeniable that Operation Focus delivered a decisive blow upon Egypt, Jordan and Syria. The opening Israeli attack not only removed Egypt's offensive capability, but also caused crippling losses to the UARAF MiG-21 and MiG-17 units. This in turn not only rendered futile any attempts to fight for air superiority

over Sinai, but also caused shock and paralysis within the chain of command in Cairo. With the UARAF out of the way, the Egyptian commanders panicked themselves and their subordinates into a defeat within the first 24 hours of the war. With Egypt out of the way, Israel was free to deal with all other major opponents as and when this was judged suitable. In summary, not only the UARAF, but also the other Arab air forces were prevented from playing an important role in the fighting, and because of this Israel won the war.

Jolted Leaders

Egypt was the first to start rectifying its miserable conduct of diplomatic and military operations, and this effort began with a series of major reshuffles within the ranks of its military and political leaders. In the light of the catastrophe, President Gamal Abdel Nasser decided to resign. His announcement, broadcast live at 18.30 on the evening of 9 June 1967, is notable in that it cited Israel's intention to invade Syria, Nasser's decision to deploy the Army in Sinai, oust the UNEF and block the Tiran Straits, and also the pressure applied by both the US and the USSR that prevented Egypt from opening hostilities. Nasser's broadcast also renewed accusations of US and British collusion in the attack on Egypt. Minutes after Nasser's speech, the streets of Cairo and Alexandria filled with hundreds of thousands of people, demanding that Nasser remain. Whether impromptu or instigated by Nasser's sympathisers, as often claimed, this outpouring of popular support proved irresistible. The president withdrew his resignation, instead accepting the resignations of Amer, Badran and of virtually all his general staff. In fact, tensions between Nasser and FM Amer reached the point where the latter was arrested on 25 August 1967 for plotting a coup attempt.[5] The C-in-C UARAF, AM Mahmoud Sidki Mahmoud, his Deputy CO, AM Abdul Amin Hafiz, and a number of other top UARAF commanders (including Afifi, Daghedi and Ismail Labib), as well as Lt Gen Mortagi (former GOC of forces in the Sinai), and even Admiral Suleyman Izzat, Commander of the Navy, were dismissed, indicted, tried and jailed for misconduct.[6] Further dismissals and arrests of lower-ranking commanders and officers followed through autumn 1967, apparently with the aim of weeding out political suspects and strengthening support for Nasser, as much as to punish those who had failed in battle. Crucial positions were taken over by officers considered to be capable but not too politically astute, such as FM Mohammed Fawzy as the new C-in-C of the Armed Forces, Lt Gen Riyadh as the Chief of Staff of the Armed Forces, and – on 11 June 1967 – the retired Lt Gen Madkoor Abu al-Ezz as the new C-in-C UARAF.[7] Thus began the complex, massive and often troublesome effort that effectively resulted in the re-establishment of the Egyptian armed forces.

What also began was the period of Nasser's maturity: he virtually abandoned promotion of his Philosophy of Revolution and tried instead to further Egyptian neutralism while attempting to heal at least some of the rifts in the Arab world and taking up the cause of the Palestinians. In the days immediately after the June 1967 War, Nasser met a number of other Arab leaders, including the Tunisian president, President Atassi of Syria, President Boumedienne of Algeria, King Hussein of Jordan, President Arif of Iraq and President Ismail el-Azhari of Sudan. This round of meetings culminated in the Arab Summit in Khartoum, between 30 August and 3 September 1967, which resulted in the declaration that there would be no peace with Israel, no recognition of Israel and no negotiations until Israel had completely withdrawn from all occupied Arab territory. Furthermore, Arab leaders agreed to subsidise Egypt and Jordan for their losses in the June War, and consolidate Arab military strength, while Nasser quietly agreed to disengage from Yemen – in exchange for Saudi Arabia ending its financial and other support for the Royalists.

Elsewhere within the Arab world, the first reaction of most governments was to look for scapegoats. A number of these were found before too long: the United States and United Kingdom, to whom they then added Israel, a number of their own – particularly military – leaders, and the Soviet Union. Their anger and frustration at all these actors was openly expressed at every opportunity, with differing degrees of success.

At least initially, no process of political and military change was initiated in Syria, which during 1967 had experienced not only a sound military defeat, but also further internal political disorder and economic near-collapse. The loss of the Golan Heights and the resulting economic damage prompted widespread popular resentment against President Atassi and General Jadid. To the surprise of many, al-Assad and his sympathisers survived through keeping a low profile on the one side, but also demanding that Syria prepare more purposefully for war with Israel, establish closer relations with Iraq and generally aid inter-Arab cooperation. However, President Atassi then went on to suffer a series of diplomatic setbacks. In the course of meetings with Soviet leaders in Damascus and Moscow it became obvious that the USSR was not interested in renewing its economic, military and diplomatic sponsorship of Syria, and instead counselled restraint and caution. During the Khartoum conference, Atassi's stridently radical position and proposals that the war against Israeli be continued by means of a widespread popular uprising, guerrilla activities and sabotage were flatly rejected, and Syria was not allocated any portion of the relief funds granted to Egypt and Jordan.

Jordan suffered the most significant losses during the war, including not only the entire West Bank with its approximately 700,000 inhabitants, the best farmland, and a number of important cities, but also most of the equipment of its Army and Air Force. For the time being, King Hussein thus found himself in a seemingly impossible position. Eventually, he and his country were saved by extensive financial aid from other Arab states, and also from the US – though not without much political unrest and a near civil war, as will be described in future volumes.

It was only in Iraq that the government of President Arif – which relied on a variety of factions in the officer corps – did not experience any problems directly related to the Arab defeat. The country broke off relations with the US and the UK, and closer links were established both with the USSR and France. However, the speed and scale of the Israeli victory prevented more than a token Iraqi participation, and, lacking borders to Israel, Iraq was no front-line state. Furthermore, politicians in Baghdad remained preoccupied by the military's inability to defeat the Kurdish uprising. Rather than the June 1967 War, it was the unrest provoked by the communists in the south and the clear military weakness in Kurdistan that threw into question the credibility of the successive military regimes that had ruled the country since 1958.

Eventually, even those Arab leaders that would never publically admit so did at least recognise the reasons for the humiliation and began to face up to the task of analysing the underlying factors. They understood that Israeli strength was real and they could not trifle with the Jewish state, and that the military defeat was caused by

a general misconduct of operations, and a lack of sufficient Arab planning and coordination. They were also aware of the effect of poor intelligence estimates, the lack of proper and realistic training, and the effects of Israel's surprise attack. Therefore, even though the power struggles in Damascus and Baghdad were to last for almost another two years, the future of the Atassi and Arif governments had effectively been sealed by autumn 1967.

Air Forces and Coup Attempts

Unsurprisingly, over time, the June 1967 War provoked or inspired coup attempts in practically all the Arab states. Many of these saw some sort of involvement by local air forces, to varying degrees. Some such coup attempts, such as the well-known cases in Iraq, Jordan, Libya, Morocco, Sudan and Syria, were to occur only years later and will be described in subsequent volumes. Others remained unknown until very recently. One such case was an attempt against Nasser, planned for 26 August 1967 by a number of UARAF and Army officers that sympathised with FM Amer. Namely, while most Egyptian officers put the blame for the debacle on Amer, there were also those who blamed their president.[8] Among the latter was Fikry el-Gindy, as of June 1967 still recovering from his accidental ejection from a MiG-17. After returning to service, el-Gindy was appointed Deputy CO of a re-established MiG-17 squadron based at the newly constructed Qwaysina air base, under the command of Faiz al-Milah. The first plan prepared by al-Milah and el-Gindy was part of a larger plot, designed in support of FM Amer. According to this plan, al-Milah and el-Gindy were to fly their MiG-17s to attack Nasser's country home in the Nile Delta, with bombs and rockets, at a time they knew he would be there. Eventually, Amer died, supposedly having committed suicide, on 14 September 1967. Many other leaders of this plot subsequently died under similarly unclear circumstances. Some of them were apparently forced into suicide, as seems to have been the case with Amer, while others were executed.

The two UARAF officers did not give up. After learning that their squadron was to provide escort for President Nasser's aircraft during his flight to the Pan-Arab Conference in Khartoum, on 29 August 1967, al-Milah and el-Gindy drew up a plan to shoot down the aircraft. However, when the time came, al-Milah cancelled the plan because there were too many other 'good and useful' people aboard the same aircraft, and he considered it immoral to kill them as well. As a devout Muslim, el-Gindy remained eager to go ahead, because he believed that the innocent victims would go straight to paradise, as 'shahids' – martyrs. Eventually, this plan was never carried out. Faiz al-Milah was apparently suspected by his superiors, but never arrested. Instead, he was sent to Nigeria with a number of other UARAF pilots, in order to support the Federal Government in a war against breakaway Biafra. El-Gindy avoided prosecution: none of those arrested ever mentioned his name and thus he avoided any repercussions, thereafter concentrating on his military duties only.[9]

Algeria was the next to experience similar developments. Following the June 1967 War, President Boumedienne became one of the strongest exponents of a continued hard-line policy towards Israel. He openly shared most of President Atassi's ideas about how the Arabs should continue their struggle. While successfully negotiating with Moscow, however, Boumedienne refused to participate in the Khartoum Summit and then found himself confronted by stiff opposition within his own country. Because of disagreements within the ruling political party, a group of Algerian officers led by the Army Chief-of-Staff, Col Tahar Zbiri, launched a coup attempt on 28 December 1967. The coup plotters managed to paralyse much of the military, but their attempt collapsed within a matter of hours. One of the major reasons for the failure of this plot was an attack delivered near Blida by several MiG-17Fs, hitting an Army brigade led by the coup plotters. The MiGs struck this unit in the open near the village of el-Affroun, without causing heavy losses but frustrating the officers involved. The latter were informed that the QJJ pilots refused to participate in the coup, but also that they disobeyed the order to bomb any of the mutinying units. In turn, this raised the question of who flew these MiGs. Many unofficial Algerian sources have suspected that Soviet advisers flew the MiGs in question; others stress that these were Algerian pilots slated to travel to the USSR for training. At least two eyewitnesses to this attack reported that it was not very precise, that it caused no collateral damage, nor any casualties among the insurgents. Indeed, it only caused just as much damage as was required to frustrate the mutineers.[10] Eventually, Zbiri was forced to flee, first within Algeria, then to Tunisia.

Although Boumedienne later pardoned Zbiri (he is still living in Algeria, receiving a state pension), this coup attempt had a major impact on the future development of the state. President Boumedienne first dissolved the general staff and personally assumed many staff responsibilities. He never considered himself a military professional, and he and his top aides never appeared publicly in uniform, but he was able to call upon the advice of many technically competent and experienced military personnel that meanwhile served in the ministries. During the following years, the management of Boumedienne and his aides prompted a number of economic development projects, which in turn gave regional military commanders powers of patronage that further boosted their political influence. Ever since, most of the governors of the Algerian wilayas (provinces) have had military backgrounds, and the military remains the critical power behind Algerian statehood. In the early 1970s the QJJ also drew an important lesson from the coup attempt and established a squadron equipped with Magister jet trainers, specialised in counter-insurgency operations.

Soviet Re-supply for Egypt

A major effort to rebuild the UARAF had been launched before the ceasefire of 10 June 1967. Undeniably, this process began with a number of fierce discussions in Cairo as well as in Moscow. Like the Arabs, the Soviet leaders had been surprised and dismayed by the outbreak of the war, and shocked by the speed and extent of the Arab defeat. As next they had to face the furious Egyptians who demanded the USSR immediately replace their demolished air arm. Moscow's first reaction was to argue that there was nowhere to land the transport aircraft that would bring replacements, since the airfields had been 'destroyed'. This standpoint changed within a matter of hours. On 8 June 1967, as the Israelis were launching their first attacks on Syrian positions on the Golan, a secret meeting between all East European communist leaders was held in Moscow. In the course of this meeting a decision was taken to compensate Egypt and Syria for the losses of their air forces and to send replacement aircraft via Yugoslavia.

A corresponding package was announced to President Nasser via the Soviet ambassador in Cairo.[11] No aid arrived during the next three days, but the situation changed completely following the visit by Algerian President Boumedienne to Moscow, on 11 June. Boumedienne frankly explained to the Soviet leadership that it would be in their best interest to provide prompt and rigid support to the Arab states, preferably in the form of emergency military aid. Always cautious, the Soviets refused to launch a military intervention. Instead, they promised to replace all the Egyptian and Syrian losses on a one-for-one basis and to *'work resolutely to eliminate the effects of aggression'*.[12] To the surprise of many, at least the first part of this promise proved to be true. On 20 June, Marshal Zakharov, Soviet Chief of Staff, accompanied by a large military delegation, visited Cairo and then Damascus. Zakharov's primary task was to determine the amount of material necessary for the immediate defence of Egypt, to arrange for it to be dispatched and to establish a Soviet military mission – led by Col Gen P. N. Lashchenko and Gen Alexander Ivanovich Vybronov – that would help the Egyptians assimilate it.[13] On 26 June 1967 a Czechoslovak military mission also arrived in Cairo, with the aim of preparing a detailed explanation for Egypt's defeat.[14]

Starting from 12 June, before the Soviet and the Czechoslovak military missions arrived, Moscow launched an emergency airlift that lasted about three weeks, including some 200 An-12 transport aircraft, each carrying a MiG-17, MiG-21 or Su-7BMK. Crated materiel that had been hastily dispersed to Yemen, where it was stockpiled for safety, was brought back to Egypt. More was to follow, and throughout the summer and until mid-October, at least two Soviet cargo ships called at Egyptian ports weekly to unload military equipment. As can be seen from the Table 4, extracted from official Egyptian documentation, with the exception of bomber aircraft, the Egyptian Air Force was back to its pre-war strength as early as of late June 1967:[15]

Table 4: Numbers of UARAF aircraft by type, pre- and post-June 1967 War[16]

Type	Before 5 June 1967	10 June 1967	Operational losses	Deliveries from USSR	Deliveries from Algeria	Deliveries from East Germany	End of June 1967
MiG-15	26	11	15	–	–	–	11[17]
MiG-17	70	26	44	93	21	30	166[18]
MiG-19	27	11	16	–	–	–	11[19]
MiG-21	100	22	78	65	20	–	98[20]
Su-7	34	1	25	–	–	–	41[21]
Il-28	34	–	34	10	12	–	30[22]
Tu-16	23	–	23	–	–	–	–
Il-14	48	29	19	–	–	–	27
An-12	22	15	2	–	–	–	15
Mi-1	6	6	–	–	–	–	6
Mi-4	21	20	1	–	–	–	26[23]
Mi-6	12	2	10	–	–	–	2
Mi-8	–	–	–	10	–	–	10
Total fighters	257	71	178	158	41	30	327
Total bombers	57	–	57	–	12	–	30
Total transports	70	44	21	–	–	–	42
Total helicopters	39	28	11	10	–	–	44

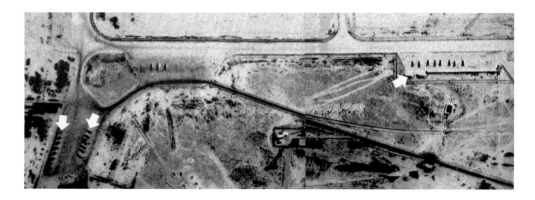

Taken shortly after the June 1967 War, this Israeli reconnaissance photograph shows an unidentified Egyptian air base with rows of newly delivered MiG-21s, as well as crates with additional aircraft waiting for their assembly. (IDF)

Such urgent deliveries were badly needed by Egypt, since the Egyptian military was on the verge of collapse and was entirely unable to protect even Cairo, should the Israelis have decided to continue their advance in a westerly direction. Although battered, the UARAF was the one force that could be brought back to working order within the shortest period of time, even though there was no dispute that the Israelis were in complete control of the air. In comparison, all that was left of the Egyptian Army was an armoured division in the process of forming, and a dozen small commando units.[24] Unsurprisingly, at least in public, the Egyptian and Syrian leaders praised the Soviet attitude and the speed with which Moscow provided this aid, and the Egyptian daily *al-Ahram* even published regular reports about the arrival of new Soviet weapons in Egypt, promising a renewed offensive within a few weeks.[25]

Investigating a Failure

As well as this major re-supply effort, much more fundamental changes were necessary to rebuild the Egyptian Air Force. On 5 July 1967 the UARAF established the Enquiry Committee, led by Brig Mustafa Shalaby el-Hinnawy, to investigate the reasons for the catastrophe of the June 1967 War. Following extensive investigation, the Committee pointed to the following problems:
- Inability of available radar network to detect any aircraft operating at altitudes below 500m (1,640ft) above the ground.
- Absence of a reliable visual observation system.
- Unsuitability of available aircraft and their armament to detect, intercept and combat enemy aircraft operating at low levels.
- Shortage of air defence weapons suitable for operations against aircraft operating at low altitudes.
- Lack of an electronic surveillance system.
- Incompetence in regards of communications, early warning and cooperation within the UARAF and between the UARAF and other branches of the military.

The same Enquiry Committee concluded that most of these problems were known as early as 1963, and that appropriate requests were issued to Moscow, but that the UARAF did not consequently insist on delivery of such equipment and the Soviets eventually refused to deliver it. Gabr Ali Gabr summarised:

'The Committee indicated that the defeat was the result of the numerous short-comings that the armed forces had suffered before and during the war, and which were mainly caused by the politicisation of the armed forces, and involving them in the Yemen operations for five years. Only four out of the final 93 pages report concerned the air force and air defence forces.'[26]

Furthermore, the UARAF had to accept the loss of four air bases in Sinai, all captured by the Israelis, as well as three along the Suez Canal, which were considered unsafe for routine operations due to their proximity to enemy positions. The remaining five air bases in the Nile Delta were completely insufficient to enable the Air Force to disperse its remaining aircraft effectively. Therefore, as early as the week after the end of hostilities, an extensive programme of construction of new air bases and dispersal airfields, and expansion of a number of older airfields (including Jiyanklis New, el-Birjat/Jabel el-Basur, Saiyah el-Sherif, Shubrakhat/ar-Rahmaniyah, Birma/Tanta, el-Mansourah, Qwaysina and the nearby Minshat Sabri and Tukh Highway Strips, Kfar Daud, az-Zaqaziq, al-Manzilah, as-Salihiyah, Qutamiyah/Wadi al-Jandali, Kom Awshim, el-Minya, Ras Gharib, Ras Shukhayr, Ras Jimsah, and Bir Abu Rahal) was launched, together with the construction of hardened aircraft shelters (HASes) on most of these. The programme is recalled by Reda el-Iraqi:

'Immediately after the ceasefire we began the work on our air bases... this was a massive undertaking necessitating the inclusion of nearly all the Egyptian construction companies (which in turn led to the cessation of all the other construction work around the country). These men were true heroes that worked without interruption for weeks. As first they erected 3m-high [9.8ft] sand berms around our aircraft hardstands. These were then covered by wooden planks. Nearby, they constructed a number of decoys of wood, filled with drums of fuel: if one of these had hit, enemy pilots would have been convinced that they had destroyed our aircraft... Then they extended the runways on all our air bases. At Inchas they even constructed a

As well as no fewer than seven air bases, the UARAF lost the services of a number of forward radar stations, crucial for its ability to detect Israeli aircraft in time to scramble its own interceptors, as well as a number of SA-2 SAM sites. This photograph shows a wrecked P-37 (ASCC codename Bar Lock) early warning radar system captured by the Israelis during the June 1967 War. (IDF, via Albert Grandolini)

new runway that is practically invisible from the air: this was used only in the case of emergency... Their work on HASes was excellent: later, during the October 1973 War, not a single aircraft inside HASes constructed by them was destroyed – not even when one HAS received a direct hit by a 2,000lb [907kg] bomb ...'

Samir Aziz Mikhail added:

'I was assigned to a re-established unit stationed at el-Mansourah, which was then a very busy place, with dozens of HASes under construction and anti-aircraft balloons chained to the ground hanging in the air all over the place. We were flying MiG-21FLs, armed with R-3S missiles only, hard to fly and equipped with a very poor radar. But our unit included some of the best Egyptian pilots and we were determined to improve our efficiency and hit back.'

It required the catastrophe of June 1967 to prompt the UARAF to finally start constructing hardened aircraft shelters on its air bases. This is the construction site of a concrete HAS on an unidentified air base, as photographed by an Israeli reconnaissance aircraft. (IDF)

An Israeli reconnaissance
photograph showing an
emergency runway and two
HASes – camouflaged as
houses – constructed near
el-Birjat (better known in the
West as Bir Ket) on the Cairo-
Alexandria highway.
(IDF)

In summary, the reconstruction of the UARAF during this period followed four
directions:
*   Development and support of the necessary manpower through training of additional
    personnel, and foremost much more intensive and realistic training of existing per-
    sonnel; re-equipment of units with aircraft and ammunition necessary to replace
    losses; establishment of new formations to further develop the combat capability
    of the Air Force.
*   Development of existing and construction of new air bases, and construction of
    hardened aircraft shelter, command, and support facilities, as well as establishment
    of 'aircraft engineering companies', responsible for maintaining air bases, con-
    structing fortifications, rapid repairs of the same, and bomb disposal.
*   Development of the industrial and technical infrastructure necessary to support
    operations of the Air Force, including the establishment of a domestic capability to
    manufacture aircraft armament, reconnaissance cameras and wireless reconnais-
    sance equipment.
*   Learning from experiences during the war in order to avoid making the same mis-
    takes again.

Return to Working Order

Most published Western accounts emphasise that after the June 1967 War, the UARAF came under strong Soviet influence and was reorganised according to the example of the Soviet Air Force. In fact, the organisational structure of the Egyptian Air Force was one aspect where Soviet influence remained minimal. While all the former UARAF air groups were renumbered and then reorganised as air brigades during the second half of 1967, generally, very little changed in regards to squadrons and the structure of other units.

In the process of the first post-June 1967 reorganisation, the newly established air brigades of the UARAF received designations consisting of three digits, the first of which designated their main purpose and the second the aircraft type they operated. As far as is presently known, air brigades operating fighters received designations starting with '2', while designations of training, transport, and helicopter brigades apparently began with other digits, such as '1', '3', '4' etc. Theoretically, air brigades that flew MiG-17s were designated in the 20x sequence, those flying MiG-19s in the 21x sequence, those flying Su-7s in the 22x sequence, and those flying MiG-21s in the 23x sequence. Some newly established brigades comprised three squadrons, but most only two, each of which was usually stationed at a different air base. For example, the Cairo West-based 'big squadron' was reorganised as Air Brigade 231 by 14 June 1967. Medhat Zaki recalls its organisation:

'One of the squadrons was based at Inchas, the other at Abu Suweir and the third unit, later re-designated as No. 12 Squadron and put under the command of Maj Amosis Azer, operated from Cairo West.'

Similarly, Barakat recalled the following details of the establishment of Air Brigade 201:

'Immediately following the June War, I was appointed as commander of a newly created No. 25 Squadron, based at Qwaysina. Another newly established MiG-17 unit was based at el-Mansourah, but I cannot recall its designation.'

As the number of operational units increased and MiG-19s were replaced by additional MiG-17s and Su-7s, several air brigades were successively re-designated and their units moved from one air base to the other quite often. Known UARAF fighter air brigades in the period 1967 to 1969 are as follows:

Table 5: Known UARAF fighter air brigades, 1967–69[27]

Air Brigade	Aircraft type	Air base	Approximate establishment/ renumbering date
201	MiG-17F	Qwaysina	June 1967
202	MiG-17F	Almaza	June 1967
203	MiG-17F	Beni Suweif	July/August 1967
211	MiG-19	Jiyanklis New	August 1967
221	Su-7BMK	Cairo West	June 1967
222	Su-7BMK	as-Salihiyah	July 1967
231	MiG-21	Cairo West	June 1967
232	MiG-21	Inchas	June 1967
233	MiG-21	el-Mansourah	July/August 1967
234	MiG-21	al-Ghardaka	August 1967

Notable in this review is the absence of bomber units. The background to this is that during July 1967 Moscow began to change its stance towards Egypt. While continuing to supply large quantities of arms, the Soviets not only began establishing greater control over their use, moderating their support, and exercising political restraint, but they also put emphasis on bolstering the *defence* of Egypt and therefore provided only 10 replacement Il-28s. Moscow refused outright to provide any replacement Tu-16 bombers. AM al-Ezz, eager not only to restore UARAF morale but also obtain the capability to hit back at Israel as quickly and effectively as possible, insisted the Soviets provide Yakovlev Yak-28 supersonic bombers. However, Zakharov and other Soviet officers eventually managed to convince Fawzy and Nasser that providing Egypt with an adequate air defence capability was paramount. Eventually, this resulted in AM al-Ezz's decision to reach an agreement with Iraq and send all of his Tu-16 crews – still nominally under the command of Hossni Moubarak – to Habbaniyah, where they continued training on IrAF aircraft. Completely unknown at that time, this measure was to prove not only critical to the future of the Egyptian Air Force, but indeed for the future of Egypt as a whole.

Despite the establishment of air brigades, and although a number of old squadrons were disbanded or at least renumbered, the squadron remained the most important organisational element and nearly all such units retained their identity, traditions and insignia. Furthermore, the UARAF maintained a number of independent squadrons, not subordinated to any air brigade but under the direct control of the UARAF HQs. One such unit was to become one of most important of the entire Air Force. Mamdouh Heshmat recalled the reasons behind the establishment of the squadron in question:

'Following the June War, I was reassigned to a MiG-17 unit based at Beni Suweif. We realised that we knew nothing about the enemy, not even about their positions along the Suez, and that we lacked even the most rudimentary reconnaissance equipment. Our early reconnaissance operations over Sinai were thus very primitive. For example, we would send two aircraft to an altitude of 10,000m [32,800ft] over the Suez, their pilots being equipped with a notepad and pencil pen only, and having the order to draw and write down everything they saw. But, we flew such missions.'

Farid Harfush explained what happened next, in turn revealing that the supposed 'reconnaissance sorties' flown by UARAF MiG-21s over Israel in May 1967 (see *Volume 2* for details) were actually nothing of the kind:

'In August 1967, we launched a major effort to improve our reconnaissance capabilities. This led to the establishment of a new unit, No. 46 (Independent) Squadron, at Inchas AB, in October the same year. This unit consisted of 16 pilots – including Lt Hossni Gad Allah and me from MiG-17s – but also Hussein Azab and Sherif Shafei. We received training in finding and recognising different types of enemy tanks and artillery, searching for and recognising enemy anti-aircraft positions [and] flying maritime patrols. We flew MiG-21F-13s equipped with reconnaissance cameras. These aircraft were actually equipped with all necessary installations before the June War, but nobody paid attention back then. After the war, relatively big cameras were installed under the right wing of our aircraft, protruding some 40-50cm [16-20in] below its lower surface. They made our aircraft heavy, slow and significantly increased fuel consumption. Furthermore, the available cameras were useful only from low level, while we found it necessary to fly at medium altitudes, even though this exposed us to all major enemy anti-aircraft weapons. We therefore

worked under very primitive conditions and found it necessary to always protect the reconnaissance aircraft with at least two other MiG-21s. Such missions were usually flown by our best pilots. Many of our sorties at that time began with a low-level pass at 1,000km/h [621mph] over Fayid AB: we realised that the enemy radar coverage of that area was poor. From there, we would turn left or right, and then climb, depending on the mission. Many of our missions brought us in direction of Kantara, Balouza, Romani, even over the Mediterranean Sea. Then we would return via Port Said to el-Mansourah or Cairo West... The mission did not end with landing and parking the aircraft within the HAS. We would then take care that the film was carefully removed from the camera, in order to make sure that nothing was damaged, and would then carry the fruits of our dangerous work to development, and then to photo-interpreters. It was important to memorise the flow of the mission and keep the photos in the same order, so as to know what they were showing, and about the potential importance of objects we photographed.'

Soviet and Czechoslovak Advisers

As the Egyptian military tried to set about reorganising itself, it was hampered by a number of problems. The first was the lack of senior officers, which was a result of purges: in all, over 800 officers – mostly senior – agreed to an early retirement, were dismissed or arrested. This process lasted well beyond the second half of 1967, as recalled by Fikry el-Ashmawy:

'After the June War, several senior UARAF officers retired voluntarily because they felt that they lacked the required experience of modern combat aircraft, needed in the new situation. Many others were sacked. But, there still remained a problem with some of these 'outdated-experience men' – in late 1967, and even into early 1968. This resulted in orders and missions which were impossible or impractical, or resulted in aircraft being lost because they ran out of fuel.'[28]

The second problem was that the available officers tended to work in a rather sluggish fashion. Before the June War, many officers came from wealthy families, with traditional backgrounds of elegance and ease. They enjoyed immense prestige. After the war, they were deprived of many privileges and had to spend their time with their units, working hard; there were no more long weekends in Cairo, as previously. When this deficit was discovered, the Egyptians asked the Soviets to take on a larger part of the reorganisation and training. At least 100 Soviet officers had already been attached to the Egyptian Army and the UARAF by 15 June, down to the brigade and squadron level, and had already caused dissent between Egyptian officers.[29] Their number was soon to increase significantly, in line with an agreement between Nasser, Fawzy and Zakharov. Carefully avoiding the signing of any defence pacts or becoming directly involved, the USSR increased the influx of its advisers, instructors and technicians to Egypt until around 2,000 were present. Retired Soviet Gen Ostrumov recalled his deployment to Egypt:

'Late one evening I received a telephone call in my flat. It was the Head of the Air Force, Gen Braiho. I was his deputy at that time. He ordered me to go the following morning to one of the airfields near Moscow, but wearing civilian clothes and, he emphasised, without any documents... There I met the Assistant Commander-in-Chief, Col Gen Sheglov, and some other generals specialised in anti-aircraft defences.

Later Zakharov and Lashenko – the Army commander of the Prikapiyskiy Region – also arrived… Out task was to travel to Egypt, learn about the military situation, to discover their [Egyptian] combat readiness and to help restore the Army, Air Force and other resources. We flew to Cairo in darkness. The lights were never switched on because the Egyptians feared that this would provoke an Israeli attack on the air base. There were just a few lights to help us land. Fortunately, we did so safely.'

Once in Egypt, Lashenko, Vybronov and the other Soviet advisers provided not only classes for Egyptian pilots and officers, but also flew with them – sometimes over the occupied Sinai.[30]

Right from the start, the Soviets found the Egyptians difficult to deal with, finding them impatient and unappreciative of the rather slow, methodical and thorough Soviet methods of training. This is actually unsurprising considering there was plenty of pre-judice on both sides, and that RAF-style traditions were still widespread within the Egyptian Air Force. Negative experiences, logic, as well as a natural sense of national pride made the Egyptians suspect that the onus of blame should not fall solely on their shoulders – instead, they found fault with the Soviet weapons and doctrine. In fact, as already described, the ranks of the UARAF were rife with allegations against specific Soviet aircraft and their armament. The Soviets tried to reassure them that their equipment and doctrine were valid, but at the same time they were anxious to find out why their weapons had failed to win the war.[31] Furthermore, the Soviets had to explain why more and longer-lasting training was necessary: for most of the 1960s, the courses the Egyptians completed in the USSR generally lasted only a few months and were designed to quickly familiarise UARAF personnel with Soviet equipment. Now that the Soviets had found the Egyptians in need of more comprehensive and intensive training, and since they were also in the process of providing more modern and more complex equipment that required ever longer periods of introduction to service, they also expected the Egyptians to change the way they went about planning and working.

Finally, before the June 1967 War ever smaller numbers of Egyptian officers were sent to Eastern Europe for training: while around 870 made the trip in 1961, only 235 travelled to the USSR, Czechoslovakia and Poland in 1966.[32] After FM Fawzy and Lt Gen al-Ezz – apparently under the influence of faulty intelligence concerning numbers of available Israeli pilots – decided to increase the number of fully qualified UARAF pilots to 800, the available training institutions that could train 50-70 new pilots annually proved entirely inadequate. Although four new flight schools – with the capability of training 300 new pilots annually – were established at Bilbeis, large numbers of young Egyptian cadets had to be sent to the USSR even for basic pilot training, while all operational pilots were sent for additional courses in air combat, each of which lasted three months.[33]

Tough Times

Before the UARAF was able to hit back at the Israelis and avenge the defeat of the June War, AM al-Ezz knew that his pilots were in bad need of much tougher and more realistic training, which would be repeated often enough for the men to have faith in their own abilities and equipment. Correspondingly, he and his subordinates began pushing their pilots very hard. Reda el-Iraqi, still assigned to the Inchas-based No. 43 Squadron equipped with MiG-21FLs, explained how and why al-Ezz excelled in his work:

'AM Abu al-Ezz was a very strong character and a strict disciplinarian. He played the most prominent role in the process of rebuilding the UARAF within the shortest period of time. He excelled at prompting the Soviets to deliver the largest possible number of replacement aircraft within a very short period of time. He agreed with the Soviets for these to assemble the aircraft after delivery and to test-fly them before their handover to us. That way our technicians were free to do their duty with the squadron and every new aircraft was combat ready within a few hours of arrival in Egypt. At that time, every single new aircraft, every piece of ammunition, mattered a lot to us. Once the aircraft were here, we began flying very intensively …'

Similarly, Medhat Zaki, who graduated from the Air Force Academy in May 1965, recalled:

'In mid-1966 I was ordered to convert to the MiG-21F-13, but we all flew very little and I collected only 21 hours on that type by the time I was assigned to Fayid-based No. 47 Squadron, during the June 1967 War… After the war I was first assigned to the 'big squadron' at Cairo West, then under the command of Maj Shahid Hassan. I was paired with Maj Fawzy Salama [newly converted from the MiG-19; authors' note], and we flew together most of the time. After replacement aircraft were delivered we flew so much, that by mid-July I already clocked 14 additional hours of flying.[34]

Qadri Abd el-Hamid recollected the situation as of late June and early July 1967:

'Those were some very though times for all Egyptian pilots. We were under great pressure to raise our standard of training. After the war, we started to fly at very low altitudes. Now we knew how to fight and were flying 50 or more hours a month in the July heat. Flying and flying… we stayed 50 days at the air base without a single day off while providing an umbrella for the Russian re-supply missions and then flying training missions too …'

El-Iraqi described the period of intensive training as follows:

'We were still terrified of a possible new strike like that on 5 June and thus we held our aircraft ready for combat all times of the day. After spending 45 days at the air base without interruption, I got 48 hours of vacation, and even then could have got a call to return to duty at any time… During these 45 days we had 20 MiG-21s at Inchas, of which four were held back as reserve. The other 16 were held at Readiness Rate 1 all the time: we were able to launch all of them within 10 minutes if necessary … Of course, such a high number of available aircraft also significantly improved our training. At first we regularly flew two, three sorties a day. After a day of break, we would intensify the training and fly six or even seven sorties. Eventually, the tempo was increased to the point where flying five or six sorties a day was 'normal' … In addition to our own training, we also trained new pilots, instructed them in tactics and technology. Many of these were fresh from training in Russia and their level of knowledge was very low as the Russians only trained them to take off and land, but no air combat… We flew and stayed at the air base so long that we had to set up new quarters for all pilots, as well as additional quarters for technicians and equipment. Most of the corresponding buildings were built underground …'

Abd el-Hamid continued:

'Eventually, we trained so hard that we began losing pilots in accidents… one of the pilots killed in such an accident was the late Maharem. He was in a more junior class than mine… we flew a dogfight session over the Cairo West training

Taken at Meliz before the June 1967 War, this photograph shows two No. 45 Squadron pilots, Qadri Abd el-Hamid (right) and Maharem. Maharem was killed during a two-versus-one air combat exercise against el-Hamid, in July 1967. At the time UARAF pilots were under incredible pressure to fly in protection of their nation, but also to train as hard as possible. (Qadri Abd el-Hamid Collection)

zone and he was number 2 with one of my classmates. Their mission was to train two-versus-one (I was solo). I succeeded in reaching an attack solution against both of them and shot them down with my gun camera before they sighted me, high above their six o'clock. After seeing me, their leader broke very hard, probably 8g, while we were all at only 300m [984ft] above the ground. Maharem attempted to follow but his aircraft went out of control. It entered a steep, nose-down, almost vertical dive, hit the ground and exploded.[35]

El-Iraqi explained one of the reasons for the high attrition rate among Egyptian pilots during the period of their very intensive training, in summer 1967:

'The MiG-21F-13 was an excellent aircraft, very special. I am convinced even today I could beat any other pilot flying another aircraft if I would fly a MiG-21F-13. But, it was also a very limited aircraft, carrying only 60 rounds of 30mm calibre … in an attack these 60 rounds were spent within two seconds. This meant that in order to hit the enemy aircraft, the pilot had to be an excellent marksman … in order to improve our skills to levels not reached even by the Soviets, we flew live-firing exercises with only 20 rounds on board. This resulted in inexperienced pilots trying to manoeuvre their aircraft very hard … pilots often experienced complete disorientation during such flights: seemingly, there was no difference between the ground and the sky. Maj Shahid Hassan pushed us very hard, until he experienced a similar situation. Following a series of hard manoeuvres, he panicked, believing he was only 100m [328ft] above ground level. Eventually, it turned out he was 4,000m [13,123ft] high! This happened very quickly and with his aircraft almost out of control … I immediately announced an emergency landing and we both landed safely. He came down and took me to the squadron ready room, asking me to explain to him everything that happened, in all honesty and without any secrets… The other prob-

lem was that even as of June and July 1967, the USSR did not supply any two-seat MiG-21s to Egypt. Under terrible pressure, we were forced to convert a large number of pilots to the type with help of nothing but theory and subsonic MiG-15UTIs ...'

Back to the Battle

After acquiring enough replacement aircraft, and once the UARAF's radar network was reinstated, al-Ezz was keen to hit back at the IDF/AF as soon as possible. He did not have to wait too long. On 1 July the Israelis moved a mechanised force on Port Fuad, on the eastern side of the northern entrance to the Suez Canal. At that time, this town was relatively isolated from the rest of Sinai, encircled by swamps and sea, but still under the control of a 30-man squadron of Egyptian commandos. Expecting their opponents to flee at their sight, the Israelis nonchalantly marched along a narrow road only to run into a small minefield and then receive a barrage of RPG-7s and recoilless gunfire in the flank while approaching the hamlet of Ras el-Aish. After losing at least six armoured vehicles and a number of men killed and wounded in the process, the Israelis shelled Port Fuad and the Egyptian positions, and even flew some air strikes, but eventually withdrew: the triangle around this town was to remain the only part of Sinai in Egyptian hands until the October War of 1973.

The 'battle of Ras el-Aish', as this clash became known in Egypt, was an important moment in the history of the Egyptian military, and one that taught it a number of lessons. It was also the signal for the start of a period in the course of which the Egyptians began to hit back at an increasingly arrogant IDF.

Emboldened by the success of the defence at Ras el-Aish, the Egyptians reached out to hit Israeli positions elsewhere in Sinai. As early as 3 July, the Israelis admitted the first act of sabotage, when a train was derailed. Two days later, the UARAF went into action, deploying 10 MiG-17s to hit an IDF camp near Qantara East, as recalled by el-Iraqi:

'That Israeli camp near Qantara East was full of soldiers that did not miss any opportunity to insult and humiliate us, to weaken the morale of our soldiers. They would swim in the Suez Canal completely naked, put up Israeli flags all around their camp, scream insults including that the Egyptian Army was defeated by an army of women ... so we decided to bomb that camp at the first opportunity.'

Following the air strike, the same site was hit by Egyptian artillery. Eventually, the Israelis admitted five killed and 31 wounded, and the IDF/AF was swift to hit back at the Egyptian artillery positions. On 8 and 9 July, MiG-21F-13s of the (future) No. 46 Squadron flew a series of reconnaissance sorties over the same area, but their efforts were largely hampered by fog. The sorties had to be repeated by Su-7s of the re-established No. 55 Squadron in the afternoon (pilots of the latter unit were able to fly visual reconnaissance only). The Israelis claimed to have shot down a MiG-21 and a Su-7 each, but the UARAF did not suffer any losses. On the contrary, in the course of repeated reconnaissance sorties flown on the afternoon of 9 July, its fighters finally brought back the first useful photographs of Israeli positions along the Canal.[36]

As tensions rose, both sides rushed to bring their weapons right up to the edge of the Canal and bombard each other at almost point-blank range. On 14 July the Egyptian Army opened artillery and mortar fire on Israeli positions near Qantara, Firdan,

Ismailia and Port Suez. The UARAF appeared hot on the heels of this attack, launching a major operation that attempted to drag Israeli interceptors into an ambush, as later described by FM Fawzy:

'After the June 1967 War, the IDF/AF started flying daily reconnaissance sorties over the western bank of the Suez Canal, well inside Egyptian airspace. Irritated by this behaviour and intending to deny the Israelis control of the airspace, AM al-Ezz prepared an action plan that envisaged minimal risk for our aircraft ... At the first opportunity, on 14 July 1967, he realised that plan.'[37]

As a pair of Israeli reconnaissance-fighters approached the southern portion of the Suez Canal in order to find the Egyptian artillery positions, the UARAF launched 10 MiG-17s. These did not manage to intercept the original Israeli formation, but then clashed with another one and claimed two Mystère IVAs as shot down (the IDF/AF denied any combat losses on that day, even though admitting that one of its Mystères crashed, killing its pilot, due to engine failure). Confident that they had prevented the Israelis from roaming the skies over the Suez freely, Egyptian confidence in the MiG-17 was considerably bolstered and morale soared. Both sides prepared for another day of similar clashes.

On 15 July the UARAF launched dozens of fighter-bombers to attack Israeli positions, causing up to 25 Israeli casualties and forcing them to withdraw their soldiers from several exposed positions. The IDF/AF reacted in force, scrambling Mirages forward deployed at the former Bir Gifgafa – renamed 'Refidim' by the IDF/AF – to intercept, and thus provoking a series of air battles. Farid Harfush reported:

'I was stationed at Cairo West and on alert duty. They launched four of us (I was number 4 in that group) and as we went east as fast as we could, we received instructions to join an air battle between Israeli and Egyptian fighters. I saw two Mirages, and reported them to my leader. We were flying supersonic at this time at an altitude of 7,000m [22,966ft]. We did a split-S and got behind the Mirages. After some hard turns, I saw my number 1 fighting with a single Mirage. So I came in and tried to protect him. My number 1 launched a missile and it hit the Israeli jet. The Mirage exploded and I didn't see the pilot bale out. My section did not suffer any losses, but some fighter-bombers from other flights were shot down.'

Following close behind the four-ship from Cairo West were six MiG-21s from Inchas. The first two MiG pilots, Ahmed Anwar and Mohammed Aweys, engaged inconclusively, but the next two attacked the same Israeli formation that had already been engaged by Harfush, as Medhat Zaki recalled:

'Maj Salama and myself were scrambled from Cairo West and ordered to fly in the direction of Ismailia, but after take-off our GCI informed us that it was not tracking any enemy aircraft and we should provide top cover for our returning fighters instead. We approached the abandoned Fayid AB ... I looked downwards and sighted a Mirage in the process of attacking a MiG-21 that was behind another Mirage, which in turn was behind another MiG. Out fighters were flown by Maj Farid Harfush from Abu Suweir and Capt Farouk Hamada from Inchas. Salama ordered me to activate afterburner and attack. I knew nothing about the capabilities of the Mirage at that time, but the fight was soon over. We approached undetected, Maj Salama fired one missile and this scored a direct hit: the Israeli pilot ejected. I hit the other Mirage and that pilot did not eject. As soon as they sighted us, the other Israelis panicked and gave up fighting. They broke and attempted to run away, but

Reda el-Iraqi in the cockpit of a MiG-21 in late June 1967. (Reda el-Iraqi Collection)

This extremely rare photograph, taken immediately after the June 1967 War, shows the right top view of MiG-21F-13 serial number 5341 flown by Reda el-Iraqi before he was reassigned to the MiG-21FL-equipped No. 43 Squadron. The old identification stripes indicate that this was one of the aircraft delivered before June 1967, camouflaged in 'sand and spinach' only a few days after the end of that conflict. (Reda el-Iraqi Collection)

Hafrush and Hamada were soon behind them. Later I learned that the Israelis lost four out of six Mirages that engaged in that air combat ...'

Short on fuel, all the Egyptian MiGs withdrew towards the west without continuing their pursuit deeper over Sinai. Medhat Zaki concluded:

'The MiG-21F-13 was very manoeuvrable – really an excellent dogfighter – but suffered from a very short range. We ran out of fuel after nearly every exercise. After every air combat with the Israelis there were always a few pilots forced to land somewhere short of their home base because of the lack of fuel. Another problem was that of our poor radars, which could not detect or track any low-flying aircraft, and then that of our thick windshield: it was nearly impossible to visually track an opponent flying directly in front of the MiG ... After this battle, we were ordered to land at Inchas. However, before reaching it a new order came: land at Beni Suweif ... it turned out that Hafrush and Hamada were out of fuel and had to make emergency landings at Inchas before us ... I ran out of fuel shortly after crossing the Nile and while still searching for Beni Suweif. Finding a solution for my situation was tricky: the Russians taught us to eject from the aircraft if something of this kind happened. But, I thought to myself, we are already lacking aircraft and I'm not going to lose this one in vain. Thus, after the engine flamed out I slowly glided towards the road, touched down quite hard, hurting my spine, but managed to stop in time. A bicycle-mounted police officer appeared, then somebody on a horse, and finally there was a big group of people around my aircraft. My injury made me cry when I attempted to climb out of my seat, but the policeman helped me out and then I was brought – on horseback – to Beni Suweif, from where they evacuated me by a helicopter to a hospital in Cairo ... Meanwhile, our brigade's leading engineer officer returned to the scene, refuelled the aircraft and another pilot flew it to Beni Suweif ... Later on, I was put under investigation by a council led by Maj Farouq Hamada because of my landing on the road. Instead of a reward I nearly got punishment. It was AM al-Ezz, proud of having such tough fighter pilots, who decorated me with the Star of Military Honour ...'

The fighting on 15 June ended the same evening, with a ceasefire negotiated by the United Nations Truce Supervision Organization (UNTSO), to which both sides had actually agreed days earlier, but not before the IDF/AF claimed nine UARAF fighters, including three MiG-17s, five MiG-21s and one Su-7, while in turn confirming the loss

Another view of the same MiG-21F-13, showing to advantage the wavy lower border of the camouflage pattern applied on the upper surfaces and sides of the aircraft, as well as its drop tank, which carries the same serial number as the aircraft. (Reda el-Iraqi Collection)

of only one Mirage (the pilot was recovered). The Mirage loss was first attributed to a SAM, and only years later as 'in air combat'. The Egyptians claimed four Mirages shot down and one damaged, in return for one MiG-17 and one Su-7BMK lost. While both UARAF pilots are known to have ejected safely, Morteza Rifai was captured and was soon on the way to join Salah Danish in an Israeli PoW camp. Capt Muhammad Abd al-Rahman managed to bail out over the Egyptian-held side of the Suez. Mamdouh Heshmat concluded:

'Our confidence improved considerably following the battles on 14 and 15 July. At first, the situation remained very tense. On most days we spent 12 hours in the cockpits of our fully armed and fuelled aircraft, parked near the end of runway, ready to launch at short notice. Eventually, we realised that the Air Force couldn't go on like that forever: we were in need of more training. Therefore, there followed a period of relaxed readiness, which we used to further improve our capabilities and skills. We flew for up to three hours and received up to eight hours of lectures in technology, tactics and armaments each day. Most of these latter were provided to groups of pilots seating barely 50m [55 yards] from their aircraft. We were left with barely one hour to eat something and get at least some rest ...'

The Egyptian pilots thus not only trained hard, but hit back hard, too. Eventually, their feeling of a smarting sense of chagrin wore off and gave way to a determination to prove their worth. In this aspect, the Soviet influence – although not crucial – proved very important for the ability of the UARAF to re-establish itself as a coherent and professional military force, and recover its morale. The Air Force was on its way to helping restore the pride of nation that was going through its hardest times, and preparing itself for the return of Sinai to Egypt.

1   According to the former CIA operative in Saudi Arabia, Robert Baer, one of the crucial lessons for the Arabs from the June 1967 War – and also the reason for the revival of Islam – was the conclusion that, 'a massive Arab military force was defeated by a small Jewish force, which was leaning on religious cohesion of its citizens'. Some Arabs, and particularly the Saudis, concluded that the Arabs must be capable of developing a similar military force based on their own religion, Islam. Concerned about its own future, yet powerful thanks to its vast oil fortune, the House of al-Saud thus began to support a network of charitable organisations and financial development of new mosques and religious schools where a new generation of young Muslims was

Arab MiGs | Volume 3

indoctrinated by the most radical interpretation of Islam. Eventually, this development led to the emergence of various forms of modern-day Islamic extremism (see Baer, *The Saudi Connection*, p133).

2   Notably, the UARAF MiG-17s and Il-28s forward deployed in Yemen also flew some 12-16 combat sorties against Royalist bases in that country, on 5 and 6 June 1967.

3   In addition to its aircraft losses, the UARAF lost almost the entire equipment of all its AAA regiments and at least four SA-2 sites and several radar stations deployed in Sinai. As far as SA-2 sites are concerned, it is known that two of these were knocked out in Israeli attacks during the war, while the equipment of two others – including all of their most sensitive elements – was captured intact. Not to ignore is the fact that the UARAF also lost four air bases and their ammunition depots in Sinai. While available US and Israeli sources differ, these indicate that between 38 and 238 R-3S air-to-air missiles (most of them in almost brand-new condition, manufactured only in 1966), and considerable quantities of Egyptian-made Sakr 76mm unguided rockets were secured intact. As already mentioned, the IDF/AF was quick to press captured Sakrs into use on the Jordanian and Syrian fronts. Later on it also modified a number of Mirage IIICJ interceptors for carriage of R-3S missiles, a story discussed in more detail in one of the future volumes of this series.

4   Churchill and Churchill, *The Six Day War*, p80 and p84; interestingly, the IDF/AF did not differentiate between such losses when crediting its own pilots with kills.

5   There is still much controversy over whether FM Amer did indeed plan a coup against Nasser after the June 1967 War. Indeed, Amer's family continues to blame Nasser and his sympathisers for removing and murdering the field marshal in order to secure their own position. While Nasser's sympathisers have so far failed to provide firm evidence about possible plans for a coup attempt, as explained further below, it is meanwhile certain that Amer's sympathisers at least did pursue such plans. What remains uncertain is whether Amer was involved or at least informed of their intentions.

6   Notably, Sidki Mahmoud, Afifi, Daghedi and Labib were brought before a military tribunal on 30 September. In theirs, as well as in nearly all the other cases, the indictments were not made public because, it was stated, the information contained might be of value to the enemy, and, 'the request to hold the trial in secret was granted'; see *al-Ahram*, 25 September and 1 October 1967.

7   For details about al-Ezz's earlier career with the Egyptian Air Force, see *Volume 1*.

8   According to an article in the Egyptian daily *al-Ahram*, from 19 September 1967, 149 persons were detained under suspicion of being involved in the Amer plot to seize control of the armed forces. For statements about FM Amer by Egyptian officers that ended up as PoWs in Israel, see O'Ballance, *The Third Arab-Israeli War*, p168.

9   Fikry el-Gindy, interview, Cairo, November 2010. For details about el-Gindy's early career and his accidental ejection from a MiG-17, see *Volume 1*. Al-Milah is still alive and today owns an Upper Nile cruise company, in southern Egypt. Additional details about his and the service of other Egyptian pilots in Nigeria will be provided in *Volume 4*.

10 M. A. (retired MiG-21 pilot of the QJJ), interview provided on condition of anonymity, 2003.

11 Shukairy, *The Great Defeat*, p32.

12 Ibid.

13 According to Russian researcher Mikhail Zhirokhov, the Soviets considered deploying no fewer than 12 fighter regiments to Egypt under the command of Gen Alexandr Ivanovich Vybronov. However, this plan proved impractical and instead Moscow limited itself to replacing UARAF losses at no cost. Zhirokhov, *The Unknown Heroes: Soviet Pilots in the Middle East, 1955–1974*, unpublished article.

14 Guy Laron, *Assessing the Damage: the June 1967 Czech Delegation to Egypt*, CWIHP.

15 Curiously enough, the situation in regard to tank deliveries for the Egyptian Army was entirely different, although the Army suffered far heavier losses than the UARAF, having lost not only nearly all of its equipment in Sinai, but also much of its personnel, including an entire armoured division, two infantry divisions and 15 out of 23 independent brigades. During the war Moscow agreed to dispatch some 200 tanks and a number

218

of vehicles to the UAR, but none of these arrived before the end of the month. Additional tanks delivered during July 1967 were part of a shipment agreed before the fighting began. Of course, the major reason for this relatively slow pace of deliveries for the Army was the weight of the equipment in question, which necessitated its transportation by ship. Given the relatively limited size of the Soviet merchant navy at the time, it proved impossible to provide all the MBTs, APCs and artillery necessary to rebuild the Egyptian Army within 12 months. A more intensive operation of this kind would have completely disrupted the work of the Soviet merchant navy and other trade activities.

16 EFM, Document No. 44. Clearly, the figures presented here are very important in regard to precisely quantifying UARAF losses during the June 1967 War, and in demonstrating that these were far lower than usually claimed by the Israelis or assumed by various Western intelligence services (and thereafter taken for granted by most published Western sources).

17 Seven of these aircraft were stored, while the other four were under repair.

18 No fewer than 52 MiG-17s were in storage as of early August 1967, of which 11 were MiG-17PF night-fighters and 26 MiG-17s (without afterburner).

19 Eight of these 11 aircraft were under repair.

20 This figure included 40 newly delivered MiG-21PFs – all of which had been previously brought up to a standard similar to the MiG-21PFM (including SPS flaps) and should therefore have been properly designated MiG-21PFS – as well as MiG-21FLs (considered 'all-weather fighters' by the UARAF), plus 19 'original' MiG-21PFMs (considered 'night-fighters' by the UARAF). Interestingly, the Egyptians tended to designate all of these variants as 'MiG-21FL'.

21 Twelve of these aircraft were in storage.

22 Ten of the aircraft still available as of late June were Il-28R reconnaissance-bombers. Note that eight additional Il-28s were stationed in Yemen.

23 A total of 16 out of 26 in service with the UARAF were assigned to the Egyptian Navy.

24 O'Ballance, *The Electronic War in the Middle East, 1968–1970*, p18.

25 Shukairy, *The Great Defeat*, p33.

26 Gabr Ali Gabr, interview, April 2005 and an unpublished document concerning air warfare between Egypt in Israel in June 1967, by the same author. Note that similar conclusions can be found throughout EFM, Document No. 44, which contains more than 50 pages related to the UARAF and its failures.

27 Based on research by Menno van der Wal.

28 El-Ashmawy, interview, New York, July 2005.

29 *Soviet Policy and the 1967 Arab-Israeli War*, p36. CIA, Directorate of Intelligence, Intelligence Report CAE-AR XXXVIII, 16 March 1970.

30 According to Zhirokhov, *The Unknown Heroes: Soviet Pilots in the Middle East, 1955–1974*, Vybronov actually flew 12 combat sorties over Sinai in MiG-17s and Su-7s during the second half of 1967, each of which had to be authorised directly from Moscow.

31 This was especially the case with the Czechoslovaks that visited Egypt in late June. Their close acquaintance with the Egyptian military encouraged the Egyptian officers to talk more openly to the Czechoslovaks, and provide very detailed explanations of their defeat. One of the details they provided in the course of such discussions was especially interesting, detailing the deployment of two Israeli Vautour fighter-bombers equipped for electronic countermeasures at high altitude over Sinai on the morning of 5 June 1967. According to the Egyptians, these aircraft suppressed the activity of the SA-2 SAMs to a degree whereby they created 'corridors' within the Egyptian air defence system, through which Israeli aircraft were able to reach their targets in relative safety. According to corresponding Egyptian accounts, this use of electronic warfare by the Israelis was far more important than the altitude at which their aircraft were able to fly. See Laron, *Assessing the Damage: the June 1967 Czech Delegation to Egypt*, CWIHP.

32 SNIE 11-13-67, p102.

33 Fawzy, *The Three-Years War*, Chapters 14 to 16.

34 Zaki, interview with Group 73, November 2009.

35 El-Hamid, e-mail interview, November 2009.

36 Neither these two claims, nor the Israeli claim for a UARAF Su-7 supposedly shot down on 11 July 1967 – and the capture of its pilot – can be verified with the aid of Egyptian sources. On the contrary, the number of Egyptian pilots that ended up as PoWs in Israel during the following six years was so minimal that their names are well known within the ranks of UARAF/EAF veterans.

37 Fawzy, *The Three-Years War*, Chapter 18.

APPENDIX I

Table 6: Known serial numbers of Iraqi MiG-19s and MiG-21s, 1960–67

Aircraft Type	Serial number	Unit	Remarks
MiG-19S	489	No. 9 Sqn	Written off at Rashid AB, November 1963
MiG-19S	498	No. 9 Sqn	
MiG-19S	500	No. 9 Sqn	
MiG-19S	501	No. 9 Sqn	
MiG-19S	502	No. 9 Sqn	
MiG-19S	503	No. 9 Sqn	
MiG-19S	504	No. 9 Sqn	
MiG-19S	518	No. 9 Sqn	
MiG-19S	519	No. 9 Sqn	
MiG-19S	520	No. 9 Sqn	
MiG-19S	521	No. 9 Sqn	Wreck at al-Assad, 2005
MiG-19S	1093	No. 9 Sqn	IrAF Museum Baghdad; post-1988 serial number
MiG-21F-13	522	No. 11 Sqn	Wreck at al-Assad, 2005
MiG-21F-13	523	No. 11 Sqn	
MiG-21F-13	524	No. 11 Sqn	
MiG-21F-13	525	No. 11 Sqn	
MiG-21F-13	526	No. 11 Sqn	Overhauled in USSR, 1981–82 then No. 27 OTU
MiG-21F-13	527	No. 11 Sqn	Overhauled in USSR, 1981–82 then No. 27 OTU
MiG-21F-13	528	No. 11 Sqn	
MiG-21F-13	529	No. 11 Sqn	
MiG-21F-13	530	No. 11 Sqn	Last seen in 1967
MiG-21F-13	531	No. 11 Sqn	Overhauled in USSR, 1981–82 then No. 27 OTU
MiG-21F-13	532	No. 11 Sqn	
MiG-21F-13	533	No. 11 Sqn	Overhauled in USSR, 1981–82 then No. 27 OTU
MiG-21F-13	534	No. 11 Sqn	c/n 741104; flown to Israel August 1966, later to US
MiG-21F-13	535	No. 11 Sqn	
MiG-21F-13	536	No. 11 Sqn	Overhauled in USSR, 1981–82 then No. 27 OTU
MiG-21F-13	537	No. 11 Sqn	Overhauled in USSR, 1981–82 then No. 27 OTU
MiG-21FL	665	No. 17 Sqn	Delivered December 1965
MiG-21FL	666	No. 17 Sqn	Delivered December 1965
MiG-21FL	667	No. 17 Sqn	Delivered December 1965
MiG-21FL	668	No. 17 Sqn	Delivered December 1965
MiG-21FL	669	No. 17 Sqn	Delivered December 1965
MiG-21FL	670	No. 17 Sqn	Delivered December 1965
MiG-21FL	671	No. 17 Sqn	Delivered December 1965

MiG-21FL	672	No. 17 Sqn	Delivered December 1965
MiG-21FL	673	No. 17 Sqn	Delivered December 1965
MiG-21FL	674	No. 17 Sqn	Delivered December 1965
MiG-21FL	675	No. 17 Sqn	Delivered December 1965
MiG-21FL	676	No. 17 Sqn	Delivered December 1965
MiG-21FL	678	No. 17 Sqn	Delivered December 1965
MiG-21FL	679	No. 17 Sqn	Delivered December 1965
MiG-21FL	680	No. 17 Sqn	Delivered December 1965
MiG-21FL	681	No. 17 Sqn	Delivered December 1965
MiG-21FL	682	No. 17 Sqn	Delivered December 1965
MiG-21FL	683	No. 17 Sqn	Delivered December 1965
MiG-21FL	684	No. 17 Sqn	Delivered December 1965
MiG-21PFM	702	No. 9 Sqn	Delivered July 1967
MiG-21PFM	703	No. 9 Sqn	
MiG-21PFM	704	No. 9 Sqn	
MiG-21PFM	705	No. 9 Sqn	
MiG-21F	706	No. 17 OCU	IrAF Museum Baghdad, 2009
MiG-21F	707	No. 17 OCU	
MiG-21F	708	No. 17 OCU	
MiG-21F	709	No. 17 OCU	Gate guard Wahda AB, 2003
MiG-21PFM	710	No. 14 Sqn	
MiG-21PFM	711	No. 14 Sqn	
MiG-21PFM	712	No. 14 Sqn	
MiG-21PFM	714	No. 14 Sqn	
MiG-21PFM	715		
MiG-21PFM	716		
MiG-21PFM	717		
MiG-21PFM	718		
MiG-21PFM	719		
MiG-21PFM	720		
MiG-21PFM	721		
MiG-21PFM	722		
MiG-21PFM	723		
MiG-21PFM	724		
MiG-21PFM	725		
MiG-21PFM	726		
MiG-21PFM	727		Operational late 1960s, later assigned to No. 27 OTU
MiG-21PFM	728		
MiG-21PFM	729		
MiG-21PFM	730		
MiG-21PFM	731		
MiG-21PFM	732		
MiG-21PFM	733		
MiG-21PFM	734		
MiG-21PFM	735		
MiG-21PFM	736		
MiG-21PFM	737		

APPENDIX II

Table 7: Known serial numbers of Iraqi Il-28s and Tu-16s, 1965–67

Aircraft Type	Serial number	Unit	Remarks
Il-28U	421	No. 8 Sqn	c/n 69808; manufactured Factory No. 30 in Moscow (MMZ); abandoned al-Taqaddum since early 1980s
Il-28U	422	No. 8 Sqn	c/n 69520; manufactured Factory No. 30 in Moscow (MMZ); abandoned al-Taqaddum since early 1980s
Il-28	423	No. 8 Sqn	Abandoned al-Hurrya AB (Mosul), before September 1980
Il-28	424	No. 8 Sqn	
Il-28	425	No. 8 Sqn	c/n 56605703; manufactured Factory No. 166 in Omsk; abandoned al-Taqaddum since early 1980s
Il-28	426	No. 8 Sqn	c/n 56605704; manufactured Factory No. 166 in Omsk; abandoned al-Taqaddum since early 1980s
Il-28	427	No. 8 Sqn	c/n 56605717; manufactured Factory No. 166 in Omsk; abandoned al-Taqaddum since early 1980s
Il-28	428	No. 8 Sqn	
Il-28	429	No. 8 Sqn	Wreck at al-Bakir AB, 2003
Il-28	430	No. 8 Sqn	c/n 56606206; manufactured Factory No. 166 in Omsk; abandoned al-Taqaddum since early 1980s
Il-28	431	No. 8 Sqn	
Il-28	432	No. 8 Sqn	c/n 56606540, manufactured Factory No. 166 in Omsk; shot down by THK F-84Fs on 16 August 1962
Il-28	433	No. 8 Sqn	c/n unknown; seen immediately after delivery in 1960, fate unknown
Il-28	434	No. 8 Sqn	c/n 56606207, manufactured Factory No. 166 in Omsk
Il-28BM	564	No. 8 Sqn	c/n 5901703, manufactured Factory No. 39 in Irkutsk; abandoned al-Taqaddum since early 1980s
Il-28BM	565	No. 8 Sqn	c/n 5901801, manufactured Factory No.39 in Irkutsk; abandoned al-Taqaddum since early 1980s
Tu-16	547	No. 10 Sqn	
Tu-16	548	No. 10 Sqn	
Tu-16	558	No. 10 Sqn	
Tu-16	559	No. 10 Sqn	
Tu-16	560	No. 10 Sqn	
Tu-16	561	No. 10 Sqn	
Tu-16	562	No. 10 Sqn	
Tu-16	563	No. 10 Sqn	
Tu-16	566	No. 10 Sqn	
Tu-16	638	No. 10 Sqn	

APPENDIX III

Table 8: Hawker Hunter deliveries to Jordan before June 1967

Variant	Original identity	RJAF serial number	Remarks
T.Mk 66A	G-APUX	800/P	Loaned to RJAF by Iraq as 800/P; served with No. 6 OCU RJAF before return to Hawker
F.Mk 6	XE551	700/A	Delivered 7 November 1958, destroyed on the ground, 5 June 1967
F.Mk 6	XE558	701/B	Delivered 1 November 1958, crashed 1 July 1960 due to pilot error
F.Mk 6	XF381	702/C	Delivered 11 November 1958, flown by Flt Lt Saif-ul-Azam, 5 June 1967; destroyed on ground at Amman IAP, 5 June 1967
F.Mk 6	XF373	703/D	Delivered 7 November 1958, crashed April 1965
F.Mk 6	XF498	704/E	Delivered 12 November 1958, destroyed on ground, 5 June 1967
F.Mk 6	XF444	705/F	Delivered 14 November 1958, destroyed on ground, 5 June 1967
F.Mk 6	XF496	706/G	Delivered 12 November 1958, destroyed on ground, 5 June 1967
F.Mk 6	XE543	707/H	Delivered 12 November 1958, crashed September 1962 due to pilot error
F.Mk 6	XF452	708/J	Delivered 12 November 1958, destroyed 5 June 1967
F.Mk 6	XF379	709/K	Delivered 11 October 1958, destroyed 5 June 1967
F.Mk 6	XF380	710/L	Delivered 10 November 1958, destroyed 5 June 1967
F.Mk 6	WW597	711/M	Probably the aircraft that crashed before delivery
F.Mk 6	WW507	712/N	Delivered 11 December 1958, fate unknown
T.Mk 66B	–	714/B	Delivered 4 July 1960, crashed 15 August 1965
T.Mk 66B	XG231	715	Delivered 19 April 1966; probably destroyed 5 June 1967
T.Mk 66B	N-249	716	Delivered 7 October 1966, survived 1967 and donated to Oman in 1975
F.Mk 6	XG159	717	Delivered 17 April 1967, destroyed on ground, 5 June 1967
T.Mk 66B	N-283	801	Delivered 1962
F.Mk 6	XF415	802	Delivered 9 August 1962
F.Mk 6	XF423	803	Delivered 1962; crashed 5 July 1962

F.Mk 6	XG132	804	Delivered June 1962; flown to Egypt by defecting pilot, 1962; returned to Jordan; survived 1967 and transferred to Oman in 1975
F.Mk 6	XG263	805	Delivered June 1962
F.Mk 6	XG268	806	Delivered June 1962
F.Mk 6	XG269	807	Delivered 31 July 1962
F.Mk 6	XG171	808	Delivered 9 October 1962
F.Mk 6	XF518	809/K	Delivered 11 September 1962; destroyed 5 June 1967
F.Mk 6	XF417	810	Delivered 3 October 1962; flown to Egypt by defecting pilot, 1962; returned to Jordan; probably destroyed 5 June 1967
F.Mk 6	XG187	811	Delivered 9 October 1962
F.Mk 6	XG257	812	Delivered n 9 October 1962
Total			29 delivered and one on temporary loan; six destroyed before 1967; 21 destroyed on 5 June 1967, two survived (both donated to Oman in 1970s)

APPENDIX IV

The story of Saif-ul-Azam's Hunter

While Saif-ul-Azam's logbook shows that he apparently flew IrAF Hunter F.Mk 59B serial number 702 during his sortie on 7 June 1967 (for a relevant scan from his logbook, see the illustration below), this detail remains questionable. According to Iraqi documentation, the aircraft in question was Hunter F.Mk 59A serial number 570.

Saif-ul-Azam explained that the CO No. 1 Squadron RJAF, who was not at Habbaniyah at the time this mission was flown, had made this entry. Furthermore, since Saif-ul-Azam is not fluent in Arabic, he could not recall whether this was indeed the serial number of the Hunter he flew that morning. The IrAF did receive a Hunter with this serial number: it was delivered in May 1967, but almost immediately broken up as a source of spares for older examples. The serial number was subsequently taken over by a newly delivered MiG-21. It is therefore possible that the CO No. 1 Squadron RJAF subsequently entered the serial number of an (already destroyed) Jordanian Hunter F.Mk 6 in its place. What is certain is that Iraqi records indicate that Saif-ul-Azam flew a Hunter F.Mk 59A that morning. Eventually, it was serial number 570 that was decorated in commemoration for the Pakistani's success in combat.

The wreckage of that Hunter F.Mk 59A was discovered in a scrap yard of the (meanwhile abandoned) Habbaniyah air base, next to a US Marine Corps compound, in March 2006, and was extensively photographed. It is unclear whether the aircraft can still be found there, or even if it remains intact.

Extracts from Group Captain Saiful Azam's Log Book

A scan from Saif-ul-Azam's logbook, documenting sorties he flew in Jordanian and Iraqi Hunters during the June 1967 War.
(Saif-ul-Azam Collection)

Another pre-delivery photograph of Hunter F.Mk 59A serial number 570 – probably the only aircraft of this type ever to have scored two kills. This photograph also provides a useful comparison of the original camouflage pattern with what can be seen in the following photographs.
(David Nicolle Collection)

As of March 2006, wreckage of three Hunters could be found at Habbaniyah.
(Tom Cooper Collection)

The first Hunter, the nose of which was still pointing skywards, was F.Mk 59A serial number 585. These two photographs show details of its forward fuselage and cockpit. (Tom Cooper Collection)

Two photographs showing the rear fuselage and the fin of Hunter F.Mk 59A serial number 585. Immediately behind it is the fin of F.Mk 59A serial number 570.
(Tom Cooper Collection)

At first glance, there was nothing special about the second Hunter F.Mk 59A – serial number 570 – found at Habbaniyah. However, a closer look revealed a very interesting detail – a double kill marking applied below the right side of the cockpit.
(Tom Cooper Collection)

Detail photos of the kill markings applied on the right side of the forward fuselage. As well as showing two 'Stars of David' in white, the inscription below them reads, 'Lt Saif-ul-Azam shot down two Zionist aircraft.'
(Tom Cooper Collection)

Two views of the rear fuselage of Hunter F.Mk 59A serial number 570: one showing general details of the camouflage, and the other recording the original serial number – badly peeling away after all the years, but still clearly legible. (Tom Cooper Collection)

APPENDIX V

Colours of Arab MiG-21s and Su-7s in the mid-1960s

As was normal for almost all air forces around the world at the time, during the late 1950s and early 1960s Arab MiGs wore no camouflage colours. The colours they did wear they received while at the factory in which they were manufactured. As in the case of the MiG-15s and MiG-17s before them, MiG-19s, MiG-21s and Su-7s delivered to Arab air forces during the first half of the 1960s were painted in a manner in which the bare metal of their construction was covered by a primer coating consisting of 5 per cent aluminium powder. As soon as this 'clear' coat was dry, another layer of 8 per cent aluminium powder was added.

The resulting effect, roughly similar to chrome silver F.S.17178, made the aircraft appear as if painted in a colour usually described as 'natural metal', 'bare metal' or 'aluminium silver' overall. However, due to differences in manufacturing methods, the use of various metals other than aluminium for aircraft skin and various moving parts in particular, and due to weathering effects (sun, engine heat, for example), there were differences in the shades of colour as it appeared on various parts of the aircraft. The heat-resistant parts of the engine's afterburner section therefore appeared in a slightly darker, heat-discoloured metal colour.

The dielectric nose cone of the MiG-21 and Su-7 was made from laminated wood and covered with plastic foil (wood is a dielectric material that easily allows radar waves to pass through it), before being painted in radome green F.S.24108. The dielectric panel on the forward portion of the ventral fin was painted in the same colour. On the MiG-21F-13 and MiG-21FL, the SOD transponder filter antenna at the top of the vertical fin was painted in the same manner as the rest of the airframe, while the MiG-21PFM had this item painted gloss dark green.

The internal bays on early MiG-21s were usually left in natural metal, but a number of aircraft had the bays and the insides of the landing gear doors painted with anti-corrosion green chromate paint. The interiors of various maintenance panels on the nose and fuselage, as well as the interior of the airbrakes, received similar treatment. The cockpit interior and the cockpit framing, as well as the instrument consoles, were painted in a light blue-green colour. The instrument panel on MiG-21F-13s and MiG-21FLs was usually in light blue-green, but semi-gloss black was also often used, and it appears that this latter became standard on MiG-21PFMs.

Maintenance instructions were all stencilled in blue and in English language, which became the standard for Soviet aircraft exported to Arab air forces during the 1960s. The only exception to this rule was the aircraft sold to Syria. Most weapons – particularly R-3S missiles – also had English labels, in black or red, and the language used was often rather rudimentary.

One example of the rather clumsy language used is that of the gun fairing on the right side of MiG-21F-13s exported to Iraq, citing, 'OBSERVING THROUGH GAS COMPENSATOR CHECK FIRE SAFETY BY SAFETY CONE LIMITS.'

Other known maintenance stencils usually applied on MiG-21F-13s were as follows:
- Directly above the front speed brake located on the underside of the aircraft and adjacent to the wing leading-edge root was a rounded panel marked 'Engine Oxygen Regulator', while a long, rectangular panel aft of this and beneath the wing root was labelled 'Aileron Control Bell-Crank.'
- Under the wing root and aft of drop tank pylon was a rounded rectangular panel marked 'Engine Accessories.'
- Immediately behind the above item was the inscription 'Attachment of Jet Engine', referring to a small and oval panel beneath.
- Aft of this was a large rectangular panel labelled 'Engine and Hydraulic System Accessories.'
- Behind the intake, positioned halfway between the fin root and the tailplane was a fairing that was pointed at both ends, marked with 'Stabilizer Control.'
- A small panel underneath it was marked with 'Jet Nozzle Actuator.'
- The bulge protruding on both sides of the fin was marked with 'Direction System NSI.'
- Two of the access panels near the fin root were labelled 'Rudder Control Bellcrank.'
- Near the leading edge of the fin was an area marked 'Hydraulic Booster' [pump; authors' note], while below it and further forward was the legend 'Pumping Unit NR-27.'
- Beneath this and a few inches from the root of the fin was the stencil 'Marker Receiver TsRP-56P', and near the leading-edge root of the fin, 'Artificial Feel System.'

Serial Numbers and Special Insignia

No unit insignia is known to have been applied on any Egyptian, Iraqi or Syrian MiG-21s (nor on any Egyptian Su-7s) in the mid-1960s.

Egyptian serial numbers consisted of four digits, and were applied on the forward fuselage with the aid of stencils – usually before delivery from the USSR. Although the first two digits usually designated the type, variant and batch of the aircraft, the last two digits were issued at random, and not in a consecutive fashion as sometimes reported.

During the 1960s the serial numbers of Iraqi MiG-21s still consisted of three digits and were applied on forward fuselage only. The serial numbers were applied in consecutive order, based on aircraft delivery.

The serial numbers of Syrian MiG-21s consisted of four digits applied on the forward fuselage and near the top of the fin. The SyAAF is known to have used serial numbers consisting of a two-digit prefix that designated the type and the sub-variant, while the remaining two digits designated the individual aircraft within a batch. Notable was

The pilot of a UARAF MiG-21F-13 in the process of making final checks and powering up the engine of his aircraft. Notable is the large number of maintenance instructions applied around the forward fuselage, all of them in blue.
(David Nicolle Collection)

the absence of any kind of national markings on the fuselages of any Syrian MiG-21s, ever since that type was introduced to service.

At least some Syrian MiG-21F-13s in service up to June 1967 had their rudders and intakes painted in red – a measure introduced following the establishment of the UAC in 1964. In addition, a few Iraqi MiG-21FLs (as well as some Egyptian MiG-21PFMs) received black anti-glare panels in front of their cockpits. Despite these exceptions, generally all aircraft of this type in service with Arab air forces received no other special markings. Other notable exceptions were a handful of Algerian MiG-21F-13s, which received a 'lightning bolt' applied on the forward fuselage (see *Volume 2*, Appendix III, p235, for an example) and all UARAF MiG-21s, which received the usual set of identification stripes, always applied in black. One set of three stripes was applied around each wingtip (on the upper and lower surfaces), with the central strip roughly two or three times as thick as the outer strips. Only two identification strips of various thicknesses were carried on the rear fuselage.

Camouflage Colours

Immediately following the June 1967 War, i.e. during the final days of the period covered by this volume, the UARAF was the first Arab air force to begin camouflaging its aircraft. Alaa Barakat's recollection in this regard was very specific, and needs little further commentary:

'Camouflage paint was applied on our Air Force's aircraft immediately after the June War. Because there was no proper paint for aircraft in Egypt, this was done with the help of car paint, very roughly, and without polishing. This colour did not shine. The paint was supplied by the Air Force HQ. Most of the aircraft based in the Nile Delta received the 'sand and spinach' colours, while those based on air bases in the desert received 'sand and stone' colours.'

These colours were applied in a random fashion, with no standardised pattern, and – at least in the case of the aircraft delivered before June 1967 and that survived that war – around, partially even over the top of the existing special markings, foremost the identification stripes. It remains unclear what colour was used to paint the undersides of these aircraft, but the few available photographs indicate various shades of a very light – almost white – blue or grey colour.

These two photographs show the wreckage of a Su-7BMK damaged in the Israeli attack on Fayid on the morning of 5 June 1967. Abandoned there by the Egyptians, it was captured by the IDF in October 1973. The aircraft never received any camouflage colours, and its wreckage thus shows the original size and position of the UARAF markings as used in 1967, as well as at least some of the maintenance stencils. (IDF)

UARAF MiG-21F-13 serial number 5211. Originally delivered to Egypt in 1962, this aircraft served with the FTU at Cairo West before being reassigned to an operational squadron. The fighter is representative of this variant as in service at the time of the June 1967 War. After at least one overhaul in Egypt it received slightly larger serial numbers, repeated on the centreline drop tank. While it is unknown whether this aircraft survived that conflict, its drop tank was sighted in July of the same year.

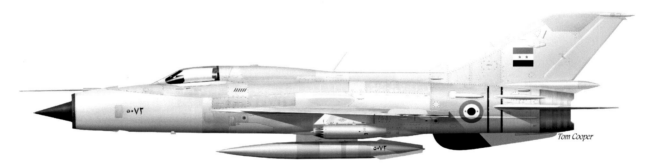

UARAF MiG-21FL serial number 5072, as operated by No. 43 Squadron before, during and after the June 1967 War. Its markings are representative for most UARAF MiG-21FLs and PFMs at that time. The aircraft is shown carrying one UB-16-57UD rocket pod, as usually deployed for air-to-ground attacks on the advancing Israelis.

QJJ MiG-21FL (formerly serving with 14e Escadron de Combat) as flown to Egypt sometime between 7 and 12 June 1967. Algerian markings – including roundels on the upper and lower surfaces of the wing, as well as the fin flash – were all removed shortly after arrival in Egypt. These aircraft apparently entered service with the UARAF still wearing their (above-described) 'natural metal' colours.

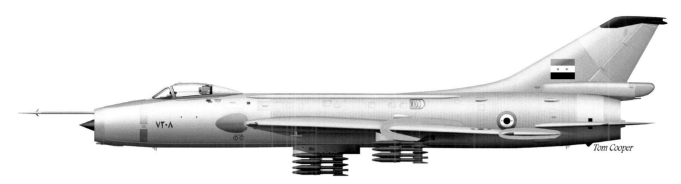

UARAF Su-7BMK serial number 7208 as flown by Maj el-Shennawy during one of three sorties he completed on 15 July 1967 (he flew serial numbers 7242 and 7108 on his other two missions on that day). The aircraft is shown armed with two launchers for Soviet-made S-3K rockets (each loaded with seven rockets), which proved prone to malfunction and non-effective in combat.

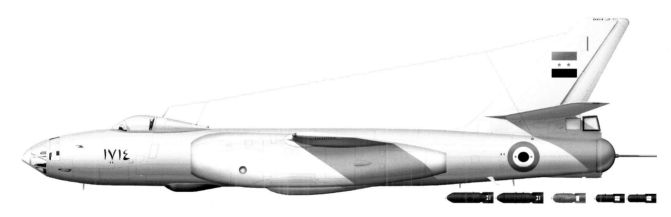

UARAF Il-28 serial number 1417, representative of the entire fleet of these light bombers in Egyptian service at the time of June 1967 War. The inset shows representative major weapons, as deployed in combat in Yemen, but also for attacks on Israeli positions on Sinai, including (from left to right) two FAB-250M46 bombs, a single FAB-100M46 and two FAB-50M46s.

UARAF MiG-21F-13 serial number 5341 as flown by Reda el-Iraqi immediately after the June 1967 War. Originally delivered to Egypt in 1965 or 1966, this aircraft survived the conflict and was one of the first to receive the 'sand and spinach' camouflage pattern (applied using car paints and without any polishing).

A reconstruction of RJAF Hunter F.Mk 6 serial number C/702 as seen in the early 1960s. The aircraft was not upgraded to F.Mk 73 standard before the June War, and appears to have been flown in action – before being destroyed on the ground on 5 June 1967 – while still wearing the relatively intact markings of No. 1 Squadron. Notable is the practice of repeating the code 'C' on the door of the nosewheel bay; in comparison, Iraqi Hunters had their serial numbers repeated in this position.

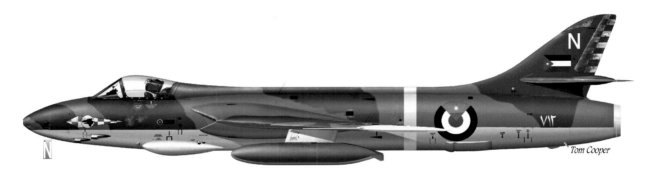

A reconstruction of the last known appearance of RJAF Hunter F.Mk 6 serial number N/712, which was not upgraded to F.Mk 73 standard before the June 1967 War. The fighter was flown in combat by Ihsan Shurdom on 13 November 1966, and by Saif-ul-Azam on two occasions on 5 June 1967. Even though the Israelis admit the loss of only one of their fighters claimed shot down by pilots flying this Hunter, it was the most successful fighter of this type in service with the Royal Jordanian Air Force.

RJAF Hunter F.Mk 73 serial number J/708 was one of eight examples upgraded to this standard and present in Jordan by the time of the June 1967 War. It received red colours on the nose and fin in accordance with a UAC-related agreement from 1964 and is shown armed with Hispano-Suiza 80mm unguided rockets. A total of 24 such weapons could be carried, installed in eight banks of three rockets each (only two of which are shown). Interestingly, one of the launchers was always installed on the outboard underwing pylon, with two others inboard, and one outboard of it. Insets show the slightly modified insignia of No. 1 Squadron and a single Hispano-Suiza rocket with its launcher.

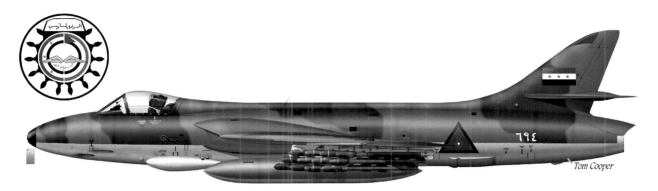

IrAF Hunter F.Mk 59B serial number 694 was part of the final batch of Iraqi Hunters, delivered in April and May 1967. Assigned to No. 6 Squadron, this aircraft was flown by the number 2 in the formation that attacked Kfar Sirkin airfield in Israel on the morning of 5 June 1967. It is shown with the armament used during that raid, consisting of four banks of three 3in unguided rockets under each wing. The inset shows the insignia of No. 6 Squadron.

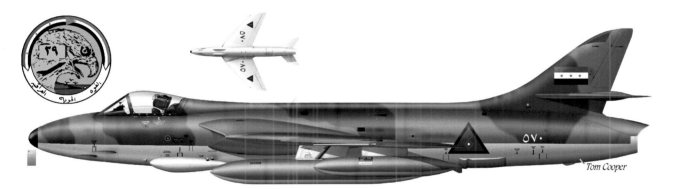

IrAF Hunter F.Mk 59A serial number 570 as flown by Flt Lt Saif-ul-Azam during the battle over H-3 airfield, on the late morning of 7 June 1967. The aircraft is shown carrying 230-Imp gal and 100-Imp gal drop tanks for a long-range CAP. Insets show the insignia of No. 29 Squadron and the size and application of the national insignia and serial number on the lower surfaces of the wing.

The same Hunter F.Mk 59A with details of two kill markings applied to commemorate Flt Lt Saif-ul-Azam's success over H-3 airfield. The application of red panels was in accordance with agreements reached when the UAC was originally established in 1964 and was common to Jordanian and Lebanese Hunters. While it is possible that the nose and the fin were painted red prior to 7 June 1967, available information indicates that this happened sometime between 1970 and 1973.

IrAF MiG-21FL serial number 682 was a new arrival with No. 17 Squadron when it was deployed to H-3 airfield with most of that unit, on 5 June 1967. It was badly damaged (indeed, claimed shot down by the Israelis) in the course of an air combat over the same airfield on the following day, but survived the mission and continued to serve until at least 1982. The inset shows the insignia of No. 17 Squadron.

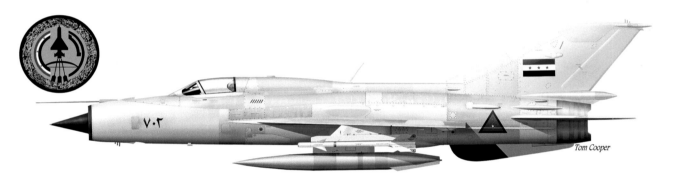

IrAF MiG-21PFM serial number 702 was the first example of this variant delivered to Iraq, in May 1967. It took over the serial number of a Hunter F.Mk 59B that was delivered around the same time, but reportedly broken up for spares immediately after. The inset shows the insignia of No. 9 Squadron, which included a silhouette of a MiG-21 instead of MiG-19 ever since that unit had been re-established and re-equipped in 1966. (For the original appearance of this patch, see artwork in *Volume 2*, p231.)

A reconstruction of the SyAAF MiG-17F flown by Adnan Madani (or Adnan Malki) when he made a forced landing southwest of Amman on 4 October 1960. This was possibly ex-Egyptian Air Force serial number 2048, or one of the few SyAAF MiG-17s that received full UARAF insignia (including identification stripes around the wingtips and rear fuselage). While it remains unknown if this aircraft survived long enough to take part in the June War, it is shown in 'makeshift' Syrian national markings (as often applied on ex-UARAF MiGs after the UAR disintegrated). It is seen in the configuration employed by most SyAAF MiG-17s that flew attacks on Israel around noon on 5 June 1967, including four twin launchers for Sakr unguided rockets of Egyptian origin.

BIBLIOGRAPHY

Aloni, S., *Israeli Mirage and Nesher Aces* (Oxford: Osprey Publishing Ltd, 2004)
ISBN 1-84176-653-4

Aloni, S., *The June 1967 Six-Day War, Volume A – Operation Focus; the Israeli pre-emptive strike of June 5, 1967* (Bat-Hefer: IsraDecal Publications, 2008)
ISBN 965-7220-09-2

Baer, R., *Die Saudi-Connection* (C. Bertelsmann, 2004; German issue of *The Saudi-Connection*, published 2003 by Random House: Santa Barbara)
ISBN 3-570-00807-X

Boufre, A., *The Suez Expedition 1956* (London: Faber and Faber Ltd, 1969)
ISBN 571-08979-8

Bowen, J., *Six Days* (London: Simon & Schuster UK, Ltd, 2003)
ISBN 13-978-0-7434-4969-4

Bull, Gen O., *War and Peace in the Middle East: the Experiences and Views of a UN Observer* (London: Leo Cooper Ltd, 1976)
ISBN 0-85052-226-9

Centre for Military Studies, *The History of the Syrian Army* (in Arabic), (Damascus, 2001–2002)

Central Intelligence Agency, *Probable Soviet Objectives in Rearming Arab States*, Special National Intelligence Estimate No. 11-13-67, 20 July 1967 (released in response to FOIA inquiry by the CIA Historical Review Program), cited as 'SNIE 11-13-67' in this volume

Cohen, Col E. 'Cheetah', *Israel's Best Defense* (Shrewsbury: Airlife Publishing Ltd, 1993), ISBN 1-85310-484-1

Cull, B., Nicolle, D., and Aloni, S., *Spitfires over Israel* (London: Grub Street, 1994)
ISBN 0-948817-74-7

Cull, B., Nicolle, D., and Aloni, S., *Wings over Suez* (London: Grub Street, 1996)
ISBN 1-898697-48-5

Dupuy, Col T. N. and Blanchard, Col. W., *The Almanac of World Military Power*
(2nd Edition), (London: Arthur Barker Ltd, 1972)
ISBN 0-213-16418-3

Egyptian Ministry of Defence, *Document 44* (Findings of the Commission tasked
with the inquiry into the reasons for the Egyptian defeat in the June 1967 War,
presided by General Hassan Metawea), excerpts published by *el-Fager Magazine*
(designated 'EFM' in footnotes of this book), Volume 14, June 2010, and HEYKAL,
H. M. *The 30 Years War* (see below for details)

Fawzy, Maj Gen M., *The Three-Years War* (in Arabic), (Beirut: Dar Mustakbal al-Arabi,
1998)

Gluska, A., *The Israeli Military and the Origins of the 1967 War*
(New York: Routledge, 2007)
ISBN 0-415-39245-4

Green, S., *Taking Sides: America's Secret Relations with a Militant Israel,*
1948/1967 (London: Faber and Faber Ltd, 1984)
ISBN 0-571-13271-5

Green, W., and Fricker, J., *The Air Forces of the World* (London: MacDonald, 1958)

Griffin, D. J., *Hawker Hunter in UK and Foreign Service*
(Morrisville: Lulu Enterprises, 2007)

Hammel, E., *Six Days in June, How Israel Won the 1967 Arab-Israeli War*
(Pacifica: Pacifica Military History, 1992), ISBN 0-935553-54-1

Heykal, H. M., *The 30 Years War* (in Arabic), (Cairo: el-Ahram Publishing &
Translation Centre, 1990), Reg. No. 5063/1990

Israeli Defence Force, *The Six Day War* (Tel Aviv: Mizraghi Publishing House, 1967)

Iraqi Ministry of Defence, *History of the Iraqi Armed Forces, Part 17; The Establish-*
ment of the Iraqi Air Force and its Development (in Arabic), (Iraq: 1988)

Irra, M. 'Drama na solnem jezere', *Letectvi & Kosmonautika*, 1999

al-Jawadi, Dr. M., *In Between the Catastrophe: Memoirs of Egyptian Military*
Commanders from 1967 to 1972 (in Arabic), (Cairo: Dar al-Khiyal, 2001)

al-Jawadi, Dr. M., *Martyr Abdel-Moneim Riad, Model of the Egyptian Army*
(in Arabic), (Cairo: Dar al-Atebaa, 1984)

JELAVIC, T., *No. 352 (Y) R.A.F. Squadron* (Zagreb: Multigraf d.o.o., 2003)
ISBN 953-97698-2-5

JONES, B., *Hawker Hunter* (Ramsbury: The Crowood Press Ltd, 1998)
ISBN 1-86126-083-0

KATERBERG, E., and GRAVEMAKER, A., 'Silah el-Jaw Ilmalki el-Urduni'/'Königliche
Jordanische Luftwaffe (RJAF)', *Fliegerrevue Extra*, Volume 15, December 2006

KONZELMANN, G., *Damaskus: Oase Zwischen Hass und Hoffnung*
(Frankfurt/Main: Ullstein Buch, 1996)
ISBN 3-548-35588-9

LABIB, A. M., *The Third Arm: A History of the Egyptian Air Force* (in Arabic),
Volumes 7 to 9

MARSHAL, T. J., 'Israeli Helicopter Forces: Organization and Tactics', *Military Review*,
May 1972

AL-MENAHIM, Maj Gen A. K., *Egyptian Wars in Modern History* (in Arabic),
(Beirut: Dar Mustakbal al-Arabi, 1990)

EL-MONEIM, A. A., *Lieutenant Colonel Salah Danish: the Only Egyptian Pilot captured in June 1967* (in Arabic), online article

EL-MONEIM, A. A., *Wolf in the Sun's Disc* (in Arabic), (Cairo: 1988)

MOUKHAD, Maj Gen M. A., *My Life* (in Arabic), (Damascus: al-Zakhira, 2005)

MUSTAFA, Gen H., *The June War, 1967, Part II* (Lebanon: Establishment for Arab
Studies and Publication, 1970)

MUSTAFA, K., *The Fall of the Golan* (Cairo: Dar al-Itisam, 1980)

MUTAWI, S. A., *Jordan in the 1967 War* (Cambridge University Press, 1987)

NICOLLE, D., and COOPER, T., *Arab MiG-19 and MiG-21 Units in Combat*
(Oxford: Osprey Publishing Ltd, 2004)
ISBN 1-84176-655-0

NORDEEN, L., *Fighters over Israel*, (Guild Publishing, 1991)

NORDEEN, L., and NICOLLE, D., *Phoenix over the Nile* (Washington: Smithsonian, 1996)
ISBN 1-56098-826-3

O'BALLANCE, E., *The Third Arab-Israeli War* (London: Faber & Faber, 1972)
ISBN 0-571-09214-4

O'BALLANCE, E., *The Gulf War* (London: Brassey's Defence Publishers, 1988)
ISBN 0-08-034747-9

OMAR, Maj Gen K. K., *Memoirs of the Iraqi Air Force CO* (unpublished document in
Arabic)

OKASHA, Maj Gen M., *Conflict in the Sky: the Egyptian-Israeli Wars, 1948–1967*
(Cairo: Ministry of Defence, 1976)

OREN, M. B., *Six Days of War: June 1967 and the Making of the Modern Middle East*
(Oxford: Oxford University Press, 2002)
ISBN 0-19-515174-7

OVENDALE, R., *The Origins of the Arab-Israeli Wars* (Harlow: Longman Group UK Ltd,
1984), ISBN 0-582-49257-2

PARKER, R. B., 'USAF in Sinai in the 1967 War: Fact or Fiction', *Journal of Palestine
Studies, Volume XXVII, No. 1/Autumn 1997* (Institute for Palestine Studies)

RAZOUX, P., *Le Guerre des Six Jours (5–10 Juin 1967) Du mythe à la rèalité*
(2nd edition) (Paris: Editions Economica, 1999)

RIAD, M., *The Struggle for Peace in the Middle East* (Consett: Quartet Books, 1981)
ISBN: 978-0704322974

AL-SA'ADON, M., *Pilot Memoir* (privately published document, 2005)

EL-SADAT, A., *In Search of Identity* (Harper & Row Publishers, Inc., 1977)
ISBN 0-060137428

SADIK, Brig Gen A., and COOPER, T. *Iraqi Fighters, 1953–2003: Camouflage & Markings* (Houston: Harpia Publishing, 2008)
ISBN 978-0-615-21414-6

SADIK, Brig Gen A., and COOPER, T., 'Nahostkrieg 1967 – Die Basis H-3', *Fliegerrevue
Extra* magazine (Germany), Volume 17/June 2007

SAFRAN, N., *From War to War: the Arab-Israeli Confrontation, 1948–1967*
(New York: Pegasus Books, 1969)

SHALOM, D., *Like a Bolt Out of the Blue* (in Hebrew), (Bavir Aviation & Space Publications)
ISBN 965-90455-0-6

SHEIF, Z., *The Israeli Military Encyclopaedia* (Amman: 1st Arabic Edition, translated
into Arabic and published by Dar el-Jaleel For Publishing, Research & Studies,
1988)

SHUKAIRY, A., *The Great Defeat; Major Defeat of Kings and Presidents* (Cairo: Arab Foundation for Publishing and Distribution, 2005)

STAFRACE, C., *Arab Air Forces* (Carrolton: Squadron/Signal Publications Inc., 1994) ISBN 0-89747-326-4

SMÝRA, F., 'Arabské MiGy-21 kontra stihaci s Mogen David', Part 1, *LiK* magazine, 1999

SOKOLOV, A, 'PVO in Local Wars and Armed Conflicts: The Arab-Israeli Wars', *VKO*, No. 2 (2), 2001

SOKOLOV, A., 'The Arab-Israeli Wars', *VKO*, No. 2 (5), 2002

TESSLER, M. A., *A History of the Israeli-Palestinian Conflict* (Bloomington and Indianapolis: Indiana University Press, 1994)

UDA, M. and IMAM A., 'A Lesson We Should Have Learned', *al-Ahali* magazine (Egypt, in Arabic), 29 June 1983, reprinted in *al-Ahram*, 29 June 2004

ZAKI, T., *Testament* (unpublished document prepared by Tahsin Zaki for his son, shortly before Zaki's death in 1990; translation provided by Mr Sherif Sharmy)

ZHIRIKHOV, M., and NICOLLE, D., 'Operation 105: des MiG-15 tchécoslovaques pour l'Egypte (1955–1956)', *Avions* magazine (France)

Various volumes of *Armed Forces Magazine*, published by the Egyptian Ministry of Defence, 1950s and 1960s; *El-Djeich* (official publication of the Algerian Ministry of Defence), various volumes from 2007 to 2009; various magazines and journals published by the Iraqi Air Force and the Iraqi Ministry of Defence, 1970s, 1980s and 1990s; *Kanatlar* magazine (Turkey), June 2003

Interviews with various Algerian, Egyptian, Iraqi, and Syrian Air Force officers, pilots, and ground personnel (see Acknowledgments and Footnotes)

Personal notes of all authors

INDEX

Dutch Aviation Society
P.O.Box 75545
1118 ZN Schiphol
The Netherlands
Fax: +31 (0) 84 - 738 3905
E-mail: info@scramble.nl
www.scramble.nl

The Dutch Aviation Society is a non-profit
organisation run totally by volunteers. For those of
you who have never heard of us, we will briefly
explain our activities.

The main activities of the Dutch Aviation Society are:

– The publication of the monthly magazine 'Scramble'.
– The publication of civil and military aviation books.
– Maintaining the aviation website www.scramble.nl.
– To organise spotter conventions.
– Maintaining and publishing from an aviation information database.

The production of the magazine, Scramble, is our core business. The magazine averages around 144 pages and more than 100
photographs from all over the world. It is published in the English language. It covers all aspects of civil and military aviation
worldwide in many separate sections.

From September 2012 you can also download Scramble Magazine to your smartphone or desktop and tablet computer

Go to the App store or Google play and search for Scramble Magazine

– Civil airport and military airbase movements from the Netherlands;
– Civil and military movements from many European airports and airbases;
– Civil aviation news word wide
– Dustpan & Brush, in depth reports about accidents and incidents;
– Military aviation news world wide
– Timetables and information on shows, deployments, exchanges and other events;
– Radio Activity (new frequencies, call signs);
– Show reports (full reports in all major aviation events);
– Full coverage of the Dutch Civil Aircraft Register;
– Trip reports from all over the world;
– A mix of large and small, civil and military articles.

And coming soon:

The Scramble database app

**Visit:
www.scramble.nl
for details**

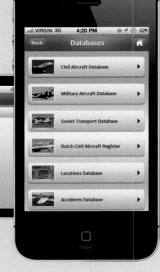

DUTCH AVIATION SOCIETY

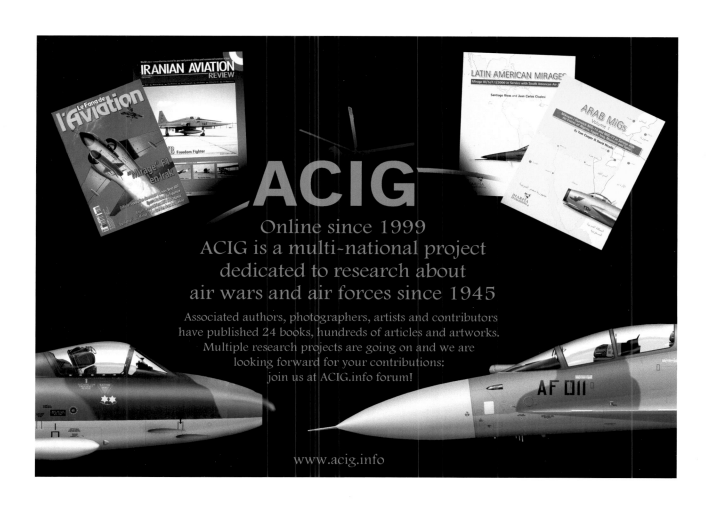

HARPIA PUBLISHING+

Glide With Us Into The World of Aviation Literature

**African MiGs, Volume 2 | Madagascar to Zimbabwe,
MiGs and Sukhois in Service in Sub-Saharan Africa**

Tom Cooper and Peter Weinert, with Fabian Hinz and Mark Lepko

256 pages, 28 x 21 cm, softcover

35.95 Euro, ISBN 978-0-9825539-8-5

Completing an in-depth history of the deployment and operations of MiG and Sukhoi fighters (as well as their Chinese-built Chengdu and Shenyang variants) in sub-Saharan Africa, Volume 2 covers 11 additional air forces, from Madagascar to Zimbabwe.

This encyclopaedic account is so far the only one of its kind to provide detailed analysis of aerial conflicts including those waged between Ethiopia and Somalia, Tanzania and Uganda, and in Sudan.

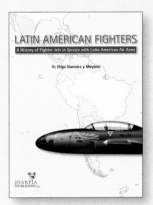

Latin American Fighters | A History of Fighter Jets in Service with Latin American Air Arms

Iñigo Guevara y Moyano

256 pages, 28 x 21 cm, softcover

35.95 Euro, ISBN 978-0-9825539-0-9

This book for the first time describes the military fighter jet aviation in Latin America. It covers the eventfull history of fighter jets in 17 countries ranging from Mexico in the north down to Argentina in the south. Each country is covered type by type in chronological order. Information on each type is being provided related to purchase, squadron service, losses, upgrades and service history. Each type ends with a table covering the number of delivered aircraft, different types and subtypes, delivery dates and known serial numbers. Each of the over 100 aircraft types mentioned could be covered with at least one picture. An appendix lists the existing plastic scale model kits in 1/72, 1/48 and 1/32 scale as wells as decal sheets in regards to the 17 Latin American air forces featured in the book.

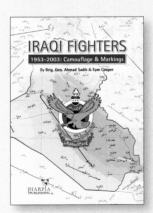

Iraqi Fighters | 1953–2003: Camouflage & Markings

Brig. Gen. Ahmad Sadik & Tom Cooper

156 pages, 28 x 21 cm, softcover

29.95 Euro, ISBN 978-0-615-21414-6

Richly illustrated with photographs and artworks, this book provides an exclusive insight into service history of 13 fighter jet types – from Vampires and Hunters to MiG-29s and Su-24s – that served with Royal Iraqi Air Force (RIrAF) and Iraqi Air Force (IrAF) between 1953 and 2003.

The result is a detailed history of RIrAF and IrAF markings, serial numbers and camouflage patterns, the in-depth history of each Iraqi fighter squadron, their equipment over the time as well as unit and various special insignias.

An appendix lists the exisiting plastic scale model kits in 1/72, 1/48 and 1/32 scale as well as decals sheets in regards to Iraqi Air Force.

www.harpia-publishing.com